THE NEW ECONOMIC NATIONALISM

THE NEW ECONOMIC NATIONALISM

edited by

Otto Hieronymi

with contributions by

Jack N. Behrman, Richard Blackhurst
Innocenzo Cipolletta, Benjamin J. Cohen
Gerard Curzon, Victoria Curzon Price, Emilio Fontela
Otto Hieronymi, Lawrence B. Krause
Nicolas Krul, Jacques A. L'Huillier, Robert A. Mundell
Keichi Oshima, André Reszler
Rimmer de Vries

M

First published 1980 by
THE MACMILLAN PRESS LTD
London and Basingstoke
Associated companies in Delhi
Dublin Hong Kong Johannesburg Lagos
Melbourne New York Singapore Tokyo

Printed in Great Britain

British Library Cataloguing in Publication Data

The new economic nationalism
1. International economic relations – Congresses
I. Hieronymi, Otto II. Battelle – Geneva
(Institute)
382.1 HF1410

ISBN 0–333–26173–9

Contents

Acknowledgements

The papers included in this book were originally presented at a three-day conference on *The New Economic Nationalism*, organised by the Battelle Research Centre in Geneva in June 1978.

The idea for the conference originated at Battelle–Geneva in late 1976, as a result of our ongoing work in the field of international economics as well as our close involvement with economic developments in Europe and around the world. It also reflected the belief that the signs of the rising new economic nationalism, which can be observed in Europe and in America, as well as in other countries, represent a serious threat not only to our future prosperity, but also to political and social stability and cooperation in both the OECD area and the rest of the world.

The plans for holding such a conference, with a concerned group of economists, officials and businessmen participating, met with an immediately favourable response both inside and outside Battelle. As it so happened, developments in 1977 and 1978 made the subject matter of such a conference even more topical than at the time when the idea was first raised.

The conference was attended by about 100 specialists from 12 OECD countries, including representatives from not only the major central banks, ministries of finance and international organisations, but also banks, industry, research establishments and universities. The formal presentations were followed by an extensive and lively discussion, which confirmed the profound concern about economic nationalism felt by a very broad spectrum of economists, bankers, businessmen and government officials.

First of all I want to thank all those who addressed and participated in the conference and whose interest and ideas gave birth to this book.

My appreciation also goes to the Conference's Advisory Committee, which included Professor Jacques A. L'Huillier, Professor of Economics, University of Geneva; Mr William McChesney Martin, former Chairman of the Federal Reserve

Board and Member of the Board of Trustees, Battelle Memorial Institute; Professor Keichi Oshima, Professor of Nuclear Engineering, University of Tokyo and former Director of Science and Technology at the OECD; and Dr Valentin Stingelin, Director, Battelle–Geneva Research Centre.

The late Professor Ludwig Erhard had originally also expressed support for the objectives of this conference: because of his untimely death he could not be a member of this advisory group.

I am particularly grateful to Dr Stingelin, who from late 1976 gave his full backing to the idea of this conference.

My most sincere thanks go to Nicolas Krul, General Manager of the Gulf and Occidental Investment Company in Geneva, who from the start accepted the role of co-organiser and to whom much of the credit belongs for the success of the conference. I am also indebted to Emilio Fontela of Battelle and the University of Geneva and to André Reszler of the Institut d'Études Européennes in Geneva for their advice and encouragement.

The successful and efficient organisation of the conference owed much to the efforts of P. Falter, C. Humbert, M. Lavergnat and F. Liebich, of the Group of Economic Analysis and Forecasting of Battelle–Geneva. They have been also very helpful in the editorial work involved in the preparation of this book.

I also wish to convey my thanks to Ambassador Cornelio Sommaruga, of the Trade Division of the Swiss Federal Department of Economy, who so kindly agreed to address our dinner session, and to the Conseil d'Administration of the City of Geneva for the hospitality that it extended to our conference participants.

The Battelle–Geneva Research Centre generously contributed to the costs of organising the conference, while the Battelle Memorial Institute has provided support related to the costs of editing this volume.

As a final word, the opinions expressed in this book do not necessarily reflect the views of Battelle or of other organisations with which the authors may be connected.

Geneva, December 1978 Otto Hieronymi

Notes on the Contributors

Jack N. Behrman. American. Luther Hodges Distinguished Professor at the University of North Carolina School of Business Administration. Major field of interest: foreign investment, economic development, and the role of multinational enterprises. Assistant Secretary of Commerce 1961–4. Consultant of the Department of State, the Treasury and other US agencies, the United Nations Center on Transnational Corporations, and ministries of other governments on problems of foreign investment and economic growth. Author of numerous articles for professional journals and some twenty books and monographs in the fields of international economics and business.

Richard Blackhurst. American. A Senior Economist on the staff of the General Agreement on Tariffs and Trade (GATT). Part-time professor at the Graduate Institute of International Studies in Geneva. Ph.D. economics, University of Chicago (1968). Co-author (with Nicolas Marian and Jan Tumlir) of two monographs in GATT's Studies in International Trade series, *Trade Liberalization, Protectionism and Interdependence* (1977) and *Adjustment, Trade and Growth in Developed and Developing Countries* (1978). Other recent publications include an article on 'International Trade and Domestic Environmental Policies in a Growing World Economy' (1977) and 'Reciprocity in Trade Negotiations under Flexible Exchange Rates' (1979).

Innocenzo Cipolleta. Italian. Research Director of ISCO (Istituto Nazionale per lo Studio della Congiuntura) Rome, where he is in charge of current economic analysis and short-term forecasting. Member of the Governing Committee of AIECE (Association d'Instituts Européens de Conjoncture Économique), of the commissions and working parties of the OECD and of the European Community dealing with the economic outlook. Author of numerous articles dealing with forecasting and business cycle analysis and of various monographs published by ISCO including *A System of Quarterly National Accounts for Italy, The Effects of the Devaluation of the Lira in 1973* and *Prices and Remuneration of Factors of Production*.

Benjamin J. Cohen. American. William L. Clayton Professor of International Economic Affairs at the Fletcher School of Law and Diplomacy, Tufts University. Ph.D. economics, Columbia University. Former research economist at the Federal Reserve Bank of New York. Former member of the Economics Department, Princeton University. Author of five books including *The Question of Imperialism* (1973) and *Organizing the World's Money* (1977).

Gerard Curzon. British. Professor of International Economics at the Graduate Institute of International Studies. On the staff of the Center for Education in International Management in Geneva. Formerly editor of the 'Journal of World Trade Law'. On the Editorial Board of 'World Development' (Oxford); on the Board of Directors of various organisations in the field of international economics, including the Trade Policy Research Centre, London. Author of a comprehensive study of GATT (*Multilateral Commercial Diplomacy*, London 1965). Recent publications (with Victoria Curzon) include 'The Management of Trade Relations in the GATT' in *International Economic Relations of the Western World 1959–1971*, Andrew Shonfield (ed.), (Royal Institute of International Affairs) and *The Multinational Enterprise in a Hostile World* (London, Macmillan, 1977).

Victoria Curzon Price. British. Associate Professor at the Graduate Institute of International Studies and a member of the faculty at the Center for Education in International Management in Geneva. Publications include *The Essentials of Integration: Lessons of the EFTA Experience* (Macmillan, 1974), and (with Gerard Curzon) 'The Management of Trade Relations in the GATT' in *International Economic Relations of the Western World 1959–1971*, Andrew Shonfield (ed.), (Royal Institute of International Affairs, 1976) and *The Multinational Enterprise in a Hostile World* (Macmillan, 1977).

Emilio Fontela. Spanish. Professor of National Accounting and Director of the Department of Econometrics at the University of Geneva. Consultant to the management of Battelle–Geneva;

Director of the Department of Applied Economics of Battelle–Geneva, 1966–73. President of the European Association of Applied Economics (ASEPELT). Associate editor of the *European Economic Review* (Amsterdam); of *Futures* (London); and of *Futuribles* (Paris). Director of *Argus* (Barcelona). He has wide-ranging experience in applied economics research, strategic planning and the development of large econometric models. Author of many publications in the fields of prices, input-output models and analysis, medium-term forecasting and corporate planning.

Otto Hieronymi. US citizen, born in Hungary. Head of the Group of Economic Analysis and Forecasting at Battelle–Geneva. In charge of Battelle's short- and medium-term forecasting programmes and responsible for large research projects in the area of international trade, regional policy and strategic planning. Ph.D. international economics, (Graduate Institute of International Studies in Geneva); was an Assistant Professor of Economics 1964–65 at the University of Dallas. Former international economist with Morgan Guaranty Trust in New York 1966–70. Publications include *Economic Discrimination Against the United States in Western Europe, 1945–1958* (Geneva, Librairie Droz, 1973) and (with A. Gabus and P. Kukorelly) *Japanese-European Trade Relations: Restrictions or Cooperation? The Case of the Automobile Industry* (Geneva, 1978).

Lawrence B. Krause. American. Since 1963 a Senior Fellow, Brookings Institution, Washington DC. He was an Assistant Professor of Economics at Yale University 1956–63 and taught at various other universities. Formerly on the senior staff of the Council of Economic Advisors, and a consultant to the State Department and the Special Representative for Trade Negotiations. Numerous publications in international economics. Recent publications at Brookings include (with others) *Asia's New Giant: How the Japanese Economy Works* (1976); (co-edited with C. Fred Bergsten) *World Politics and International Economics* (1976); and (co-edited with Walter Salant) *Worldwide Inflation: Theory and Recent Experience* (1977).

Nicolas Krul. Dutch. General Manager of the Gulf and Occidental Investment Company in Geneva. Financial adviser to the Government of Qatar and economic policy consultant to several governments. Member of the Scientific Committee of the

International Center for Monetary and Banking Studies, Geneva. Previously Chief Investment Strategist and Economist for Lombard, Odier & Cie. Ph.D. international economics (Graduate Institute of International Studies in Geneva). Author of two books and numerous articles on money and finance.

Jacques A. L'Huillier. Swiss. Professor of Economics and Director of the Department of Political Economy at the University of Geneva and at the Graduate Institute of International Studies. Vice Chairman of the Swiss Federal Commission on Current Economic Conditions. Publications include *Théorie et practique de la coopération économique internationale* (Paris, Génin Librairie de Médicis, 1957) and *Le Système monétaire international, aspects économiques* (Paris, Armand Colin, 1971).

Robert A. Mundell. Canadian. Professor of Economics at Columbia University. Educated at the University of British Columbia, Ph.D. in Economics from the Massachusetts Institute of Technology and the London School of Economics. Formerly Professor of Economics at the University of Chicago, the Graduate Institute of International Studies, Geneva, and at the University of Waterloo, Ontario. Former consultant to the World Bank, the Board of Governors of the Federal Reserve System, the US Treasury and the European Communities. Author of numerous books and articles including *International Economics* (1968); co-editor with A. Swoboda, *Monetary Problems of the International Economy* (1969); and *Monetary Theory: Inflation, Interest and Growth in the World Economy* (1971).

Keichi Oshima. Japanese. Professor of Nuclear Engineering at the University of Tokyo. Formerly Director for Science, Technology and Industry of the OECD, 1974–6; now a member of the Advisory Panel of the OECD Interfutures.

André Reszler. Swiss, born in Budapest. Professor at the Graduate Institute of European Studies and Director of the European Cultural Center in Geneva. Ph.D. in political science (Graduate Institute of International Studies). Professor at Indiana University, 1968–75. Author of numerous articles and several books, including *L'Esthétique anarchiste* (1973); *Le Marxisme devant la*

Culture (1975); and *L'Intellectuel contre l'Europe* (1976) (all translated into several languages). Editor of *Cadmos*, a quarterly review dealing with European issues.

Rimmer de Vries. US citizen, born in the Netherlands. A Senior Vice President of Morgan Guaranty Trust, New York, in charge of the International Economics Department, which is also responsible for the monthly review *World Financial Markets*. Prior to joining Morgan Guaranty in 1961, he was a foreign research economist with the Federal Reserve Bank of New York. Graduated from the Netherlands School of Economics, Ph.D. in economics (Ohio State University).

Introduction

One of the consequences of the profound changes that have occurred in the international economy since the late 1960s has been a gradual revival of economic nationalism throughout the world. The ultimate disintegration of the post-war international monetary system has led almost inexorably to a widening rift between strong and weak currency countries, between inflationary and non-inflationary economies and between the rich and the poor both in the developed and in the less developed world. The slowdown in economic activity and the persistent high level of unemployment throughout the OECD countries have added to protectionist pressures for the sake of individual industries and sectors as well as for balance of payments reasons.

While the revival of economic nationalism has been a *cause* and a *consequence* of the crisis of the 1970s, it is also the single most important issue influencing the outlook for the 1980s in both the developed and developing countries.

Economic nationalism is a complex phenomenon. It goes beyond traditional efforts to protect domestic production through tariffs or other restrictions; it includes dumping, export subsidies and various forms of 'beggar-my-neighbour' policies. Certain types of industrial policy, as well as so-called voluntary export or import agreements, are among its contemporary manifestations in the developed market economies. In the 1970s, as in the 1930s, *monetary nationalism* has been its most pervasive and, so far, its most disruptive manifestation. The concern with the revival of economic nationalism and with its potential consequences for the world economy was shared by all the speakers at the conference in June 1978; it is this concern for the future of the liberal economic order which is the common theme of this book.

The speakers and the participants at the conference came from a wide variety of professional, national and geographic backgrounds. In planning the conference's programme, however, a systematic effort was made to show the complexity of the phenomenon and the interdependence of the different manifestations of modern economic nationalism. The realisation of this objective has provided the main interest of the conference both for the organisers and for the participants, and is the basis, we hope, for the unity of the present volume.

Speakers and participants at the conference were seeking answers to three fundamental questions:

– What is the relationship between the shocks and changes that have occurred in the 1970s in the world economy and the revival of economic nationalism, and, in particular, what is the link between monetary disorders, floating exchange rates and protectionism?
– What will be the objectives and instruments of trade policy in the future, and will there be in the area of trade a similar metamorphosis or breakdown of the post-war order as had occurred in the international monetary system?
– Is the rise of economic nationalism a temporary phenomenon only, to be followed sooner or later by a restoration of a more stable and liberal international economic order, or if not, will economic nationalism, some time in the 1980s, lead to the kind of conflicts and social and political disasters as had been experienced in the past?

There are no uniform answers to these three questions in the present book, and none was provided by the participants in Geneva. This may be partly due to the fact that there is as much disagreement among experts about the very characteristics of *today's* international economic order as there is about the system or order of the future. One of the reasons why it is so difficult to forecast the future is because it is so hard to know and find a consensus about our present position. The lack of common answers to these basic questions, however, has also more fundamental causes. The papers in the present volume show that a central aspect of today's economic nationalism is the loss of common objectives, of a common vision of the future; it is the breakdown of the consensus on the basic features of economic order.

In the last ten years there has been a new emphasis on 'strength' (and the reintroduction of military terminology) in international economic relations, as well as profound changes in the perception of *national* or *particular* interests as distinguished from *international* or *common* interests. This trend has been noticeable in relations not only between the industrialised and developing countries, but increasingly also among the members of the OECD. The reference to strong and weak countries has become common not only in Europe, but also in the context of Europe, Japan and the United States. Depending on the issue (income, inflation, trade or balance of payments) and on one's point of view, each of these countries and areas is alternatively seen as the victim or the villain of the international economic system.

The revival of economic nationalism is not limited to the 'weak' countries; nor can a sharp separation be drawn according to size. Small *and* liberal countries can also be nationalistic: the fact that Switzerland managed to achieve a significant reduction in its labour force without a rise in unemployment is a case in point. The German government and central bank have been consistently the strongest supporters within the European Community of liberalism and free trade. Yet, by focusing their policies and reform proposals on a system that would permit isolating the German economy from outside influences, they have also contributed to the breakdown of the gold exchange standard and to the spreading of monetary nationalism.

In the debate on economic nationalism it is often difficult to distinguish expectations and the perception of events from actual developments and interests. Britain and Italy have probably suffered the greatest losses from the international crisis and the reversal of European integration in terms of output, the transfer of resources and instability; yet, in both countries inward-looking policies still tend to predominate; there is even growing pressure for outright protectionism in Britain. There was not much favourable echo at the conference to the concept of organised free trade launched by France. This approach, which also finds many supporters outside Europe would accelerate rather than decelerate the trend towards the fragmentation and the growing cartellisation of the world economy. The ambiguous position of Japan was also noted at the meeting: while a latecomer to trade liberalisation, Japan is among the countries that have reaped the greatest benefits from free trade and the opening of new markets. Yet, beyond price competitiveness, the difficulty of penetrating the Japanese market is known to all, and Japan continues to follow a defensive policy in both trade and monetary matters.

The role of the United States and the nature of American policies is a major theme of this book as it dominated much of the discusssion at the conference. By abandoning its post-war position in favour of international stability, the United States was considered by most of the participants as the major factor in the revival of economic nationalism. This view had little to do with traditional anti-Americanism: it rested on the conviction, expressed by the majority of the European speakers and participants, that there is a direct link between floating exchange rates, monetary nationalism and the rise of protectionist pressures. Flexible exchange rates are no substitute for protection: the growing gap between inflationary and non-inflationary countries and the instability and uncertainty engendered by floating are sources of unemployment and of the increasingly defensive (and protectionist) attitude in both surplus and deficit countries. In the face of this criticism some of the American speakers continued to argue in favour of 'perfect' floating. The thesis that central banks should make no attempt to maintain exchange rate stability was strongly defended by some, although not all, American participants. They argued that fixed exchange rates are a chimera: the refusal to seek a new common *and* stable international monetary order is realism and not economic nationalism. The search for stability ('interference' with alleged 'fundamental market forces') *is* the expression of the nationalistic policies of non-US central banks.

A similar argument developed (although not along national lines) about the direction and the content of the new trading system among the Western industrialised countries and between the OECD and the advanced developing nations. It was recognised that no final break has occurred so far with the principles of a liberal world trading system. Yet, it was the conclusion of the conference that the threat of a relapse into protectionism *is* real, and it is by no means certain how long and to what extent the proliferation of restrictive new commercial practices can be reconciled with the present degree of interdependence in the world economy. In fact, strong fears were expressed at the conference that the process of integration may have been reversed and that we are moving towards a fragmented pattern of trade relations both among the developed and the developing countries.

None of the speakers and participants questioned the initial assumption of the organisers that *there has been a dangerous rise in economic nationalism since the late 1960s*. It was also the conclusion of the meeting that without a serious concerted effort the present trend will continue with disastrous consequences both for *national* and *international* prosperity.

The conference took place shortly before the Bremen Summit of the European Community and the Bonn Economic Summit of the leading OECD nations. Bremen saw an initial agreement to reverse the process of monetary disintegration in Europe; at Bonn protectionism was firmly condemned.

Developments since the summer of 1978 have borne out the conclusions of the conference: the legitimate concern about the rise of nationalism, but also the realisation of the difficulty of reversing the current trend of events. The concepts of *solidarity* and *stability* are still far from being fully accepted in Europe as the discussions and progress on the European Monetary System seem to have stopped at the level of foreign exchange market interventions. Similarly, the implementation of the Tokyo Round agreements despite the summit commitments is still far from certain.

* * * * * *

Part I of the present book explores the origins of the new economic nationalism, the relationship between monetary nationalism, floating and protectionism, and the problem of nationalism in the context of domestic and international financial markets.

Recent trends in trade policies and their impact and the trade policy outlook are dealt with in Part II. It also contains a detailed discussion of the problems of adjustment faced by producers as a result of the growth of international trade.

Part III starts with an analysis of past trends in world trade and a forecast for the 1980s, with particular attention being paid to the relationship between the OECD countries and the so-called advanced developing countries. Part III also deals with the role of multinational companies, of industrial and technology policies in shaping trade relations in the future. The book closes with an appropriate reminder that *economic* nationalism is part of the broader phenomenon of *nationalism*.

Chapter 1 describes the gradual metamorphosis of the post-war domestic and international economic order. The collapse of the gold standard was as much due to *apparent* as to *real* conflicts between domestic and external interests. The open conversion to monetary nationalism has been at the root of the crisis of the 1970s. It is argued that floating and protectionism are expressions of the same futile attempt to isolate the national economy from outside influences. This trend can be reversed only if a new consensus on economic order is established among the leading OECD countries (including the European Community, Japan and the United States) based on the principles of *stability*, *solidarity*, and *economic efficiency*. This new consensus will also have to mean the return to a system of fixed exchange rates.

In Chapter 2, *Monetary Nationalism and Floating Exchange Rates*, Robert Mundell deals with the consequences of the introduction for the first time in human history of an entirely managed monetary system without any external or objective constraints. Mundell argues that the unilateral break with the gold exchange standard by the United States and the introduction of floating exchange rates have brought less rather than more autonomy for the rest of the world. He also points out the fallacy of trying to restore balance of payments equilibrium through a system of flexible exchange rates.

In Chapter 3 on US monetary policy Benjamin Cohen argues that American monetary policy is not becoming nationalistic since it has always been nationalistic. Cohen sees the best chance for a return to greater international monetary stability in the responsible behaviour of the United States and in the improvement of the coordination for economic policies among the members of the OECD.

In Chapter 4 on US balance of payments policies, Rimmer de Vries puts up a spirited defense of floating exchange rates and of the internationalist character of American policies. He argued in June 1978 that the dollar was overvalued against some of the major currencies (his remarks brought some ruffles in exchange rates the Monday following the conference). While pointing to the inflation in the United States as a major problem, he also stands by the official thesis that central bank interventions in foreign exchange markets, because they allegedly delay the correction of fundamental disequilibria, could lead to more protectionist policies in the United States.

In Chapter 5 Innocenzo Cipolletta deals with a key issue of the current economic disorders: the impact of floating exchange rates on the weak currency countries. Using the case of Italy as an example he persuasively argues that the introduction of flexible exchange rates, far from providing greater autonomy for more effective growth policies, has been a major factor in the slower growth and the weakening of the Italian economy. Thus, the revival of protectionism, in the case of the weak currency countries, can be directly linked to the current international monetary system.

In Chapter 6 on financial markets and economic nationalism, Nicolas Krul examines a vast range of national interventions and their impact on welfare and on the efficient functioning of financial markets. While there is a good case for some of these controls, they often do not achieve the expected effect. Distortions resulting from nationalistic policies tend to reduce the allocative efficiency of financial markets and tend to maintain the cost of financing in most countries at an artificially high level.

In the first chapter of Part II, Richard Blackhurst argues that 'a majority of the domestic and international economic problems which have plagued the world economy in recent years can be traced to an inadequate pace of adjustment in patterns of production and trade in the industrial countries'. He also reminds the reader that the dichotomy between domestic and international interests is a false one, and that import restrictions also mean restrictions on exports and thus a loss of jobs.

In their paper on 'The Multi-Tier GATT System' (Chapter 8) Gerard and Victoria Curzon pay tribute to the unprecedented and unexpected success of trade liberalisation among the industrialised countries. While they feel that the achievements of the GATT system are fairly robust, they also warn of the pitfalls that are still lying ahead in the form of non-tariff barriers. They also feel that the next major challenge will be the integration of at least some of the developing countries into the liberal world trading system on a reciprocal basis.

In Chapter 9, Jacques L'Huillier uses the example of the Multi-Fibre Agreement to analyse the role of escape clauses in the GATT system and the welfare effect of so-called voluntary export restrictions. As do others, he criticises the discriminatory character of the safeguard measures.

Part III begins with Chapter 10 in which Emilio Fontela analyses the relationship between international trade and economic growth in the past and in a future perspective. Whereas the expansion of trade was a major factor of growth for the rich countries, this was not the case in the less developed world. In the future, Fontela suggests that a new impetus to growth is likely to come to the OECD countries from the growth of trade with the most rapidly industrialising developing countries. By once more leaving aside the poorest countries in the world, will the new system be any more just or equitable than the old one?

In his paper (Chapter 11) on *Europe and the Advanced Developing Countries*, Lawrence Krause demonstrates that the oil crisis did not slow down the rapid growth of production and trade of the advanced developing countries. While he does not dispute that the progress of these countries may also have potential benefits for the European countries, he points out the need for more flexible and more dynamic industrial and social policies. Without being unduly pessimistic he believes that 'the world economy is likely to be less tidy and less manageable in the future. Institutional changes will reflect the new constellation of power and new methods of negotiations may have to be developed'.

In Chapter 12, Jack Behrman presents the case of multinational enterprises as a new form of international industrial integration. The distribution of the benefits from trade and of the international division of labour is increasingly biased according to nationalistic objectives. So-called industrial policy is becoming an important instrument in this process. 'Without the use of the capabilities of the multinational enterprises', Behrman argues, 'the search for nationalistic gains and a re-distribution of the benefits will push the world still further toward mercantilism.'

According to Keichi Oshima in Chapter 13, governments today are increasingly inclined to promote technological progress and to regulate the transfer of technology in accordance with narrowly defined national objectives. In order to reverse this trend, which can be harmful to all concerned, it is not sufficient to stop at the level of general principles: in order to be effective, international cooperation must deal with specific issues and problems.

In the last chapter of the book, André Reszler looks at what is positive and what is negative in the idea of nationalism. In historical terms nationalism is a relatively recent phenomenon. While in many instances it may be the last defense against a loss of identity, all too often in the past nationalism became arrogant and aggressive, and ultimately destroyed the very values it aimed to uphold. It is on this note of concern, on the difficulty of distinguishing between 'good' and 'bad' nationalism, that he joins the other authors in their preoccupation about the destructive potential of economic nationalism.

Part I: Monetary Nationalism, Protectionism and the Balance of Payments

1 The New Economic Nationalism

Otto Hieronymi

THE REVIVAL OF ECONOMIC NATIONALISM

The 1970s have witnessed an open revival of economic nationalism. This development has been in apparent contrast with the progress and the unexpected success of world-wide economic and financial integration of the last 30 years.[1]

The increased calls for protection, the frequent derogations from the rules of free trade, the erratic monetary and fiscal policies are often seen as resulting from the profound shocks and structural changes that have occurred since the late 1960s. In fact, the sharp fluctuations in exchange rates, demand and prices have all led to a more defensive attitude on the part of governments, unions and businessmen and can be directly linked to the adoption of a broad range of protectionist measures throughout the OECD countries.[2]

Ten years ago economic nationalism was mainly an issue in the context of the developing countries.[3] Most of the nations which had only recently obtained *political* independence sought to achieve *economic* independence through protection and the pursuit of nationalistic development policies. The most heralded and most successful act of economic nationalism in the 1970s was the dramatic oil price increase of six years ago. Also, in the first half of the 1970s, visions of the 'new international economic order' referred primarily to the North–South debate and the relations between rich and poor countries.[4]

Yet, today the issue of economic nationalism has once more become the central concern and responsibility of the Western developed countries. The revival of protectionism has been linked to changes in the real world, in production, trade and employment. It has been, however, also a sequel to *monetary nationalism* and to the breakdown of the fixed exchange rate system.[5] The crisis of the 1970s – as was that of the 1930s – has been the crisis of the liberal economic order. The upheavals in the 1970s have been the result of the break in Europe and in the United States with the post-war consensus on economic order.[6] It is still widely hoped that the upsurge of economic nationalism may turn out to be a passing phenomenon. However, the breakdown of order has also led to changes in the perception of real or alleged national interests. The story of the revival of economic nationalism cannot be entirely read in the history of economic events. It is the thesis of this article that the trend of ideas has been an important factor behind the metamorphosis and the threatening breakdown of the post-war economic system: without returning to a new common vision, economic nationalism will increasingly shape the course of future events.

ECONOMIC INTEGRATION AND GROWTH

It has been said that there is a *natural* tendency towards protection: the instinct of businessmen and governments is *against*, not *for* free trade and more competition. All government policy is meant to promote national prosperity and to safeguard national interests. The essence of economic nationalism lies in the efforts to achieve this objective through (i) shielding the national economy against outside influences and (ii) aggressive and discriminatory policies against foreigners. Economic nationalism, as *all* forms of nationalism, tends to emphasise the real or apparent conflict of interests between one's own country and the rest of the world.[7] According to the doctrine of economic nationalism the costs (in terms of social and economic stability and friction, and in terms of policy harmonisation) tend to outweigh the benefits of economic and monetary integration.

Economic liberals have argued since the eighteenth century that integration *is* in the national interest: the increase in efficiency and in prosperity which it brings, if its benefits are equitably distributed, will outweigh the social and economic costs of adjustment.

The post-war efforts of the United States and of the European governments to establish a world economic order based on the rejection of the principles of economic nationalism proved to be successful beyond all expectations. The degree of integration, the freedom of trade and payments achieved by the 1970s exceeded the hopes of the most ardent advocates of free trade. The exceptional record of growth and spreading prosperity since World War II has furnished an impressive proof of the theorem that

– trade liberalisation and international trade are a major source of growth, and
– economic growth promotes trade, and it is only in a dynamic or growing economy that the constant adjustments required by international trade and foreign competition can be accomplished without excessive social tensions or political opposition.

While quantitative estimates of economic growth for a more distant past are subject to fairly wide margins of error, there is no doubt that the record of growth of output *and* trade in the 1950s and 1960s had no parallel in previous economic history.[8] Growth and prosperity were quite widespread in geographic terms also, with virtually all the industrialised countries participating in this process. Even the countries plagued by the well-known stop–go cycles, experienced on the whole a sustained growth of production and a more rapid expansion of trade. Moreover, the post-war period witnessed a general convergence of economic conditions and living standards among the OECD countries. Although differences in wealth and productivity between individual countries (or the regions in the various countries) were not expected to disappear entirely in the foreseeable future, there was a general tendency up to the early 1970s for economic differences to decrease, rather than increase.

Despite the setbacks of the last decade, including the rise of unemployment and of economic uncertainty, trade and production continue to grow: the credit for today's unprecedented prosperity and for the resilience of our economic structures can be largely attributed to the lowering or elimination of tariffs, the banning of quantitative import quotas, the achievement of currency convertibility, the liberalisation of the movement of capital and labour, the control of cartels and the promotion of competition, that is to say *to the success of integration in the world economy*.

THE FOUNDATIONS OF THE POST-WAR ECONOMIC ORDER

The conditions for the integration of the world economy were provided by the emergence of a consensus on economic order in the Western industrialised countries in the aftermath of World War II. This consensus was related both to the internal sphere and to the interdependence between the domestic and the international economy. Transcending economic theory and specific policies, as well as national boundaries, the new economic order was based on the principles of *stability, economic efficiency and solidarity*. These fundamental principles could be recognised behind the complex rules, institutions and policies in the international economy and they were at the root of the objectives and policies pursued by the individual governments.

The apparent consensus on basic objectives was not the product of a single school of thought. In fact the post-war period saw rather sharp differences at the level of both economic theory and government policy, in the United States as well as in Europe, with respect to the merits of specific objectives and the appropriate means to attain them.[9] The experience of the 1930s and of the immediate post-war years provided, at the level of both theoretical insight and of political will, the main source for defining the essential features and for bolstering the emerging post-war economic order. The fear of economic instability, unemployment, protectionism and currency speculation, and ultimately the fear of war, all played a role in this process.

The notion of *stability* covered the efforts to avoid unemployment and excessive fluctuations in economic activity, as well as the objective of stable prices and exchange rates.

The principle of *economic efficiency* had several dimensions. It involved the efficient use of productive resources, the bolstering of the market economy and of the effective functioning of the price system, and limitations on cartels and direct government planning. In the international area it involved non-discrimination and the gradual elimination of barriers to the free movement of goods, services, labour and capital.

The new economic order did not mean a return to nineteenth century Manchester capitalism. The essential complement to the objectives of stability and economic efficiency was the principle of *solidarity*. In the international area it involved foreign aid and balance of payments assistance. At the national level, solidarity implied the introduction or strengthening of social security legislations, unemployment benefits and various forms of adjustment or reconversion assistance for individual industries or regions. Both in the domestic and in the international area solidarity went beyond charity or assistance to the victims of competition: it implied the idea of a common economic future. The vision of a common economic future was the ultimate foundation of domestic *and* international economic order, of the success of reconstruction and of European and world-wide integration.

The success of post-war policies aiming at both stabilization *and* increased prosperity helped maintain and strengthen the commitment to a common economic order: the pursuit of conflicting domestic and external policies and the abandoning of the vision of a common future led to the gradual revival of economic nationalism and the current crisis of economic order.

DOMESTIC VS. INTERNATIONAL ECONOMIC ORDER

The origins of the crisis of economic order date from well before the 1970s. The issue of economic nationalism was never fully resolved even in the industrialised countries. There has been a marked dichotomy between economic theory, economic policies and the trend of events throughout the post-war period. The *real* or *alleged* conflict between domestic and external policy objectives and the degree of autonomy of national governments have been at the centre of the economic policy debate of the last 30 years.[10]

In the 1950s, which were a period of rapid growth *and* effective world-wide stabilisation, there was a strengthening and spreading of the idea that some inflation was necessary for growth. It was only a minority of economists and governments which adhered to the assumption that inflation was not necessary but was inimical in the long run to growth. It was widely argued, that balance of payments discipline was highly onerous because it reduced the autonomy of national authorities to pursue effective growth and full-employment policies. Yet, the spreading of the fallacy of a permanent dollar shortage[11] coincided with the strengthening of the external payments position of the European economies. The growing acceptance of the view that it is difficult, if not impossible, to achieve simultaneously full employment, price stability and external equilibrium represented first a *theoretical*, and subsequently a *de facto*, break between the objectives of domestic and international economic order.

The 1960s witnessed the great debate on the reform of the international monetary system; under the impetus of the theories of Professor Triffin, the big scare of a world-wide liquidity shortage came into being.[12] The fear of a potential shortage of liquidity which dominated the reform debate was a logical extension of the idea of a dollar shortage and of the preoccupation with the excessive burden of the adjustment process (hence the need for increased liquidity). The discussions about the reform of Bretton Woods, like the theories of the dollar shortage, were dominated by the fear of deflation. To recall the inflationary bias of the reform discussion, it should be noted that the debate about liquidity creation flourished during a period that saw the birth and uncontrolled growth of the Eurocurrency markets; the system of Special Drawing Rights was designed and set in motion at the start of the most explosive growth of international liquidity in economic history.

Initially exchange rate flexibility was not a central issue in the debate on the reform of the international monetary system. With the uncontrolled growth of international liquidity and currency speculation, however, the complaints about the difficulty of maintaining exchange rate stability began to grow.[13]

Despite the unprecedented (and largely unexpected) success of world-wide economic integration, there was a further insistence in the 1960s on the alleged need for greater economic policy autonomy of individual national governments. For over 20 years the system of stable exchange rates, of quota and tariff liberalisation, and of currency convertibility was based on the assumption of *converging* (rather than *conflicting*) objectives of domestic growth and stability and international stability and trade. Yet, simultaneously with the progress of integration, the conflict theory of the balance of payments, which tends to emphasise the contradiction, rather than the harmony between domestic and external objectives, was gaining further ground both in deficit and surplus countries. Whereas American and British economists considered 'external discipline' a major obstacle to effective growth policies, in Germany the 1960s witnessed the search for policies to deal with the problem of 'imported inflation'. Thus, international economic *solidarity* increasingly came to be seen as a burden rather than as an advantage.[14]

The Bretton Woods system was gradually undermined by inflationary policies pursued in the United States and several other OECD countries, by the unwillingness to control the growth of the Eurocurrency markets and by widespread currency speculation. It was, however, also weakened by the reform debate and by the lessening belief and decreasing commitment to a joint search for domestic and external *stability* in both 'inflationary' and 'non-inflationary' countries.

Today's international monetary system is the result of the reform discussion, although the system bears little resemblance to most of the proposals put forward during the 1960s. By stressing the wrong issues—for example liquidity *creation* instead of liquidity *control*, increased *flexibility* instead of *stability* – much of the reform discussion was not only redundant but positively harmful. By trying to increase, rather than reduce, the real or apparent autonomy of national monetary and fiscal policies, the reform discussion reinforced, rather than weakened, the trend towards the revival of monetary nationalism.

MONETARY NATIONALISM AND FLOATING EXCHANGE RATES

The breakdown of the gold exchange standard and of fixed exchange rates was not the outcome of systematic planning, but of crisis developments.[15] However, the devaluation of the dollar, the gradual introduction of floating exchange rates and ultimately the Jamaica Agreement, not only resulted from the pressure of events; they also reflected theoretical views and interpretations of (i) the impact of exchange rate changes on balance of payments adjustment, (ii) the expected additional freedom to be gained by national authorities under flexible exchange rates, and (iii) the alleged compatibility of a system of floating exchange rates with a liberal world economic order. While initially some of these views were confined to abstract discussions, from the mid-1960s on, there was an interpenetration between popular prejudices (in particular by participants in the foreign exchange markets) and the theories (influenced by these prejudices) of writers on international economic matters.

The first point (embodied in the original articles of the Bretton Woods Agreement) was the apparent need for periodic exchange rate adjustments also under a system of fixed exchange rates. Such changes were thought to be required by shifts in competitive conditions and were to restore equilibrium in the current account of the balance of payments. These views – widely held in the 1960s – were largely at the root of the speculation against the pound sterling, in favour of the mark and ultimately against the dollar: they led to the devaluation of the pound in 1967, the revaluation of the mark in 1969 and the devaluation of the dollar in 1971.

For a host of reasons (which include changes in productivity and in inflation rates *following* revaluation or devaluation) the impact of exchange rate changes on the current account since the 1960s has been neutral or negative; that is to say, the opposite of what was expected by governments and the foreign exchange markets. The notion of 'fundamental disequilibrium' given as a guideline by the IMF, the Bundesbank and all the leading central banks to participants in the foreign exchange market has so far escaped qualitative or econometric definition (although not for a want of trying).

Flexible exchange rates were also seen as an arm against speculation induced by expected changes under the par-value system, as well as against erratic capital movements due to differences in interest rates required by balance of payments adjustment. *Monetary nationalism*, the attempt to *insulate* the economy from outside influences in the monetary sphere, was first invented in the 1930s in an attempt to cope with the problem of *imported deflation*.[16] The incipient monetary nationalism of the 1960s and the monetary nationalism enshrined in the revised articles of the IMF Agreement have attempted to cope with both the threat of *imported deflation* and the problem of *imported inflation*.[17]

Speculation in the 1970s, however, became greater and wilder than ever before. The record of the last ten years has exploded the theory of 'smooth' adjustment through flexible exchange rates. The hope that under floating there would be less need for *wanted* external reserves (that is to say, wanted by the suspect countries), and for *unwanted* reserves (by Germany, Switzerland and other virtuous countries) turned out to be unfounded.[18]

Smooth adjustment and the autonomy of domestic policies under floating proved to be illusory also in a more fundamental sense. Notwithstanding the shortcomings of traditional demand management under fixed exchange rates, floating has *reduced*, rather than increased, the effectiveness of fiscal and monetary policies in maintaining or restoring external *and* domestic equilibrium. The symmetry, the sharing of the burden of balance of payments adjustment, which existed under fixed exchange rates, has disappeared under flexible exchange rates. A balance of payments surplus tends to push up the exchange rate and thus helps maintain price stability; an external deficit, through the downward pressure on the exchange rate, has in turn an inflationary impact.[19] This perverse effect is reinforced by speculative capital movements. Since a current account deficit is a sign of 'disequilibrium', a depreciation is anticipated. The record has shown that exchange rate speculation overrides interest rate differentials; thus under floating, once a 'fundamental disequilibrium' is suspected, capital movements *reinforce* rather than *soften* the effect of the trade and current account imbalance. Whether it is a small or large country (including the United States), under floating, it takes a larger dose of *deflation* in a deficit country, or of *inflation* in a surplus country, to restore external balance than under a system of fixed rates.[20] While floating exchange rates provide less rather than more autonomy, they at all levels further the sensation of growing apart, of the separateness of the national economies.

Originally, the advocates of exchange rate flexibility lived in a world of neat alternatives: it was *either* protection *or* changes in exchange rates.[21] Whereas trade is at the basis of the international division of labour and of the world's prosperity, changes in exchange rates are a small price to pay for safeguarding the freedom of trade and payments.

Related to the difficulty of closing the gap between 'virtuous' and inflationary countries (and in the 1980s maybe it will be *deflationary* countries), the gravest consequence of floating is likely to be its role in the revival of protectionism. The fallacy of the argument that there was no link between *monetary nationalism* and *protectionism*, and that one was a substitute for the other, had been pointed out over 40 years ago.[22] While floating is the international monetary system of economic nationalism *par excellence* (it reflects the same desire for shielding the national economy in the monetary field, as tariffs, quotas, export subsidies, etc. do in the field of trade), it is not a substitute for protectionism. This has been shown by the record of the 1930s and of the 1970s, and has been correctly recognised by the new advocates of protectionism both in Britain and France who want both flexible exchange rates and protection against the rest of the world.[23] In fact, monetary disorders, amplified by flexible exchange rates, have become by now the principal source of protectionist pressures.[24]

THE TREND TOWARDS PROTECTIONISM

In the field of international trade no crisis has occurred thus far on a scale that would be comparable to the breakdown of international monetary order. Although increasing attention is being focused on the rise of protectionism, in both absolute and historical terms there is still an astounding degree of freedom of trade and of foreign investments in the world economy. Tariffs have been substantially reduced and quantitative restrictions have been banned on the bulk of international trade. Virtually free trade prevails among some of the principal trading nations. Compared not only with the chaotic conditions of the pre-war years, but also with the era of free trade in the second half of the nineteenth century, today's trade barriers appear to be very limited.

The present degree of integration and freedom of movement of goods, services and of factors of production (both labour and capital) are the result of a 30 year evolutionary process (including the General Agreement on Tariffs and Trade, the initial OEEC, European integration and successive GATT tariff cuts culminating in the Kennedy Round). It is a sign of the achievements and of the institutional strength of integration, that neither the monetary disorders, nor the drastic changes in the terms of trade (namely that caused by the oil price increase), nor the world-wide inflation have eradicated the official commitment to the principle of trade liberalisation. Concrete manifestations of this policy have been the pursuit of the GATT Tokyo Round negotiations (covering not only customs duties but also so-called non-tariff barriers), and the opening of talks between the European Community and prospective new members.

There are, however, also disquieting signs in the trend of trade policies, and the frequent official warnings on this subject cannot be fully ascribed to negotiating tactics in the final phase of the Tokyo Round. Today for the first time since the late 1940s, there are good reasons to be concerned about the threat of a relapse into protectionism.

In recent years there has been a growing tendency in the United States and in several Western European countries to view the rise of imports as a direct threat to domestic employment. The list of sectors claiming special treatment and protection is getting longer and longer: it includes farmers as well as major industries, such as steel, textiles and clothing, shipyards, chemicals and consumer electronics. There is also open or concealed pressure for protection in the automobile industry.[25] The number of bilateral or multilateral agreements involving import restrictions, or so-called voluntary export restraints, has increased considerably in the 1970s. Such agreements, covering broad sectors or specific products, are voluntary in name only. This trend implies a *de facto* cartellisation of international trade for the products and areas concerned. A more concealed form of protectionism is to be found in various export subsidies provided by numerous governments and administrative obstacles to imports. These have become more, rather than less, difficult to overcome, even in the industrialised countries.

The restrictions and the pressures for more protection involve not only trade between developed and developing countries, but also trade between highly industrialised areas. There is considerable strain in Japan's relations with its OECD partners, growing acrimony between the United States and the European Community, and there are actual measures, as well as further plans, to limit the freedom of trade within Europe. In contrast with the system of general preferences *in favour* of developing countries, there is a growing tendency to discriminate *against* the exports of the most successful developing countries, despite the fact that they still account for only a small share of trade in manufactures.

It has been argued that the world economy and world trade have been the victims of their own success. The problems of adjustment to foreign competition, created by the rapid, and for 30 years virtually uninterrupted growth of world trade and by the systematic reduction of trade barriers, have not been all solved either through productivity improvements or through switching into new lines of production. To some extent, developments seem to confirm tariff theory, which holds that the elimination of the final obstacles to trade is the most painful, because usually the weakest producers are protected the longest. The expansion of world trade and the rising prosperity had also inflated expectations and led to a belief that the real problem of the highly industrialised market economies was too much prosperity. A downturn, or even a halt in growth, was considered to be unlikely, despite the growing nostalgia for a less hectic life and economy.

The world-wide inflationary boom of the late 1960s and early 1970s was fuelled not only by the domestic and external deficits of the United States, but also by the confidence of governments and of monetary authorities in expansionary policies and a lack of concern about the danger of inflation. Thus, the recession and the rise of unemployment of the mid-1970s could be interpreted as correctives to the inflationary excesses of the first half of the 1970s. At its origin the revival of protectionist pressures could be linked to difficulties of adjustment at the national and international level. The current trend, however, seems to involve adjustment problems that go beyond a normal reaction to an inflationary boom. Their magnitude is the result of the general crisis of economic order.

In the first place, an important objective of economic integration had been the lessening of differences not just in economic conditions and policies, but even in the behaviour of trade unions across countries. As noted above, throughout the 1950s and 1960s remarkable progress had been achieved in this respect; greater equality in living standards and social conditions had been attained in the industrialised countries. Since the late 1960s and early 1970s there has been a halt, or even a reversal, in this process of integration. Dissimilarities in monetary and fiscal policies, in social behaviour and the considerable deterioration of labour relations in a number of countries have been partly responsible for this change. Growing labour tensions and differences in responses to inflationary developments have also contributed to breaking up the monetary solidarity within Europe as well as between Europe and the United States. The fact that today Europe and the world are once more divided into a group of strong currency and a group of weak currency countries tends to weaken the expression of common interests and common vision with respect to commercial policy.

An important consequence of the monetary disorders of the early 1970s was the size of the oil price increase of six years ago.[26] Since 1973 individual OECD countries have been trying to adjust their foreign trade pattern in such a manner that at least part of the higher oil bill should be financed through increased exports to, and diminished imports from, other OECD countries. Whereas some countries (for example Japan) have been more successful than others in implementing such a policy, for the OECD countries as a whole this policy obviously could not work. As a result, there has been a sometimes latent, sometimes open, tendency to penalise through trade restrictions those countries that manage to strengthen their trade balance at the expense of the rest of the OECD countries.

The perpetuation of the gap between inflationary and non-inflationary countries also tends to create differences in economic behaviour and in the speed of reaction to changes in demand, in competitive conditions and in the external environment in general. Experience has shown that, under the pressure of revaluation, productivity improves faster in the surplus countries than in the deficit countries. This has an impact not only on the rate of inflation but also at the level of individual sectors, often leading to requests for protection in the countries whose currency has *depreciated*.

Through the transmission and amplification of monetary disturbances, floating exchange rates have become a major source of uncertainty in the world economy. This uncertainty, which permeates all levels of economic decision-making (fiscal and monetary policy, management and investment decisions, labour as well as households) also slows down the search for bold, new solutions to structural problems and has a dampening effect on economic activity. Floating also has a destructive impact on the price mechanism and on the relationship between domestic and foreign prices. Because of the wide fluctuations in exchange rates, and the politicisation of much of the discussions about the appropriate exchange rate structure, there are frequent and sudden changes in relative prices and competitive conditions in individual industries. Whereas the substantial changes in exchange rate relationships have diminished the effectiveness of relatively low tariffs, the actual or potential changes in exchange rates have prompted calls for more effective protection of specific industries.

Michael Heilperin's assessment of over thirty years ago is being borne out by current trends. He wrote in 1946:

> Exchange rate stability is important from the point of view of both international trade and finance. That importance is greatest, contrary to popular opinion, from the long-run point of view. In the short-run it is possible to make certain safeguarding arrangements. In the long-run, however, such 'hedging' is of no avail. As regards current trade, this is a short-term transaction and therefore fairly immune to exchange fluctuations. But the international division of labor . . . is a long-run proposition. . . . The need for adaptation and the resistance to adaptation are difficult enough to cope with in practical

economic policy without aggravating the problem through monetary instability.[27]

While floating has not been the only factor behind the revival of protectionism, it is in the process of destroying the remaining basis of the liberal international economic order through its impact on uncertainty, prices and ultimately on growth.

ECONOMIC NATIONALISM AND THE ROLE OF GOVERNMENT

An important source of today's protectionism is the tendency, in deficit and surplus countries, to seek remedies for the actual or anticipated hardships caused by external disorders through government regulations, spending programmes or outright nationalisation.

In the first half of the twentieth century there was a direct link between the spreading of economic nationalism and the growing role of governments in economic life, both in collectivist and market economies. With the progress of economic integration, however, a dichotomy developed between the increasing domestic economic responsibilities of governments and the delegation of sovereignty or *de facto* limitation of government autonomy in the external field, not only in Europe, but in all OECD countries.

Economic prosperity and growth have been the principal domestic political issues after the war. Governments have increasingly assumed the credit for favourable economic conditions and the blame for poor performance. This growth of the governments' weight in economic life can only be partly explained by ideological considerations. It has been an expression of the increased role of economic objectives among *national* objectives. A central feature of Western history has been the argument about the distribution of power and responsibilities between individuals and various levels of government. Throughout history there were certain decisions which were made by the central government. As recently as the nineteenth century and early twentieth century – even in the most liberal nations – there was relatively little decentralised control over questions of war and peace. Economic decisions, however, were decentralised and only a very few aspects of economic policy were centrally controlled. Today, notwithstanding the instantaneous nature of nuclear weapons, the decision-making process about war and peace has become much more diffused and open.

Government budgets currently represent an unprecedented share of national income (even in wartime they hardly reached comparable levels). Beyond transfer payments and direct expenditures, governments exercise direct or indirect control over an additional vast range of economic decisions. The increased expectations from this broader involvement of governments in economic matters have not had, however, the expected results. This is as true for Germany and Switzerland, as it is for Britain, Italy or the United States. Whereas since the war governments have played a useful role in a number of areas (promoting economic integration, full employment and greater security and justice), their policies have resulted in more, rather than less, inflation and have often been a source of economic inefficiency. Government economic activity and government spending have been subject to the law of diminishing returns both in planned economies and in liberal, market economies. In most of these latter there has been also a drop in the quality of government services and a disenchantement with the growing weight of government, a well-known phenomenon in Eastern Europe.

The most far-reaching failure of governments, at a time when they have been trying to regulate almost all aspects of economic life, has been in the area of international monetary order. The collapse of the fixed exchange rate system may have occurred under the real or alleged pressures of market forces. The acceptance and advocacy by the major central banks of a permanent system of floating exchange rates represents, however, the abdication of one of their principal, traditional responsibilities, namely maintaining domestic *and* external monetary stability. Whereas Keynesian economics and policies have largely contributed to the breakdown of Bretton Woods, the intellectual respectability of the system of floating exchange rates is the result of the elevation of *conservative monetarism* in its turn to the level of dogma.

Initially flexible exchange rates were advocated by socialists, who argued that they represented a superior form of protection, and by conservatives, who had become disenchanted with the central banks' record with monetary management. For Professor Friedman and his followers, flexible exchange rates were to prove the superior ability of private traders to set and maintain a true market price over what they considered to be central bank price-fixing. Although most of the economists in favour of floating were convinced free traders, from the start theirs was an essentially nationalistic view of the world economy. By praising the separation of markets they undermined both the principle of solidarity and stability. They broadened, rather than reduced the scope for arbitrary government intervention, and thus weakened the foundations of the market economy.[28]

THE ATLANTIC RIFT

The rise of economic nationalism is often seen as a result of growing divergences, starting in the 1960s, on economic, monetary, political and military matters between Europe and the United States. The origins of the various streaks of anti-Americanism in Europe go back to the early post-war period. Also, in the aftermath of the Vietnam War (enhanced by European indifference or outright hostility to the American effort) a more 'hard-nosed', inward-looking attitude began to predominate in the United States in international economic matters. There is also a vague feeling (based on a serious misreading of the economic history of the 1960s) shared by American officials, businessmen and academic economists, that Europe has benefited more than the United States from the post-war international economic order; as a result there is a need for a more aggressive American policy to defend American interests at home and abroad.

The Atlantic rift also has a European dimension. The convergence of domestic and external policies, of economic, social and political norms of behaviour among the countries of Western Europe, was interrupted in the late 1960s and began to be reversed during the 1970s. This development was the result of a different impact on the 'North' and the 'South' in Europe of world-wide phenomena which partly originated, or were at least amplified, in the United States. At the economic level the concepts of *stability* and *solidarity* have been increasingly given a nationalistic, rather than a European or Atlantic interpretation.

Despite the strains on the Atlantic Alliance, the growing-apart in Europe, and the unsolved issues between Japan and its partners, political nationalism appears so far in the OECD nations to be singularly harmless: it appears to be of little importance if compared either with the nineteenth century or with the 1930s. Political nationalism in the nineteenth century was both ethnic and imperialistic; in the 1930s it was racist and imperialistic. In the 1970s political nationalism in the Western countries is largely defensive; it is of the kind that announces: 'we want to maintain our values and identity, we want less foreign entanglement'. But, there is also a strong feeling in the United States, in Britain, in Switzerland, in Japan and in Germany that more emphasis has to be put on the safeguarding of national economic interests.

While there are analogies between the economic and, in particular, the *monetary* nationalism of the 1970s and the 1930s, for the time being the differences, especially in the field of trade, continue to predominate. The belief in the irreversibility of economic interdependence is still strongly held, and there is considerable institutional opposition to protectionism.

At present institutional inertia works in favour of liberal trade policies. This inertia includes the fortunately cumbersome decision-making process in trade matters in Europe and the United States, the network of mutually binding commitments and the fear of retaliation, and the fact that trade policy is a 'messier business' than international monetary matters. The institutional inertia works at the level of international organisations as well as the public and the national governments. It also has an important dimension at the level of ideas; today the government officials dealing with international trade matters are still by and large free traders. This is in sharp contrast with the prevailing attitude in central banks and banks. The conversion to the doctrine of floating exchange rates (the view that the possibility *and* desirability of fixed exchange rates are part of a long-forgotten past) at the *technical level* has been quasi-universal in the United States and Britain, and to a large extent also on the Continent.[29]

The rise of protectionism and the increased respectability of protectionist theories are of more recent date. The conclusion of this article is that the impact of the ideas of 'new Cambridge' or organised free trade, of 'voluntary export and import agreements', of countervailing duties, of selective safeguards, of regional blocks, 'spheres of influence' and of discrimination against developing countries or of protective industrial policies cannot be assessed in a short-term perspective only. At present they still seem to represent exceptions or minority views. Their potential threat for the future, however, has to be seen in the light of the destructive experience with the gradual metamorphosis of the objectives of the international monetary system.

THE SEARCH FOR A NEW CONSENSUS

The revival of economic nationalism has not been a temporary occurrence. Either the continuation of the present economic trend (the persistance of inflation, unemployment and uncertainty) or a cataclysmic event (a protracted world-wide recession) could bring about an ultimate break with the liberal economic order in the field of trade as well. At the political level, at least in Europe, there seems to be an increased awareness of this threat. The most disturbing feature in this situation is still the attitude of the United States; there is a continued leadership vacuum in international economic matters, which cannot be concealed through regional arrangements.

Today, as after World War II, a new consensus on domestic and international economic order is needed. This consensus can be based, beyond the complexity of daily issues and real or apparent conflicts of interests, only on a vision of a common economic future for *all* the OECD countries.

This new consensus does not mean a return to the past. In order to be durable, however, it has to include the principles that provided the basis for the success of world-wide integration.

The issue of monetary *stability* is the central theme of the preoccupation about the future. Continued inflation and/or isolated attempts at deflation could accelerate the crisis of credit structures, inducing a chain reaction of bankruptcies and a world-wide depression. Stabilisation, aiming at the stability of prices and exchange rates, has to be the result of a joint plan and concerted action. It cannot be the result of sporadic and half-hearted exchange market interventions. While such a plan may require a partial return to gold or the creation of composite reserve assets, it has to include, in order to be effective, not only Europe, but the United States and Japan.

It should be noted that stability also means full employment; the full utilisation of resources (including labour) is the best guarantee for both growth and price stability. The impact of the crisis and the cost of stabilisation vary among the major OECD countries. Without effective *solidarity* the chances of success are limited. In financial terms the requirements would be still well below the potential loss of output or the amounts mobilised in exchange market interventions. The true sense of solidarity, however, will mean above all a renewal of the belief in a common future.

Economic efficiency will be a central concern of the 1980s. The main structural impact in Europe and the United States of the crisis of the 1970s has been not the predictable breakdown of the management of demand (of the fiscal and monetarist type), but the negative impact of events on the elasticity of supply. The calls for protection mean a fear of competition: with *or* without restrictions, the coming decade will see increasing competition. The views of a cartellised world of businessmen and economists are as far removed from reality as the daydreams of a world economy based on barter were 30 years ago. In order to sustain *economic efficiency*, solidarity both on a domestic level (in regional policy, in favour of the unemployed, etc.) and on an international level must not be weakened, but reinforced.

The return to a new consensus may still be blocked at the political level, but there is also a growing danger that once more, as in the 1950s and 1960s, economic theory is falling behind the trend of events. Through the continued search for the perfect system of floating exchange rates, the econometric measurements of the natural rate of inflation in individual countries and through Malthusian discussions on how to save work and reduce efficiency, the economics profession, despite its free trade convictions, may contribute to making economic nationalism the permanent order of the future.

NOTES

1. The views expressed in this paper are those of the author, and are not to be attributed to Battelle.
2. There is a rapidly growing literature dealing with the various aspects of the threat of protectionism. Cf. for example, Richard Blackhurst, Nicolas Marian and Jan Tumlir: *Trade Liberalization, Protectionism and Interdependence*, (Geneva: GATT Studies in International Trade, November 1977); International Monetary Fund, Trade and Payments Division, *The Rise in Protectionism* (Washington, DC: July 1978). A recent study carried out at Battelle–Geneva dealt with this problem in the European–Japanese context. Cf. André Gabus, Otto Hieronymi, Pàl Kukorelly, *Japanese–European Trade Relations – Restrictions or Cooperation? The Case of the Automobile Industry* for The Top '70 Study Group (Geneva 1978).
3. Cf. Harry G. Johnson (ed.), *Economic Nationalism in Old and New States* (Chicago: The University of Chicago Press, 1967).
4. Cf. for example 'North–South Relations: An Uncertain Future', *Annals of International Studies*, Vol. 7, Geneva 1976, and literature quoted therein. It is

generally recognised that the slow progress in the international discussions on how to improve the position of the developing countries is due, to a significant extent, to the increased problems faced by the developed countries in the 1970s.

5. The most systematic discussion of monetary nationalism and of the link between monetary nationalism and protectionism is still provided by Professor Hayek's 1937 Geneva lectures: Friedrich A. Hayek, *Monetary Nationalism and International Stability* (New York: Reprints of Economic Classics, A. M. Kelley, 1964, first published 1937).
The close relationship between monetary and so-called real phenomena is an important feature of general economic theory, and of balance of payments theory in particular. Time and again this relationship has been denied or misrepresented, as in the IMF report quoted above, according to which 'available evidence suggests that payments imbalances or fluctuations in exchange rates have not been a major factor in the increasing resort to trade restrictions'. (*The Rise in Protectionism*, op. cit., p. 52).
6. Otto Hieronymi, 'Growth and Economic Order: The Long-Term Outlook' *Annals of International Studies*, Vol. 8, Geneva, 1978, pp. 51–9.
7. The expression 'economic nationalism', first coined in the 1930s, refers to the attempts to control as far as possible a country's external economic relations; it implies the pursuit of policies aimed at a reduction or a break in a country's economic interdependence with the rest of the world. The 1930s witnessed the most extreme forms of economic nationalism in Communist and National–Socialist totalitarianism. Harry Johnson argued that 'the infiltration of ideas from central Europe into the Anglo–Saxon tradition did a great deal to implant the habit of thinking in nationalistic rather than cosmopolitan terms in the Western economic tradition . . .' (Johnson, op. cit., p. 131). Since the 1930s, however, Anglo–Saxon economics has been a major source of nationalistic theories and policies. On the role of Keynesian economics in the spreading of economic nationalism (a factor that is also recognised by Johnson) cf. Michael A. Heilperin, *Studies in Economic Nationalism* (Geneva: Librairie Droz, 1962) and Wilhelm Röpke, *International Economic Disintegration* (London: William Hodge, 1942). In the 1960s and the 1970s Anglo–American monetarism became part of a similar phenomenon.
8. Cf. Simon Kuznets, *Economic Growth of Nations. Total Output and Production Structure* (Cambridge, Mass.: The Belknap Press of Harvard University, 1971).
9. There was considerable scepticism about the chances of success of a liberal economic order, especially in the United Kingdom and in the Scandinavian countries, largely, although not exclusively, under the impact of Keynesian economics. Cf. Seymour E. Harris, *The New Economics* (New York: Reprints in Economic Classics, A. Kelley, 1965, first published in 1947); Thomas Balogh, *Unequal Partners*, Vols. I and II (Oxford: Blackwell, 1963). In the 1940s there were many who believed that the future of the world economy lay in the rational organisation of international *barter*. According to Ragnar Frisch, 'it is chimerical to believe that the strangulation produced by the payments effects will be eliminated by lowering tariff barriers and restoring a freer organisation of world trade'. (Ragnar Frisch, 'On the Need for Forecasting a Multilateral Balance of Payments', *American Economic Review*, September 1947, p. 539).
10. On the debate on the conflict between domestic and external objectives cf. Otto Hieronymi, *Economic Discrimination Against the United States in Western*

Europe 1945–1958. Dollar Shortage and the Rise of Regionalism (Geneva: Librairie Droz, 1973) pp. 37–61, and the literature quoted there.

11. Donald MacDougall's famous *World Dollar Problem* was published in 1957 (London: Macmillan); as late as 1960 MacDougall continued to warn of the threat of a dollar shortage. Donald MacDougall, *The Dollar Problem; A Reappraisal*, Essays in International Finance, No. 35 (Princeton: 1960). Cf. also Hieronymi, *Economic Discrimination*, op. cit.
12. Cf. Robert Triffin, *Gold and the Dollar Crisis* (New Haven: Yale University Press, 1960).
13. In Germany, the Council of Economic Experts (Sachverständigenrat zur Begutachtung der Gesamtwirtschaftlichen Entwicklung) began to advocate exchange rate flexibility at an early date as a means of 'aussenwirtschaftliche Abschirmung' (protection against outside influences). Cf. for example the Council's *Jahresgutachten* (Annual Reports) for *1966/67* and *1967/68*. In their views about the need for 'Abschirmung' they were seconded by the Minister of Economics Schiller, although not by the entire policy making establishment.
14. For internal political reasons, the unwanted increase in dollar holdings by European central banks in the 1960s was never officially called *foreign aid* to the United States. Had the European governments officially accepted to give *foreign aid* to the United States, which they were *de facto* doing, this might have given them added political leverage to reduce the inflationary bias of the international monetary system. Such an open manifestation of Atlantic *solidarity*, even though it was in the interests of the European countries, was unthinkable not only in France, but also in Germany.
15. According to Richard Nixon, the principal mover in the decisions of August 1971 was John Connally, who also headed Nixon's list of the 'men who understood the intricate complexities of economics'. Nixon, comforted by the subsequent popularity of floating in the United States, considers that the decision 'to close the gold window and let the dollar float . . . turned out to be the best thing that came out of the whole economic program' of August 1971. (*The Memoirs of Richard Nixon*, New York: Grosset and Dunlap, 1978, pp. 519–20).
16. Cf. Hayek, op. cit and Heilperin, op. cit.
17. The United States was the principal mover behind the return to monetary nationalism and the drive towards a system of national currencies without any stable link to each other or to gold. As noted by the IMF's Legal Counsel, 'the United States sought to eradicate from the Second Amendment [of the IMF Articles] any obligation to convert foreign official holdings of a currency and to avoid any impression that the United States would be willing ever again to undertake such a commitment in relation to the dollar.' (Joseph Gold, *The Second Amendment of the Funds Articles of Agreement*, Washington, DC: International Monetary Fund, 1978, p. 13).
18. The Bundesbank's official dollar holdings (expressed in German marks) amounted to DM70 bn in September 1978 compared with DM30 bn at the end of 1970, and an average of about DM10 bn in the second half of the 1960s.
19. Under the present system there is a mercantilistic preoccupation with the current account. Despite the spreading of monetarism, the *global character* of the balance of payments (the sum of all incoming and outgoing payments) seems to be lost on most operators in the foreign exchange markets. On the sector

approach to the balance of payments, cf. Otto Hieronymi, *Economic Discrimination*, op. cit., pp. 54–61.

20. Some of these limitations were noted in Robert Mundell's article 'Capital Mobility and Stabilization under Fixed and Flexible Exchange Rates' (1963), reprinted in Richard E. Caves and Harry G. Johnson (ed.), *Readings in International Economics* (London: George Allen and Unwin, 1968) pp. 487–99. On the cost of adjustment and the greater burden of the weak currency countries, cf. also Otto Hieronymi, 'The New Economic Order: The Need for Increased Growth in the Developed Countries', *Annals of International Studies*, Vol. 7, Geneva 1976. Otmar Emminger, while an ardent advocate of floating, also recognises the lack of symmetry in the burden of adjustment under the present system. Cf. Otmar Emminger in Robert Mundell and Jacques J. Polak (eds.), *The New International Monetary System* (Columbia University Press, 1977) pp. 4–7.
21. Cf. Milton Friedman, 'The Case for Flexible Exchange Rates' in *Essays in Positive Economics* (Chicago: University of Chicago Press, 1953) and James Meade, 'The Case for Variable Exchange Rates', *Three Banks Review*, 1955. As recently as 1976 'Professor Corden remarked that floating exchange rates had spared the world a multitude of trade restrictions which, in a fixed-exchange-rate world, would have been imposed by governments trying to cope with the emergency balance-of-payments situation arising from the oil price increase. Instead of trade restrictions governments had resorted to a superior method of adjusting to a payments imbalance.' In Harry G. Johnson, *Trade Negotiations and the New International Monetary System*, Gerard and Victoria Curzon (eds.), (Geneva: Graduate Institute of International Studies, 1976) p. 34. This argument confuses the ability of strong currency countries to correct the terms of trade by revaluing their currencies, and the increased burden that fell on the weak currency countries as a result of the combined impact of the oil price increase *and* devaluation. For the same fallacy cf. the IMF report quoted above.
22. 'It is an illusion that it would be possible, while remaining a member of the international commercial community, to prevent disturbances from the outside world from reaching the country by following a national monetary policy such as would be indicated if the country were a closed community.' (Hayek, *Monetary Nationalism and International Stability*, op. cit., p. 71).
23. The impact of erratic exchange rate movements on free trade is shown by the case of Switzerland. Despite the country's liberal tradition and despite the fact that Switzerland has had the largest current account surplus in terms of GNP in the world, the meteoric rise of the Swiss franc has led to widespread calls for protecting the export industry through export subsidies, split exchange rates, etc.
24. Jean-Marcel Jeanneney, *Pour un nouveau protectionisme* (Paris: Seuil, 1978) and Francis Cripps and Wynne Godley, 'Control of Imports as a Means to Full Employment and the Expansion of World Trade: the UK's Case', *Cambridge Journal of Economics*, September 1978, pp. 327–34.
25. Cf. *Japanese–European Trade Relations*, op. cit.
26. The commodity inflation of 1973 was made possible and was feeding on the uncontrolled growth of liquidity which had been the result of the disintegration of Bretton Woods. At the time of the oil price increase, flexible

exchange rates still gave the temporary illusion that the balance of payments adjustment process had become less painful. By raising the price of oil step by step, the OPEC countries were testing both the strength of this illusion and the political will of the OECD countries to resist their pressure. Under the system of fixed exchange rates, when the impact of balance of payments disturbances on real aggregates was more apparent, it would have been inconceivable for the OPEC countries to propose and for the OECD countries to accept the quadrupling of the price of oil in such a short time span.

27. M. A. Heilperin, *The Trade of Nations* (London: Longmanns, Green and Co., 1946) p. 50.

28. It is also interesting to note the contradiction between the generally sceptical views of these conservatives on government and central bank performance, and their belief and prediction that governments would not try to take advantage of the apparent freedom provided by flexible exchange rates to pursue inflationary policies.

29. Harry Johnson's dictum that 'fixed rates produce the times of crisis, and floating rates resolve them', (Harry Johnson, 'The Future of Floating Rates' in E. Claasen and P. Salin, (eds.), *Recent Issues in International Monetary Economics*, (Amsterdam: North–Holland, 1976, p. 417) became the conventional wisdom of the 1970s. It is as firmly believed in by the Italian Communist Party (cf. *Unita*, 3 December 1978, quoted in *Le Monde*, 10 December 1978) as by the ORDO liberals in Germany (cf. Alfred Bosch, Walter Eucken Institut, 'Nationale und internationale Aspekte der deutschen Stabilisierungspolitik', *Neue Zürcher Zeitung*, 2/3 December 1978).

2 Monetary Nationalism and Floating Exchange Rates

Robert Mundell

The international economic system has changed a great deal over the past decade. To understand it we have to keep renewing our evaluation of its evolution. We must find the similarities between the past and the present in order to predict the world of the future – if we are optimistic enough to think we can say something about the future. We must seek the similarities between the present and the past while recognising the differences.

In some cases, the differences are obvious while the similarities are concealed. That has been the experience of the turbulent twentieth century in the monetary area. In other cases, the differences are very hard to find and the similarities are obvious. That happens when the world has a more unified monetary system, as in the ordered nineteenth century. The nineteenth century, like the thirteenth century, was a century of relative order. The twentieth century, like the fourteenth century, is a century of disorder, and this disorder appears on the surface. It is revealed most dramatically in the monetary system which has been changing its form over and over again. Yet underneath these changes are some invariants.

Since 1971, we have moved through three or four different international economic systems. In eight years we have had more experience with international monetary systems than Alfred Marshall had in his whole lifetime. Marshall said in 1912 that he never tired of repeating the fact that the most important thing one could say about currency was that it is unimportant! He stressed the unimportance of currency because in his world of convertible currencies the gold bloc acted as a single monetary unit. Notwithstanding his extensive knowledge of monetary events,

Marshall did not see the need to do much pioneering work in monetary theory because, in his time, he saw no real problems in monetary theory. His greatest novelty was his development of symmetallism – a basket of gold and silver – which is the forerunner of the SDR. But it was the monetary turbulence of the 1920s and the great depression of the 1930s that produced Keynes.

In the twentieth century we have had such confusion in the monetary system that everybody seems to be a monetary expert. In fact, we are faced with so many monetary experts and so many explanations for each problem that it is difficult to judge who is right and who is wrong. We have champions of both fixed and flexible exchange rates, advocates of the gold standard, the dollar standard and the SDR standards; monetarists and fiscalists, optimum currency area specialists, integrationists and so on. Those of us who grew up on the gold exchange system, when the world was stable, used to be able to call ourselves monetary experts; today the public might be forgiven for doubting whether we really are monetary experts anymore.

THE BREAKDOWN OF BRETTON WOODS

If we ask ourselves how historians will perceive the cause of the breakdown of the gold exchange standard in 1971, we can come up with a variety of opinions. A first answer would be that the system broke down in 1971 because of the shortage of gold. A second explanation is the inflation generated by the US deficit. A third reply is the decline of the United States political leadership in NATO. A fourth is the challenge with which Western Europe confronted the Americans in August 1971 by its request for gold. A fifth answer is distress at inflation in Western Europe supposedly imported from America. A sixth explanation is the political conflict behind the distribution of the burden of balance of payments adjustment between the United States, on the one hand, and Japan and Europe, on the other. A seventh is the breakdown of monetary discipline and the rise in inflationary expectations caused by the creation of Special Drawing Rights leading to an expected shift in the global money supply function. An eighth is the social revolution in the United States in 1968, as well as the passage of power from a generation of inflation haters to one of inflation lovers spreading gradually over the entire world. A ninth is the uncontrolled explosion of the Eurodollar market and the growing recognition of the huge profits to be made from Eurobanking. A tenth is the expectation in Western Europe that the weakening of the dollar would promote a movement towards monetary union, based on a Eurocurrency.

I stop at ten only because ten is, Arabically speaking, a round number. Actually, all these explanations are part of a syndrome; in fact, they may be parts of one explanation. The question now is, when we have an explanation how do we know that it is valid? It seems to me that our explanation is viable when it enables us to make some sort of prediction about the future – without this *predictive* aspect, our explanation is meaningless. We don't understand the past unless we can predict the future. That is the only way in which historians can ever tell effectively whether they have an accurate explanation of what has been happening. Following this line of reasoning, we can ask why the gold exchange standard broke down in 1971. We can also ask why it broke down in 1931. Was the breakdown in 1931 the same as the breakdown in 1971? Could we have predicted the actual events following 1931? If we could have predicted the breakdown in 1931, could we have predicted the breakdown in 1971? If that were possible, then we might be able to say that history may repeat itself, since five years after the breakdown of 1931, we had a tripartite agreement and a movement back towards fixed exchange rates and a renewed gold standard. Having observed these events in 1931 and 1936, then, we can expect something to happen five years after 1971.

In fact, in 1976, a new international exchange system was created, under the Jamaïca Agreement. This was not a restoration of the fixed exchange system, but rather a new system of managed flexible exchange rates. But then one can ask why the world moved towards flexible rates in 1976, yet back towards fixed rates in 1936. If we can come up with a plausible explanation, then we can say that we are beginning to understand the underlying forces separating these systems from others.

To begin with, there is a *superficial* difference between the experience of the 1930s and that of the 1970s. The 1930s experience took place during a period of deflation, while the 1970s experience occurred during a period of inflation. In a certain sense, however, the preceding statement is false. Why do we call the 1970s a period of inflation and the 1930s a period of deflation? Because the price of goods in terms of gold went down in the 1930s, but in the 1970s the price of goods in terms of gold also went down. Thus, using the same criterion, the 1970s turn out to be just as deflationary as the 1930s. If we still do our accounting in gold, then it turns out that we are living in a period of deflation, depression and unemployment. We can define the contemporary period as inflationary only if we adopt a dollar psychology towards the present and a gold psychology towards the past. However, if we adopt a sterling psychology towards the 1930s – that is, use sterling as our unit of account – then the 1930s turns out to have been a period of stability or even inflation, rather than one of deflation. The same kind of logic can be applied to the 1970s. All that is required is flexibility of thought.

I do not mean to say that the 1930s was a world of inflation. What I really mean to say is that from the viewpoint of a sterling-centric world, the collapse of sterling in 1931 created a period of *relative* inflation, compared with what the rest of the world was experiencing at the time. At no point in the 1930s was the world, as a whole, freed from gold. Great Britain, the flagship country, went off the gold standard in 1931, but the United States and the Continental block remained on. Even when the United States went on to floating rates for a year in 1933, the Continental block remained on gold. Then the United States returned to gold, and the Continental block also continued to change its parities with respect to gold. Throughout that entire period, there was continual experience with the gold universe, despite all the chaos of the thirties and even though we eventually moved up to a higher plateau of prices, based on the increase of the dollar price of gold in 1934.

Even in 1971, the gold standard was not completely abandoned. Only in 1973, with the second devaluation of the dollar, was an actual agreement made to denominate currencies not in gold, but in SDRs. There was thus a sequential movement away from dollars because at that point the SDR was fixed and had a gold weight guarantee. The final movement away from gold occurred only through the stripping of the SDR of its gold value.

Going back to our comparison of the 1930s with the 1970s, although in 1976 we did not return to a tripartite agreement, an attempt was made to fix the dollar/mark rate, which lasted about 12 months. This can be seen as close to a bipartite agreement, and an attempt was also made to tie in the yen. So the tripartite agreement of 1936, based on the franc, sterling and dollar triangle, repeated itself in 1976, but this time includes the principal currencies of the 1970s: the dollar, the yen and the mark. Although we can find similarities between these events, the important point is that the main characteristics of the 1930s and the 1970s are different only if we alter our analytical basis and change the central feature of the system from a gold to a dollar universe.

ECONOMIC NATIONALISM AND THE DOLLAR UNIVERSE

It is reasonable for us to adopt a dollar universe and certainly it is more than resonable for Americans to adopt a dollar universe because the dollar is their currency. But what is most important is that there is no longer any sense of a unified monetary system, as there was under the gold standard. The spread of the dollar psychology has been such that everyone speaks in terms of a dollar universe and that, I think, is the basic reason why we have not gone back to the fixed exchange rate system.

In 1912 Irving Fisher advocated that the US adopt a compensated dollar – in other words, that the US go off the gold standard, stabilise commodity prices and thus let the currency go on to a floating rate system. Now at that point, the United States was not considered to be the dominant economy nor was the dollar a dominant world currency. So it was simply a case of one very big nation going off the world system: the US would bow out of the inflation/deflation discipline of gold. In 1925 Irving Fisher came back to the same idea. At that time, the US was still not universally *viewed* as a dominant world power, so the idea was still nationalistic. The fact was that the US was even then beginning to replace Britain. Keynes in his *Tract on Monetary Reform* pointed to some kind of variable exchange rate standard, but after the UK had ceased to be the dominant power. James Meade also advocated floating rates for Britain when that country was no longer the economic flagship for the rest of the world. Milton Friedman advocated floating rates for the United States and the world in 1950, at a time when he did not perceive the US dollar as a dominant world currency. At that point, his idea still represented both nationalism and conservatism.

Today, however, it is only in the United States that one finds the idea that all countries and all currencies are more or less the same. Nobody in Western Europe thinks any longer that the dollar is just another currency. It was the US Treasury in the 1970s that pushed the idea of a clean floating exchange rate system, with the idea that the peso or the Venezualan bolivar was on the same footing as the

US dollar. Only a few American economists have held this belief. I think they are dead wrong on this issue of symmetry. I do not think that even Milton Friedman any longer believes that a floating exchange rate system can be viable in a dollar-dominated world. If there is a dollar-dominated universe, then the exchange rate system is more fixed than ever before, because the other currencies have lost their monetary properties.

What sets the United States apart from other countries, however, in today's world, is that its freedom of action is limited, to a great extent, by the dollar's focal role. If Canada for example, decides it does not want to inflate along with the United States, it can operate as an independent nation. But the United States is unable to operate like this because it is just like Gulliver in the universe. Gulliver might want to be just like everybody else, so he tells himself he has become a Lilliputian. Nobody else believes him, however, because if he stamps his foot, he shakes up the whole island – which is, in fact, the whole world.

The big difference with the world of the 1930s is that today we are operating in this dollar-dominated universe from the standpoint of financial transactions. In the 1930s much of the world functioned on a dollar mentality, but there was also a more international system in operation.

Man cannot live in a world of fundamental chaos. The only way to make order out of the chaos of the 1930s was to fix exchange rates, so as to establish at least some framework of monetary stability in terms of a given currency. What we see today is what appears on the surface to be monetary instability, but, if examined more deeply, turns out to be an undercurrent of deep and abiding stability, underlying the whole system of the dollar mentality and the dollar unit of account. For better or for worse, we have to face the fact that at present we are still living in a dollarised world. American production may not offer the same development potential it once did, but the monetary and financial economy is still based on the set of relative prices that move with the American dollar. We are living in more of a dollar universe today than we were in the 1950s or the 1960s, and this tendency is increasing as currency instability rises, and reserves held in dollars, near dollars and Eurodollars increase.

We may use any other unit of account, be it Swiss francs or old masters, and price all goods in terms of that other unit. From the standpoint of the way the system behaves, however, these alternative units of account cease to be currencies and we are confronted with the underlying mainstream of the dollar universe. The mark is just a way of translating one set of price information into another. Ultimately, it is currency exchange rates that set relative price levels. If we look at the trade flows and all the other real elements in the system, if we translate everything into dollars, we will find that we have, in a sense, abolished international monetary theory, since we insist that the other markets have become unimportant. What ultimately brought about the dollar universe in which we are living is that people wanted to have flexible exchange rates so as not to have to maintain the dollar standard. They wanted to move towards a new system. But the world would not allow that to happen. If dollar accounting became universal, flexible exchange rates would be irrelevant except as a numeraire for special credit transactions.

The gold exchange standard was a way of putting a check on the dollar money supply. It operated through the convertibility discipline. But when the dollar gold standard broke down, the check to it also broke down and the Federal Reserve System became the world's central bank producing the world's effective reserves. The Federal Reserve System dominates and indirectly runs the financial world economy: all other currency systems have become satellites of the dollar system.

This is not an ideal world. I would like to see a world where there is a check on the US financial economy and on the Eurodollar market. I would like to see a global monetary system incorporating discipline reinstated again. I would also like to see fixed exchange rates, to control foreign monetary expansion, and a convertibility regime, with some control over the monetary expansion power of the dominant currency, which is still the US dollar. But our new system will have to involve more sharing of control and authority than the previous system.

AUTONOMY OR DEPENDENCE?

Joan Robinson once called the International Monetary Fund an episode in the history of the dollar. Under fixed exchange rates this may already have been the case, but it may even be more so, in a fundamental sense, under flexible exchange rates, because the International Monetary Fund has become the monitor for credit transactions operating through the Eurodollar market. It is now the lender that sets the rules; and so control not only still resides with the United States, but to an extent never experienced under the more formal legal apparatus that existed previously.

Therefore, the attempt of the world economy to break away from the dollar mentality, through any one of these political experiments, has only led to the reinforcement of the dollar system. This is because no alternative to the dollar has been prepared. Floating exchange rates give each country 'monetary freedom'. But monetary freedom for what? Simply the monetary freedom to set an independent rate of inflation. Countries can now determine their own rates of money supply, their own rates of monetary expansion and their own interest rates, but those interest rates do not count any more since the nature of the game has changed.

If Switzerland today were to decide on an annual rate of monetary expansion of 50 per cent there would be a flight from Swiss currency, of course, and drastic inflation due to the decline of confidence. But eventually the Swiss inflation rate would settle at 50 per cent higher, and so all interest rates in Switzerland would be about 50 per cent higher than they are at the present time. The Swiss, however – certainly the most intelligent people in the universe judging by the heights to which their currency soars – would quickly find that they would no longer be calculating in their own currency: they would simply continue doing what they are doing now, which is, to a very large extent, calculating in dollar terms. If the Swiss franc goes up by 10 to 20 per cent and the Swiss do not expand the money supply to keep pace with the demand for money, then the Swiss franc will keep going up, rather than down. If the Swiss produce a lot of money, the value of the franc will go down and interest rates will climb; if they produce just a little bit of money, then expectations of a future appreciation of the franc will lead to very low interest rates, below the dollar rates. The universe will become homogenous in real terms.

There is an interest rate parity doctrine in the financial sphere analogous to the purchasing power parity theory established by Gustav Cassell in the commodities sphere. Two points stand out when we try to integrate these into a coherent economy system. First of all, a historical point I would like to emphasise is that we have focused in recent years a great deal of attention on the fixed and flexible exchange rate systems. Personally, I do not consider that aspect to be as important any more as another issue. I think what is far more important is the big revolution that came about in 1971 –

the year of the Smithsonian Agreement, which President Nixon called the most important monetary agreement in the history of the world. Economists tend to scoff at such sweeping generalities and, in any case, the Agreement broke down 15 months later. But I am inclined to think that President Nixon was close to the truth in his description of the Smithsonian Agreement. It was important not because it led to an agreement, but because, *for the first time in the history of the world*, the international economy had endorsed a purely managed system in which the monetary system based on paper and credit was divorced from the commodity system represented by a precious metal. The money supply function of the world was free to shift rightwards to a degree unknown for the previous three thousand years.

Since August 1971, there has been no direct link in reality between gold, and therefore commodities, and the currency system. After December 1971, the world economy accepted the notion of a pure currency system unconnected to commodities. This represents, to my mind, a revolution in human history: a revolution, I think, for the worse, but a revolution all the same. It was an important freeing of the system from its bondage to commodities. The Smithsonian System was still a fixed exchange rate system, but it gave the world freedom to inflate money supplies because of fixed rates by management at the wrong rate in excess of real growth. All the countries of the world had to inflate together, but they could now choose a rate of inflation that was independent of the production of gold, which used to be able to make the value of money go where it wanted to. This marked a fundamental change from the world of *gold standard expectations* in which inflation had traditionally brought about correction, disequilibrium, the need for a cure and therefore the expectation of a reversal of this trend. The 1971 Agreement introduced the idea not only of a potentially *permanent inflation*, but also of a possibly *permanently increasing inflation*. It meant that we would never go back to the world of the 1950s or of the 1960s when interest rates had been very low.

Today, of course, interest rates can be lowered to all kinds of negative levels: you can get Swiss franc interest rates to fall if you stop printing francs and then make everybody move into francs through the expected appreciation of the franc; Switzerland then makes all franc interest rates negative, while the exchange rate is expected to go up.

Interest rates are based on the current international level of inflation. That is the fundamental picture and that is what is affecting the real economy through an immediate impact on interest rates. All interest rates then become affected by this new inflation psychosis, because if inflationary targets are expected to be reversed as a result of a complete change in the money supply function of the economic universe, then there is no more ceiling on interest rates. As interest rates go up and uncertainty about the rates rises, then capital market issues on the long-term end of the spectrum will dry up, resulting in a shortening of the whole economic universe in the process of production. Long-term capital can no longer be floated in terms of national currencies, there is a shortening of all issues and these become the symptoms of a capital shortage that is endemic all over the world. The shortage of long-term finance due to uncertainty has shortened the period of production and the durability of capital assets.

In a certain sense, there is a capital shortage all over the world right now: no one is able to project interest rates any more because there is no longer any basis for predicting the value of money – the concept of a global money supply function has been eroded. Two changes in the global money supply function have occurred in the 1970s. First of all, the idea of a ceiling on the rate of global monetary expansion has disappeard. The second point concerns the movement toward floating exchange rates. This point is less important than the first. It is, however, more relevant from the standpoint of this paper on economic nationalism, since the underlying predicate of fixed rates is a common rate of inflation. Floating exchange rates mean that countries can choose their own monetary inflation rates and, therefore, their own interest rates, and when they choose that, the whole information milieu becomes quite different. Flexible exchange rates to some extent create national information areas. What is confusing is that our theory has always told us that if we have a system of floating rates and countries can choose their own inflation rates, they will become insulated from the inflation of other countries. That is correct both in theory and in practice, if we understand the information problem correctly.

If information were nationalised, then all newspapers would take information only from national newspapers, which are always domestically oriented. If people in Switzerland were to read only Swiss papers and Swiss journalists only looked at national reports of what the Swiss central bank and money supply were doing, then they could predict national interest rates. However, when people read about inflation in foreign newspapers, they tend to confuse the information that comes from dollar interest rates. If you read the *New York Times*, the *Wall Street Journal* or the *Washington Post*, you learn something about what is happening in the dollar universe and dollar inflation seems to fit. But if you want to understand what is happening to inflation in France, you might be under the illusion that all inflation is likely to pick up, in France as well as elsewhere. The transmission, however, does not operate through the monetary mechanism but through the transfer of information and through the faulty reading of that information. Can we expect the public to be sophisticated monetary analysts when economists disagree?

The same syndrome has pervaded our universe of economics. In economics, at present, important topics of conversation are multilateral surveillance, control of the balance of payments, which country should move forward, which should move back, and at what rates, and what policies should be undertaken with respect to money supplies and exchange rates. All this, however, should be a completely national phenomenon under floating rates if the theory of isolation were credible. If there is no overlapping or confusion of information processes, a country should be free to determine its own inflation rates. If there is no transmission of information from abroad, the country is independent in the course of action it decides to follow. Kuwait and Saudi Arabia, for example, are two important countries in the world oil pricing picture. But if they want to let the dinar or the riyal appreciate by 20 per cent a year or depreciate by 50 per cent a year, nobody cares (and nobody should care). What, then, is the purpose of any multilateral surveillance? We should let each central bank see to it that its currency runs the way the country wants it to run and let every country have its independence, if that independence is a reality and not a myth. But it is a myth.

With closed information networks and no money or capital movements, independence would be possible. 'Independence' would mean the ability to set distinct national rates of inflation as measured by changes in the value of domestic currency. But that kind of independence may not be very valuable, except perhaps as a means of altering fixed price contracts and therefore changing – at least once – the distribution of wealth. This device was once regarded as immoral by the previous generations, since it amounted to a breach of faith. The global shift to the left – the new populism – has altered that ethical stance. But one can take advantage of the creditor class only once or twice in a generation. After that the advantages of monetary nationalism rapidly disappear. This applies not just to the distribution between the rentier class and the debtors, but also to the success of inflation as a device for lowering real wages and increasing real effective demand in order to deal with unemployment. Almost nobody believes anymore in the inflationist solution to unemployment for the simple fact that wage rates keep up, and sometimes precede price inflation.

The conclusion to which this leads is that our universe is dominated in two ways that cause monetary independence to be more of a myth than a reality. It is dominated not just by US economic power and by the dollar, which is widely and increasingly held outside the US, but also by the economic information that comes from the United States. The sole purpose of a flexible exchange rate system is to allow monetary nationalism to exist. That monetary nationalism is not worth much, for economic performance, anymore.

FLOATING AND PROTECTIONISM

The last part of my discussion concerns economic nationalism. A commonly held fallacy is that exchange rate changes can be used to shift unemployment from one country to another; it was once called a beggar-my-neighbour policy. At best, this holds true for wage-contract periods, but those are always short-term now since real salaries can be eroded for only short periods without inducing a supply response.

I have referred to multilateral surveillance, which is international and stems from the fact that people are not willing to live in a world of pure floating rates. The monetary authorities are unwilling to put into practice the principle of monetary independence because the dollar system automatically creates monetary interdependence. Multilateral surveillance is the result of an attempt to somehow manage the spillover effects of that system. In the real world, this is a phenomenon that works towards economic nationalism because of the short-run problem of the contractual basis. For example, a fall in the exchange value, such as the devaluation of the dollar, temporarily changes real wages, the flow of goods and international competitiveness during the period in which contracts are being adjusted. In that sense, it leads to pressures for economic controls in countries whose currencies are appreciating, and ultimately to a breakdown in free trade. This pattern, however, is part of the information mix-up that is created as people apply models that no longer exist in relation to the real world, and because of the different timing of price changes of goods, services and capital.

Such a system is due to the incorrect separation of information about the clean world of economic nationalism and pure monetary nationalism. However, if each country inflated at its own desired rate, and all prices moved together, there should be no reason to impose exchange or trade controls because of changes in the exchange rate. In a homogeneous universe, the exchange system does not affect the trading system. It is only through the 'noise' of the system that comes from rigidities, different speeds of adjustment and information frictions that last for one or two years through contract arrangements.

There is no reason, in theory, for an ideal system of flexible exchange rates to lead to economic nationalism in the trade sphere, if we keep in mind that the flexible exchange system does one thing only – it can give us differential inflation rates and thus differential monetary goals.

There is also an erroneous belief that exchange rate changes and tariff changes are substitutes for each other, from the standpoint of protectionism. They are not. Exchange rates cannot duplicate a tariff system, because exchange rates are a monetary phenomenon and not a real phenomenon. Abba Lerner's 1936 article on the symmetry of import and export taxes testifies to that. Tariffs or export taxes lower the level of trade while exchange rate changes induce (or are caused by) price differentials and relative money growth rates.

THE FALLACY OF BALANCE OF PAYMENTS ADJUSTMENT

Exchange rate changes (coupled with proportionate monetary expansion) only alter the rate of inflation. Now the choice of an exchange system essentially means a choice of monetary rule. If you have a flexible exchange system, it means national monetary rules, national inflation rates, national interest rates and, therefore, national capital markets. These are nationalistic components. Fixed rates mean a common monetary rule, and thus – within a regional or global area – common inflation rates, common interest rates and area-wide capital markets.

Agreeing on a common money is not equivalent to agreeing on fixed exchange rates. Agreeing on a common money with convertibility means not only agreeing on the same exchange, but also on a specific inflation rate, a specific rate of common world monetary expansion and a common capital market, in the sense of a common global interest rate. According to some political theories, the nineteenth century was a century of peace because the common capital market was interdependent based on the monetary rule of gold. However, as new countries appeared that system outgrew itself and broke down.

An exchange system is not an adjustment instrument for the balance of payments, except in a narrow short-run sense; rather it is a mechanism for establishing differential exchange rates and price levels. And flexible exchange rates become a cause of economic nationalism for two reasons: first, because they disrupt the common money element and capital markets, which have always been instruments of global cooperation; and, secondly, because they create the false illusion of adjustment through exchange rate devices.

Two points should be made here concerning the US balance of payments and adjustments. First of all, we have to be very careful about the way in which we identify exchange rate changes as a mechanism for adjusting the US balance of payments even in the short run. Devaluation of the US dollar will not correct the US balance of payments because the US balance of payments depends not only on US monetary policy but is also a function of foreign liquidity requirements, which are outside the control of the United States. The US balance of payments is defined in terms of foreign acquisitions of dollars. If foreign central banks buy dollars, then there is no way in which the United States can correct or stop that behaviour unless it is by denying these countries access to the US or Eurodollar capital market. So long as the US dollar is the principal medium of international exchange, other countries will want to acquire US dollars. At the present time, they are acquiring dollars at the rate of approximately $40 billion a year, which means that the US has to have a balance of payments deficit of $40 billion a year.

Secondly, suppose that foreign central banks decide that they are not going to acquire US dollars for liquidity purposes. Then the US balance of payments problem will be solved, no matter what happens to the exchange rate. If the central banks decide to hold marks, then the Bundesbank will have a balance of payments deficit. If they hold yen, then the Japanese will have a deficit. On the other hand, if the United States decides to buy marks and to impose upon Germany the role of reserve currency, then it will shift that deficit on to Germany regardless of what happens to the dollar exchange rate.

However, if all central banks stay out of the foreign exchange market and move towards a system of floating rates – not a system that I particularly like, but one that many people once liked – then the US balance of payments deficit will be zero. The US balance of trade deficit will be exactly equal to net US borrowing minus transfers abroad, and if foreign countries decide to lend to the United States, then the US will have a balance of trade deficit. If the United States decides to lend abroad, the US will have a balance of trade surplus. If the OPEC countries, for example, decide that they have enough liquidity and stop buying dollars, then there is no balance of payments deficit, but if they decide they want to hold US bonds, then the US will have a balance of trade deficit. If they decide to hold extensive US liquidity instruments of any kind – whether land shares or banks or companies – then the US balance of trade deficit will not be corrected. The US will be unable to correct its balance of trade deficit in other currencies because other countries want to acquire the financial instruments that the US is selling.

As regards the British economy, I have argued for a long time that Britain is much better off with a fixed exchange rate. I think that devaluation was a mistake, and I even go so far as to agree with Hawtrey and Harrod that the 1949 devaluation only led to the excessive stop–go inflation policy of the 1950s, without abolishing control. The Hawtrey and Harrod view of the world, in my opinion, turned out to be very sound in interpreting British monetary policy in the nineteenth and twentieth centuries. After all, Britain had 300 years of comparative price stability with fixed exchange rates, but it has had three or four big devaluations of the pound sterling all in the past 30 years. And this is the period when Britain turned from a monetarily stable country to a monetarily unstable country. These devaluations have not helped the British economy, they have only got it into difficulties.

There is no way in which the pound sterling can be rationed, because nobody knows what the pound sterling is. Feaveryear writes that, in 1817, Sir Robert Peel asked an accountant how he defined the pound sterling and he replied, 'Well, I don't know how to define it, Sir, but every gentleman in England knows what it is.' I think that was true in 1817, and perhaps in 1925, and maybe even in 1950, but I do not think that it is true today.

Looking at Italy, which has faced many problems, I think that the Italian adjustment to the oil crisis would have been better without the devaluation and with fixed exchange rates. I disapproved of the appreciation of the lira in 1971, as well as its depreciation later on. I do not think that the devaluation of the lira helped the Italian adjustment in real terms, although I confess it may have helped lower the real salaries of government workers before the indexing of wage rates. The most important casualty was the decline in confidence in the currency after 20 years of stability.

This shows why the balance of payments cannot be adjusted simply by flexible exchange rates. The decline of the dollar will not stop foreign banks and the public from buying dollar assets, and that demand will be greater the more a belief is spread that the dollar will rise in the future. As long as other countries buy more dollar assets or lend to the US than US residents are willing to invest or borrow abroad, the US balance of trade will be negative.

THE END OF FLOATING?

The final point that I want to make is that the experiment with floating rates has, in my opinion, been a failure. This has been evident since 1971 and the experiment should be abandoned as soon as the international monetary authorities agree on a common international monetary unit to replace the dollar, or at least to internationalise it by putting it under the supervision of an international body.

Even today, there are still lingering doubts over the definition of the SDR; this legal question leaves an opening for the world to return to a gold-centred universe if it wants to. Many people believe that in the 1980s, given the high price of gold, there will be a return to some form of gold standard, but now the SDR is also in the game. In a legal sense, there is still a symbolic element of gold remaining in the system due to the maintenance of an official gold price for valuing reserves held by central banks.

What I would recommend, however, would be to invent a new

currency, a new basket that would be a takeover from Alfred Marshall's symmetallism – only we would be dealing not with metalism but paper currencies. A new basket could be composed of one dollar, plus one mark, plus perhaps 100 yen, which would constitute a new unit of account. I suggest using a dollar plus a mark, because that gives about a two-to-one ratio strength of the dollar to the mark, with the mark representing the expansionary force. The yen tends to move with the mark and would give a strong base to the unit of account. An alternative would be to base the new basket on weighted elements of the Big Five.

This would be a composite currency, but not a sixteen-currency basket like the SDR, which no one can predict because one cannot forecast the monetary policies of sixteen central banks. It is much easier, however, to predict the monetary policies of two central banks, and for that reason a currency based on a dollar-mark basket would be of great convenience as a unit of account for the pricing of oil, airline fares, etc.

The German and American central banks would then move toward rather stable exchange rates, in terms of this new currency, and ultimately all exchange rates could move into place. Then, the only remaining problem would be to place some control over the monetary expansion of the basket currencies, with IMF endorsement. This represents my own line of thinking, rather than a return to a bipartite or tripartite agreement fixing the dollar to the mark or the yen at a particular rate. If a European currency develops, the European zone of stability would create the basis for a new arrangement by which fixed rates between the dollar and the mark would establish a general movement back to a Smithonian-type arrangement. That would constitute an important first step toward international monetary stability and pave the way for the all-important second step of anchoring the super-currency monetary expansion rates to a global commodity basket (such as gold) or a system of multilateral surveillance stabilising money expansion rates.

3 United States Monetary Policy and Economic Nationalism

Benjamin J. Cohen

Is United States monetary policy becoming more nationalistic? In this chapter I shall argue that American policy is *not* becoming more nationalistic – for the simple reason that *it always has been nationalistic*. In international monetary affairs, America has always acted out of an instinct for self-interest. That has not changed. What has changed is the willingness of other countries to acquiesce in America's pursuit of its self-interest: others no longer see this as being in their own interest as well. And so what they once regarded as world leadership by the United States, they now brand as economic nationalism. In fact, this says more about changes in their own attitudes and perceptions – and about changes in the international monetary system in general – than it does about the specifics of United States monetary policy. It is not so much the *content* as the *context* of American policy that has really changed.

I

The above remarks will be substantiated in the remainder of this chapter. But to begin with, it would be useful if I make clear what I mean by the two key phrases of my initial question.

Monetary policy. In the domestic context, where the underlying structure of the monetary system normally tends to be relatively stable, monetary policy can be understood simply to describe the use of variations in the quantity of money and/or level of interest rates to tighten or ease monetary conditions and hence to lower or raise aggregate demand. In the international context, however, things tend to be a bit more complicated. Unlike the domestic monetary system, the underlying structure of the international monetary system cannot be assumed to be stable, even for comparatively short periods of time. In this context, therefore, monetary policy must be understood to operate on two levels, not just one – on the level of 'structure' as well as on the level of 'process'. (Process-level refers to the conduct of policy *within* a given set of institutions and 'rules of the game'; structure-level refers to policies designed to *change* given institutions and rules of the game.) At the process-level, monetary policy operates (in conjunction with fiscal policy) to achieve the purposes of *macroeconomic management*; its principal concerns are the rate of real economic growth and/or unemployment, the rate of inflation, the balance of payments and the exchange rate. At the structure-level, by contrast, monetary policy operates to achieve the purposes of *monetary reform*, its principal concerns being the mechanism of balance of payments adjustment and the mechanism for creation and control of the supply of international reserves and payments financing. When speaking of monetary policy, it is important to keep both these levels of operation in mind.

Economic nationalism. There tends to be an ambiguity about this phrase. Popularly it is understood to apply to any policy motivated by pursuit of self-interest. But by that definition virtually all policies must be described as nationalistic, since virtually all states have well defined policy objectives – economic welfare, political security, domestic autonomy, international prestige – and purposefully design and implement their policy instruments to achieve them. What, then, is the problem? The problem – and the source of the ambiguity – is the lack of a qualifying adjective. Economic nationalism may be, broadly speaking, either 'malign' or 'benign'. Malign nationalism seeks national goals relentlessly, even at the expense of others; benign nationalism, by contrast, is prepared to compromise national policy priorities where necessary to accommodate the interests of others. The difference between these two types of nationalism lies in the willingness of a country to identify its own national interest with an interest in the stability of the overall international system. Benign nationalism acknowledges a connection between self-interest and systemic interest, malign nationalism ignores or denies it. When speaking of economic nationalism, it is important to keep this distinction in mind as well.

II

Having defined these two key phrases, now consider again our initial question: is United States monetary policy becoming more nationalistic? The answer, I have suggested, is that American policy has always been nationalistic. But in that case, to paraphrase Gertrude Stein, what is the question?[1] The question is, is the nationalism of United States policy becoming more malign?

The reason that American policy has always been nationalistic is that while the United States is clearly the paramount state actor in global economic relations, and has been throughout much of the twentieth century, it is also one of the world's most closed national economies, whose main orientation is still basically inward rather than outward. These two facts combine to establish a fundamental American bias toward maintenance of policy autonomy in monetary matters. As a leading economy, the United States naturally prizes its ability to act unilaterally to promote objectives believed to be in the national interest. As a closed economy, the United States accords a lesser priority to external considerations relative to domestic policy needs. The key objective of American policy, therefore, has always been to minimise any balance of payments constraint on the government's decision making capacity, in order to maximise the country's self-interested freedom of action in domestic and foreign affairs. That was, of course, the great advantage of the old Bretton Woods system from the United States' point of view. Because of the central role of the dollar in monetary affairs, there was relatively little effective external discipline on American policy autonomy. Ever since the breakdown of the Bretton Woods system in 1971, America's manifest goal has been to preserve as much as possible of the special privileges it had learned to enjoy in the years after World War II. At both process-level and structure-level, American policy since 1971 has continued to be framed with that basic vested interest in mind.

But that does not mean that American policy has been, or is necessarily becoming, malign. To understand why this is so, it is necessary to go back to first principles – in this instance, to the so-called '$n-1$ principle' of international monetary theory, also known as the 'redundancy problem'.[2] In a world of n sovereign states and currencies, there are only $n-1$ exchange rates. Therefore, only $n-1$ balance of payments policies (be they expressed in terms of exchange rate targets in a floating world or in terms of reserve targets in a pegged-rate world) can be independently determined. One country (the nth country) is redundant. If all n countries try to set their policies independently, these policies will almost certainly be inconsistent (technically, the system will be overdetermined), and, as a result, the stability of the system itself will be threatened. To preserve monetary stability, some means must be found – some organising principle – that will ensure consistency among national policies and reduce the risk of policy conflict. The history of international monetary relations is written in the succession of attempts by the international community to find such an organising principle.[3]

In theory, four alternative organising principles are possible. These are

1. *Automaticity*. A self disciplining regime of rules and conventions binding for all nations (for example, a gold standard or pure floating exchange rates).
2. *Supranationality*. A regime founded on collective adherence to the decisions of some autonomous international organisation (for example, a world central bank).
3. *Hegemony*. A regime organised around a single country with acknowledged responsibilities (and privileges) as leader.
4. *Negotiation*. A regime of shared responsibility and decision-making.

In practice, only one of these four has ever actually succeeded for any length of time in preserving international monetary stability. That one is the principle of hegemony, which underlay operation of both the classical gold standard in the last decades before World War I and the Bretton Woods system in the first decades after World War II. In each case the monetary system was effectively organised around a single hegemonic leader – Great Britain in the earlier period, the United States in the later. In both cases the comparative lack of policy conflict was directly attributable to the stabilising influence of the dominant national power.

Recent historical analysis has amply demonstrated that the classical gold standard, far from being the politically symmetrical system of conventional textbook models, was in fact distinctly hierarchical, dominated at the top by Great Britain, the supreme economic power of the day.[4] Stability in the gold standard was ensured through a trio of roles that only Britain at the time had the resources to play: (i) maintaining a relatively open market for the exports of countries in balance of payments difficulties; (ii) providing contracyclical foreign long-term lending; and (iii) acting as lender of last resort in times of exchange crisis. These were not roles that the British deliberately sought or even particularly welcomed. As far as the Bank of England was concerned, its monetary policies were dictated solely by the need to protect its narrow reserves and the gold convertibility of the pound. It did not regard itself as responsible for global monetary stabilisation. Yet this is precisely the responsibility that was thrust upon it in practice – acquired, like the British Empire itself, more or less in a fit of absence of mind. This was truly a hegemonic regime, in the sense that Britain not only dominated the system but also gave monetary relations whatever degree of inherent stability they possessed.

A parallel role was played by the United States after World War II. As dominant then as Britain had been in the nineteenth century, America rapidly assumed the same three managerial roles – in effect, taking over as money manager of the world. Since international monetary reserves were everywhere in short supply, the United States itself became the residual source of global liquidity through its balance of payments deficits. At war's end, America owned almost three quarters of the world's existing monetary gold, and prospects for new gold production were obviously limited by the physical constraints of nature. The rest of the world, therefore, was more than willing to economise on this scarce gold supply by accumulating dollars instead. The United States was accorded the unique privilege of liability-financing its deficits; the dollar became enshrined not only as the principal 'vehicle currency' for international trade and investment but also as the principal reserve asset for central banks. In the early post-war years, America's deficits became the universal solvent to keep the machinery of Bretton Woods running. The Bretton Woods system became synonymous with a hegemonic regime centred on the dollar.

In effect, the United States became the world's *n*th country, abjuring any balance of payments target of its own. Other countries set independent payments targets; consistency in global monetary relations was ensured by the fact that America could be counted upon to play a passive role in the international adjustment process. American policy was freed to concentrate largely on domestic stabilisation objectives. Its only express international monetary objective was to maintain the fixed dollar price of gold – although, implicitly, the United States also had an obligation to manage its domestic policies with the needs of the rest of the world in mind. Given America's weight in the global economy, conditions inside the United States inevitably had a considerable influence on the pace of economic developments elsewhere as well. America was the balance wheel of the world economy. (The only recourses other countries had to adjust to movements of the balance wheel were either to modify their balance of payments targets or else to alter the par values of their currencies against the dollar and gold.) Keeping the balance wheel moving stably was what the responsibility of being world money manager was all about.

Like the British in the nineteenth century, the Americans did not deliberately seek this responsibility. On the other hand, unlike the British, once they found themselves with it, they soon came to welcome it, for reasons that clearly were not unrelated to self-interest. Being money manager of the world fit in well with America's newfound leadership role in the Western Alliance. The cold war had begun, and the United States perceived the need to promote the economic recovery of potential allies in Europe and Japan, as well as to maintain a sizable and potent military establishment overseas. All of this cost money: the privilege of liability-financing deficits meant that America was effectively freed from all balance of payments constraints and could spend as freely as it thought necessary to promote objectives believed to be in the national interest. The United States could issue the world's principal vehicle and reserve currency in amounts presumed to be consistent with its own policy priorities – and not necessarily those of foreign dollar holders. Foreign dollar holders conceded this policy autonomy to the United States because it also contributed directly to their own economic rehabilitation. America's pursuit of self-interest was seen as being in their interest as well.

In effect, an implicit bargain was struck. Washington's allies acquiesced in a hegemonic system that accorded the United States special privileges to act unilaterally to promote American interests. The United States, in turn, condoned its allies' use of the system to promote their own economic prosperity, even if this happened to come occasionally at the short-term expense of the United States.

American policy was demonstrably nationalistic – but it was a nationalism that could credibly be described as benign rather than malign. The situation was characterised best by a phrase that became fashionable near the end of the Bretton Woods era: 'benign neglect'. The United States acknowledged the connection between its own interest and the stability of the overall system – and acted accordingly.

III

Since the breakdown of the Bretton Woods system, the United States has continued to act in a demonstrably nationalistic fashion. At the process level, America's monetary policy has continued to be focused almost exclusively on domestic stabilisation objectives. During the Bretton Woods period, the Federal Reserve routinely sterilised the internal monetary consequences of external deficits: that has not changed since 1971. Nor has there been any significant change in the priority accorded domestic considerations in the management of the nation's monetary aggregates and credit conditions. (The raising of interest rates in December 1977 in response to the accelerating depreciation of the dollar was a highly unusual exception.) Likewise at the structural level, American policy continues to be motivated by a desire to preserve as much freedom of action in monetary affairs as possible. This explains, for example, America's strong support of the present regime of floating exchange rates. (Floating rates are especially convenient to a large, closed economy like the United States.) It also explains America's determined resistance to all global reform proposals that might reduce the central reserve role of the dollar. Why submit to more external discipline than necessary? Such an attitude obviously underlay Washington's expressed preference in the Committee of Twenty both for a 'tight' adjustment process (presumably intended to relieve some of the pressures to alter domestic American policies that might arise in the event of future payments deficits) and a 'loose' settlement system (presumably intended to allow more cumulative deficits in the future). Suspension in 1971 of the dollar's convertibility eliminated the one major weapon that foreign governments had for restricting America's freedom of action. The United States has not been eager to submit to effective new constraints on its decision making capacity.

At only one point, however, has America's persistent nationalism threatened to become malign rather than benign. That was in the pivotal year 1971, when the Bretton Woods system was brought down by America's own aggressive actions. Toward the end of the 1960s, the United States had begun to feel severely constrained by a growing threat of conversions of official dollar balances into gold. Although most observers agreed that the dollar had become overvalued, America felt powerless to alter the value of the dollar unilaterally. (All the United States could do was alter the dollar price of gold: it was up to other countries to make the devaluation effective by intervening in the exchange market at appropriate new rates in terms of their own currencies.) Yet America also felt powerless to persuade surplus countries to revalue. And meanwhile the US deficit was widening rapidly. Ultimately it was the Americans themselves who decided to force the issue, by the measures announced on 15 August. The purpose of these measures – in particular, the 'temporary' suspension of the dollar's convertibility and the 10 per cent surcharge on imports – was to compel the major surplus countries to accept a mutual exchange rate adjustment that would correct the over valuation of the dollar. That purpose was ostensibly accomplished by the currency realignment agreed upon at the Smithsonian Institution in December 1971.

Although the currency realignment itself collapsed in little more than a year, the Smithsonian Agreement was successful at least in defusing a potentially nasty political confrontation. By the time the Committee of Twenty was established in mid-1972, United States policy had already returned to its more traditional posture of benignity. American policy makers were frankly shocked by the disruptive consequences of their own actions. John Connally (the combative Treasury Secretary who was the chief architect of the 1971 measures) may have cared little about avoiding destabilising behaviour. But his successors have been only too cognisant of the close identity of America's interests with the stability of the system as a whole. In the years since, they have needed little encouragement to try to act more 'responsibly' in monetary affairs.

If the nationalism of American policy has not changed, what then *has* changed? What has changed is the system itself – more specifically, the conditions required to organise and maintain a hegemonic system like Bretton Woods. Two conditions are essential. First, hegemonic leadership must in fact be 'responsible' – that is, the economic policy of the world's money manager must truly be stabilising, imparting neither inflationary nor deflationary impulses to the rest of the world. And second, hegemonic leadership must be regarded as 'legitimate', generating neither resentment nor policy conflict over the benefits and costs of the system. Today, neither of these conditions may be said to be satisfied.

Consider the first condition. What assurance is there that the United States will in fact always act 'responsibly'? The answer is – no assurance at all. America's policymakers may indeed be cognisant of the country's role as balance wheel of the world economy; they may be fully aware of the obligation of the world's money manager to provide a stable standard of economic performance (especially price performance) around which other countries can organise their own policy priorities. But there is still no certainty that such an obligation will actually be honoured – precisely because, by definition, in a hegemonic regime there is no effective external discipline on the leader. Given the absence of any formal deterrent, the possibility always exists that, sooner or later, accidentally or deliberately, the leader will take advantage of its special position to initiate policies that destabilise the world economy. In the case of the United States, this is indeed precisely what did happen following escalation of military hostilities in Vietnam after 1965. Before 1965, America clearly had the best long-term record of price stability of any industrial country; even for some time after 1958 the United States could not be justly accused of 'exporting' inflation, however much some governments were complaining about a dollar glut. But then President Johnson made a decision to fight a war in Vietnam and a War on Poverty simultaneously. As a result, America's economy quickly began to overheat. The virus of inflation began to spread, and ultimately the whole world was infected, setting the stage for the dramatic events of 1971. In the years since, America's policy seems to have regained some semblance of 'responsibility'. But now the genie is out of the bottle. American leadership has proved once to be destabilising. Can anyone doubt that history might one day repeat itself?

In any event, American hegemony is no longer regarded as legitimate. Objective circumstances have changed too much since the years immediately after World War II when the foundations of the Bretton Woods system were laid. In those days the United States bestrode the world economy like a colossus. Other countries may have had reservations about America's leadership role; weakened as they were by war and destruction, however, they were hardly in a position to question it. Today, by contrast, the political and economic conditions that originally made American hegemony acceptable – or, at any rate, tolerable – no longer exist. America's relative position in the international hierarchy has declined enormously. Foreign economies are no longer so weak and uncompetitive as they were immediately after the war, and foreign governments (in Europe, Japan, and even OPEC) are no longer satisfied to accept a political role subordinate to that of the United States. America's leadership role has come under increasing challenge. The United States is still acknowledged as *primus inter pares* in the world economy. But it is by no means still universally accepted as *primus motor*.

Proof of these changed attitudes and perceptions can be found in the current debate between the United States and its major allies over the so-called 'locomotive' approach to recovery from the 'Great Recession' of 1974–5. As always, America's own monetary policy – which until recently was generally expansionary in tone – has been guided essentially by domestic considerations. But since expansion at home could credibly be argued to aid recovery abroad also, the United States has been urging other 'locomotive' economies like Germany and Japan to follow America's lead, stimulating their own growth rates as well, in hopes that this would help to pull weaker economies out of the general stagnation that has persisted since 1975. Once, America's leadership in this regard might have been heeded. Today, however, it is resisted. The result is frustration and deadlock. Germany and Japan argue that further expansion of their economies may be neither desirable (because of the inflationary pressures that might be generated) nor even possible (because of domestic political and institutional constraints on policy); and that in any event the stimulative impact on weaker economies would probably be comparatively small. Instead, they criticise the United States for allowing its balance of payments to get out of control and its currency to depreciate sharply in the exchange markets. In some quarters, America is even accused of trying to use dollar depreciation to gain an unfair competitive advantage – malign nationalism at its worst.

But *is* this malign nationalism? I would argue, rather, the reverse – that America's relatively passive exchange rate policy is precisely the posture required to resolve the global redundancy problem in today's floating rate world. In fact America is still playing the *n*th-country role in the international monetary system.

Other countries pursue their independent payments targets through direct or indirect intervention in the exchange market; the residual of all their targets emerges in net movements of the dollar's effective exchange rate. This is the main reason why serious inconsistency in monetary relations has been avoided since the breakdown of the Bretton Woods system.

Not that this should be surprising. A country still as large and powerful as the United States needs little incentive to avoid destabilising behaviour whenever possible. Its ability to disrupt is too evident; as American policy makers since John Connally have recognised, the nation's self-interest is too closely identified with stability of the overall system for them to try deliberately to act 'irresponsibly'. (This of course does not rule out accidental 'irresponsibility'.) Smaller and less powerful countries, by contrast, need a correspondingly greater incentive to act 'responsibly', since the identification of self-interest and systemic interest is for them relatively less clear. One of the few luxuries afforded small countries in an international hierarchy is the privilege to pursue narrow national priorities without regard for the stability of the system as a whole. Such 'free-rider' behaviour does not threaten systemic stability so long as it is indulged in only sporadically or by just a few countries. But it can be threatening if indulged in by a greater number of countries, and it may be very threatening indeed if indulged in systematically by countries further up on the scale of size and power – countries like Germany and Japan, for example. If such countries fail to recognise the damage they can do by pursuing goals divergent from the interest of the system as a whole, stability in international relations will be very. difficult to preserve.

Essentially, this is the problem that we face in monetary relations today. Conditions are no longer propitious for an American hegemony, yet Germany and Japan have so far resisted America's blandishments to share in the responsibility for global monetary stabilisation. Some organising principle, as I have argued, is necessary to ensure consistency among national policies and reduce the risk of policy conflict. If the community of nations is unwilling to submit to the rigours of automatic rules or a world central bank, then, in current circumstances, the solution must be found in a regime of shared responsibility and decision making. Some means must be found to enable the locomotives all to pull in the same direction. If not, the train may never leave the station.

NOTES

1. Stein, on her deathbed, is reported to have muttered: 'What is the answer?' When no one replied, she continued: 'In that case, what is the question?' – and died.
2. The '$n-1$ principle' or 'redundancy problem' was first enunciated by Robert Mundell. See his *International Economics* (New York: Macmillan, 1968), pp. 195–8.
3. The problems of international monetary organisation are treated at greater length in my book *Organizing the World's Money* (New York: Basic Books, 1977). I have drawn from this source for some of the arguments developed in the present contribution.
4. See, for example, C. P. Kindleberger, *The World in Depression, 1929–1939* (Berkeley and Los Angeles: University of California Press, 1973).

4 The International Approach Towards the US Balance of Payments Problems

Rimmer de Vries

The United States is criticised frequently for employing essentially nationalistic policies in dealing with its balance of payments problems. Bankers in this country, in particular, have accused the United States of benign (and even malign) neglect in its external economic and financial policies. They believe that the United States has not taken its international economic and financial responsibilities seriously.

In this regard, it is frequently asserted that the United States has been talking down the dollar in order to promote its exports and its own economic growth, a policy that is reminiscent of the 1930s. It is also pointed out that the trade and current account deficits of recent years have been mainly the result of the sharp rise in oil imports, reflecting wasteful consumption of energy in the United States. Rather than drastically curtail its use of energy, the United States is criticised for promoting its exports in order to pay for the high cost of oil imports. Another criticism is that while the United States is running a large current account deficit, it has nevertheless permitted substantial net private capital outflows to occur, which further depressed the dollar in the exchange markets. As a result, in order to prevent their currencies from revaluing too sharply, foreign monetary authorities intervened quite heavily, and the exchange risk on their dollar holdings, they believe, should be shared to a large extent by the United States.

The present US balance of payments policies are much more

balanced and internationalistic in character than these views imply, but they could assume a more nationalistic nature if present policies do not yield results in the next year or so.

ORIGINS OF THE PAYMENTS DEFICIT

Before discussing US balance of payments policies, let us first analyse briefly the origins of the US balance of payments deficit. The current, large deficit has emerged rapidly. In 1977 the United States ran record deficits on trade and current accounts – \$31 bn and \$20bn, respectively. A year earlier, these deficits had amounted to only \$9bn and \$1½bn, respectively, and in 1975, record surpluses had been achieved. In fact, the merchandise trade balance deteriorated more than \$50bn in a two-and-a-half-year time span from a \$9bn surplus in the fourth quarter of 1975 (seasonally adjusted annual rate) to a \$45bn deficit in the first quarter of 1978. Over this two-and-a-half-year period there has been a change in the factors contributing to the trade balance deterioration.

At the beginning, the rapid growth of US oil imports was the principal factor underlying the US trade balance deterioration. The value of imports rose from \$8bn in 1973 to \$29bn in 1975 and to \$45bn in 1977, a worsening of \$37bn over four years. There is no question that oil imports have been the single, most important factor for the rapid emergence of the US trade deficit. However, the rise in oil imports is not due to wasteful energy consumption. About two thirds of the increased oil import bill between 1973 and 1977 can be attributed to higher oil prices, about one sixth to the steady decline in domestic production of crude oil before 1977 (when the Alaska pipeline was opened) and only the remaining one sixth to increased consumption, which is quite small considering the rapid economic growth the United States has been experiencing. Conservation, together with Alaskan oil beginning to flow and destocking, have been responsible for the fact that oil imports peaked at an annual rate of \$48bn in the first quarter of 1977 but declined in later months to make the bill stand at an annual rate level of \$40bn (see Table 4.1).

Instead, the rapid trade balance deterioration since the first quarter of 1977 did not come from a further deepening of the oil import deficit but from the worsening of the manufactured goods trade balance. This balance changed from a surplus of more than

TABLE 4.1: US Trade and Current Account Balances ($bn)

	1975	*1976*	*1977*	*1978/Q1*
Merchandise trade balance (FAS)	11.01	−5.87	−26.55	−38.72
By product:				
Agricultural and Other (net)	11.48	9.56	7.13	6.85
Fuels (net)	−22.01	−29.71	−40.35	−37.12
Manufactures (net)	20.52	12.81	4.54	−11.94
By area:				
Industrial Countries	8.81	3.61	−4.50	
Canada	0	−2.13	−3.64	
Japan	−1.70	−5.36	−8.17	
EEC	6.26	7.56	4.35	
OPEC Countries	−6.32	−12.46	−19.01	
Non-OPEC LDCs	6.28	0.21	−5.51	
Communist Countries	2.20	2.58	1.60	
Trade balance (BOP)	9.05	−9.30	−31.24	−44.80
Services balance	7.12	13.38	16.02	
Military transactions (net)	−0.88	0.37	1.44	
Direct investment income (net)	7.52	9.77	11.53	
Transfers (net)	−6.83	−5.41	−4.84	
Current account balance	9.34	−1.3	−20.2	

$10bn in the first quarter of 1977 to a deficit of $12bn in the first quarter of 1978, a deterioration of $22bn, all at seasonally adjusted annual rates. This swift and drastic change resulted from the relatively small increase in US manufactures exports – only 5 per cent – and the rapid increase in manufactures imports – over 35 per cent – between these four quarters.

There is some controversy about the reasons for the pronounced weakness of the US manufactures trade balance. At least three factors can be identified that have contributed to this weakness. First, compared with other industrial economies, the United States has experienced considerably faster economic growth in recent years. In 1976, the US economy grew at a rate of about 6 per cent, while the growth rate for the other principal industrial countries was about 4½ per cent. In 1977, this estimated 1½ per cent gap widened to more than 2 per cent, despite the slowing of the US growth rate to about 5 per cent. In 1978, the US growth rate is projected to be about 4 per cent, but the other industrial countries are unlikely to record an average rate much better than 3 per cent. Thus, the gap is expected to continue at about 1 per cent. Slow growth abroad has depressed demand for US exports, while relatively high growth in the United States has stimulated import demand.

Second, the international competitiveness of US manufactures appears to have deteriorated in recent years. The chart shows that from mid-1974 to mid-1976, the period of relative dollar strength, the real effective dollar exchange rate – the dollar's trade-weighted exchange rate change adjusted for inflation differentials – rose more than 10 per cent. From mid-1976 to November 1977, the real effective exchange rate of the dollar changed very little. The weakening of the competitive position of US manufactures was due both to the relative strength of the dollar and to the fact that wholesale prices of manufactures rose on the average somewhat faster in the United States than abroad.

Third, US bilateral trade with the non-OPEC developing countries swung from a \$6bn surplus in 1975 to about a \$5½bn deficit in 1977, which was the first bilateral trade deficit with these countries to occur since World War II. This swing reflected a rapid increase in US imports from these countries of about 25 per cent a year and a relatively slow growth in US exports to these countries of less than 5 per cent a year. The import surge can largely be accounted for by two developments: (i) heavy importation of manufactured products from such countries as Brazil, Mexico, Hong Kong, Korea, Malaysia, Philippines, Singapore and Taiwan, and (ii) relatively high commodity prices, particularly for coffee. The slow US export growth to these countries occurred despite the relatively strong economic expansion in the non-OPEC LDCs, averaging about 5 per cent per annum during the last two years. US exports to the LDCs are heavily concentrated in Latin America – comprising 50 per cent of US exports to the non-oil LDCs – and several key Latin American countries embarked on stabilisation programmes in 1976–7 that slowed their import growth. Therefore, the change in the US trade balance with the non-OPEC LDCs probably reflects mainly increased competitiveness of the latter.

It should be noted, however, that the poor US trade performance over the last few years was counterbalanced to a modest extent by the rise in net income from services. In the area of invisibles, the United States registered surpluses of more than $13bn in 1976 and $16bn in 1977, compared with only $7bn in 1975. The strong showing of the invisibles continues a trend that began in 1973, and is mainly due to the growth of net direct investment income, which accounted for more than 75 per cent of the 1976–7 surpluses on services transactions and for about 50 per cent of the $9bn improvement from 1975 to 1977. Net receipts on military transactions accounted for about 30 per cent of the increase of the surplus. Because of the favourable trend in net services income, the current account deterioration was not as large as that of the merchandise trade balance.

What can be said about the behaviour of the capital account during the time when the current account moved into record deficit? Contrary to frequent assertions that the United States experienced huge capital outflows in 1977, *net recorded* capital outflows in 1977 were considerably smaller than in 1976. In 1977, these outflows, that is, all capital transactions other than US Government credits, changes in liabilities to official institutions of industrial countries, and 'errors and omissions', amounted to only $1.6bn compared with $5.6bn in 1976. As Table 4.2 indicates, in 1977 US direct investment capital outflows changed little, US purchases of foreign securities dropped sharply, increases in US bank loans abroad were nearly halved, and increases in claims on foreigners by US non-bank institutions dropped to a negligible level.

There is, however, evidence that exchange market uncertainties created a significant reversal of the traditional leads and lags in international payments. This is mainly reflected in the 'errors and omissions' item of the balance of payments, which moved from a $10bn surplus in 1976 to a $3bn deficit in the United States in 1977. Furthermore, short-term bank loans to foreigners were at a rather high level in both the fourth quarter of 1977 and the first quarter of 1978.

The available statistics, therefore, suggest that capital outflows of an autonomous nature narrowed in 1977, but that there were apparently some important short-term capital outflows in recent quarters mainly associated with exchange market uncertainties engendered by the shift in deterioration of the US trade and current accounts. They thus contributed to the needed exchange rate adjustment. In conclusion, unlike the situation in the early 1960s,

Table 4.2: US Capital Flows ($bn)

	1975	*1976*	*1977*	*1977/Q4*	*1978/Q1*
Private direct investment:					
US abroad	−6.3	−4.6	−5.0	−1.5	n.a.
Foreign in US	1.4	2.2	1.5	−0.2	n.a.
	−4.9	−2.4	−3.5	−1.7	n.a.
Private portfolio investment:					
US purchases of foreign securities	−6.2	−8.7	−5.4	−0.7	−0.9
Foreign purchase of US securities	5.1	4.0	3.6	0.5	1.3
	−1.1	−4.7	−1.8	−0.2	0.4
US bank claims/liabilities:					
Claims on foreigners	−13.5	−20.9	−11.7	−9.9	−5.9
Liabilities to foreigners	0.6	11.0	6.7	3.0	−0.3
	−12.9	−9.9	−5.0	−6.9	−6.2
US nonbank claims/liabilities:					
Claims non-affiliated foreigners	−1.4	−2.0	−0.1	0.2	n.a.
Liabilities to non-affiliated foreigners	0.2	−0.6	0.0	0.1	n.a.
	−1.2	−2.6	−0.1	0.3	n.a.
Official investments by developing countries:					
OPEC countries	7.1	9.3	6.8	1.0	1.2
Non-OPEC LDCs	0.5	4.7	2.0	0.7	0.0
	7.6	14.0	8.8	1.7	1.2
Recorded net capital flows listed above	−12.5	−5.6	−1.6	−6.8	n.a.
US government credits	−3.5	−4.2	−3.7	−0.7	n.a.
Official investments by industrial countries (i.e. net exchange market intervention)	−0.7	3.9	28.7	13.9	13.6
Changes in US reserve assets[a]	−0.6	−2.5	−0.2	0.0	0.2
Errors and ommissions	5.7	9.9	−3.0	−2.2	n.a.

Note: [a] Minus sign denotes increase

when the current account was in substantial surplus and the deficit was mainly stemming from autonomous capital outflows, the current US balance of payments problem is centred in the trade account, not in the capital account.

US POLICY RESPONSE

The US approach to its present balance of payments problem has evolved considerably since 1977, probably reflecting the swiftness with which the problem emerged and the changing perceptions of the problem. At first, the United States almost solely stressed coordinating the expansionary fiscal policies of the major industrial countries. Soon after the Carter Administration took office, its representatives urged Germany, Japan and other industrial nations to follow the United States in pursuing expansionary policies in an effort to reduce the high levels of unemployment, to stem the tide of trade protectionism, and to prevent the emergence of a significant growth rate differential among these countries. Obviously, a sizable growth gap could bring about substantial imbalances in trade and current accounts, which, in turn, could lead to exchange market pressures. In advocating this approach, the United States was one of the leading proponents of the so-called locomotive strategy promoted by the OECD.

The locomotive strategy, however, ran into a number of problems. First of all, Germany and Japan were reluctant to pursue more expansionary policies, partly because of their concern about a rekindling of inflationary pressures that could result from a coordinated 'big push', and partly because of structural limitations to their economic growth potential. Second, there was growing skepticism about the rebalancing effects that coordinated fiscal policies could have. A recent OECD study, for instance, has concluded that a major reflationary programme by the OECD member countries other than the United States – a programme which would completely eliminate the growth gap differential – could only result in about a $4.7bn improvement in the US current account balance. Finally, the recent resurgence of inflationary pressures in the United States has resulted in the Carter Administration assigning a high priority to fighting inflation. In fact, Charles Schultze, the Chairman of the Council of Economic Advisers, recently stated that the recommendation of the OECD

Secretariat calling for joint stimulation of the industrial economies, no longer could be endorsed by the United States due to its rising inflation and its large trade deficit. It appears, therefore, that the United States has just about abandoned its original policy approach on the balance of payments.

Instead, the US strategy to deal with its balance of payments problem has become much more comprehensive and balanced. US external policies now emphasise the need for (i) new energy legislation to contain the growth of oil imports, (ii) a national export policy, (iii) improved operation of the flexible exchange rate system and (iv) fighting inflation.

As far as energy policy is concerned, the Carter Administration's National Energy Plan, presented in April 1977, aimed at reducing oil imports by 1985 to 7m bpd from over 8m bpd at present. With additional voluntary conservation, oil imports could be brought down to 6m bpd in 1985, according to the plan. In contrast, without any energy legislation, the administration contends, oil imports could reach 16m bpd by 1985. The major means for achieving this reduction in future oil imports is increased energy conservation. This was to be accomplished mainly by a gradual rise in domestic oil and gas prices to world levels through the imposition of various taxes on heavy energy users and tax incentives. The plan also provides incentives to stimulate greater use of non-oil energy (mainly coal) and to increase domestic oil production – although many analysts do not consider the production incentives to be adequate.

As the Carter proposals now stand in Congress, four out of five major parts have been agreed to by the Senate-House conferees and are awaiting full congressional approval. The four parts deal with natural gas pricing, industrial conversion from oil and gas to coal, restructuring of utility rates to penalise heavy users and incentives for home conservation. However, the most critical proposal of the Carter Plan – the tax on domestic crude oil to raise its cost to consumers – is in danger of not being passed.

On balance, most political analysts believe that some sort of new energy legislation, perhaps with some oil price increase, will eventually be approved in 1978. This, together with existing legislative measures (mainly those mandating car gasoline consumption levels) could contain US oil imports to around 11.5m bpd by 1985 – or to about $56bn at current oil prices. Therefore, a better US energy policy, though vital and necessary in order to prevent the trade balance from worsening severely, is nevertheless likely to be insufficient to reduce the trade deficit.

With the realisation that oil imports are going to stay high and that they are partly responsible for the secular rise of imports as a per cent of GNP, the US Government has recently embarked on a complete review of its trade policy. According to Commerce Secretary Kreps, the Administration is committed to the development of a national export policy 'for the first time in US history'. A cabinet task force under her direction is to present its recommendations to the President shortly. The scope of the report apparently will be broad, dealing with trade financing, near-term industrial and agricultural export development and promotion, possibilities for reducing obstructive government regulations, promotion of basic research and development, and eventual reform of the US industrial structure to deter imports and promote exports in the long run. Some of the report's proposals are expected to focus on tax changes, including accelerated depreciation of physical facilities to serve export markets and tax credits for the establishment of new foreign sales offices or the creation of new export product lines. Medium-size companies may receive special attention. The export opportunity information system may also be expanded and improved. Again, the rationale behind such a national export policy is clear: the structural rise in US imports must be matched by a structural rise in US exports. Existing government regulations that impede US exports may have to be revised and US industry must be made more aware of new and existing export opportunities.

While a national export policy may be helpful in reducing existing government impediments and in improving fiscal and financial incentives to exports, the main thrust behind any export drive must come from enhanced price competitiveness. This can only be accomplished by reducing the real effective exchange rate of the dollar. Since the dollar's effective appreciation by about 10 per cent in real terms between the spring of 1974 and the fall of 1977, it has slipped about 4 per cent (see figure 4.1). To many, this is a surprisingly low figure, but it reflects, in part, the adverse inflation differential the United States has recently experienced and also the 10 per cent depreciation of the Canadian dollar against the US dollar. Canada receives a very large weight in the dollar's effective rate calculation because Canada accounts for some 40 per cent of US manufactures trade with other major industrial countries. Accordingly, the US dollar in real terms is now about 3 per cent below March 1973 levels.

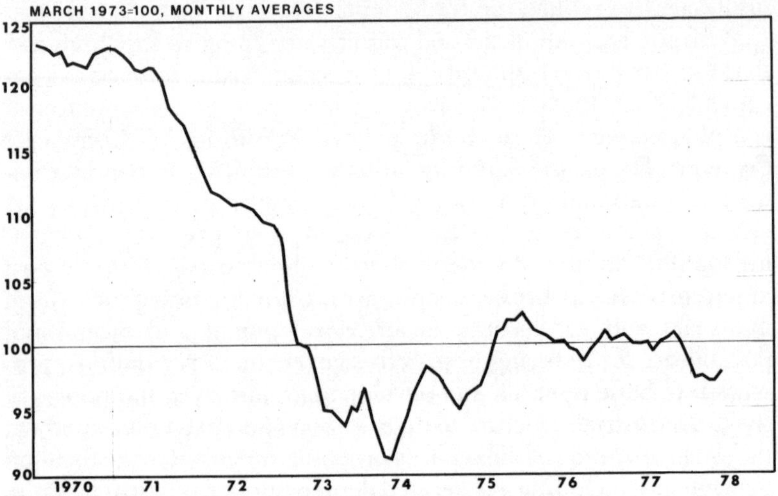

FIGURE 4.1: Real effective dollar exchange rate change March 1973 = 100, monthly averages

The US stance toward exchange rate policy has changed very little since flexible exchange rates were adopted in March 1973. US Government policy adheres to the understanding reached at Rambouillet in the fall of 1975 whereby central banks may intervene to moderate or smooth abrupt changes in exchange rates and to keep exchange markets orderly, rather than to intervene to resist fundamental market forces (for example inflation differentials, structural factors such as changes in secular trends in oil production, changes in relative growth rates). In view of the fundamentals, it is actually remarkable that the real effective depreciation of the dollar has amounted to only 4 per cent over the past nine months and has not reversed even half of its appreciation in the preceding three years.

This depreciation of the dollar, small as it has been, cannot have a lasting effect unless it is backed up by a well-designed stabilisation plan. Since the winter of 1977–8, the US Government has shifted its domestic economic priorities away from reducing unemployment towards curbing inflation. Expansionary fiscal and monetary policies have reduced the unemployment rate in the United States from a peak of 9.2 per cent in May 1975 to about 6 per cent in May 1978. Capacity utilisation in manufacturing has moved up from about 73 per cent in 1975 to 83 per cent in 1978. While the 6 per cent unemployment rate is still high compared with rates in the 1950s and 1960s, there is a growing belief that the full-employment unemployment rate in the United States is considerably higher today due to the changing composition of the US labour force. In fact according to some experts, the unemployment rate in the United States today may be within 1 per cent of full employment. As economic activity approached full employment, inflationary pressures accelerated from less than 5 per cent in 1976 to about $7\frac{1}{2}$ per cent at the moment.

According to recent statements by CEA Chairman Schultze, in order to curb inflationary pressures and the large trade deficit the United States now appears to be ready to accept a 4 per cent real growth rate in 1978, compared with the original Administration target of between $4\frac{1}{2}$ per cent and 5 per cent. On the fiscal front, President Carter has decided to delay by three months the effective date of the proposed income tax cut, and to reduce its net amount from $25bn to less than $20bn. Congress has also approved a budget for fiscal 1979 with a projected deficit of $51bn, nearly $10bn lower than that foreseen a few months ago. In addition, since mid-April 1978 the Federal Reserve has raised the Fed funds rate target from $6\frac{3}{4}$ per cent to $7\frac{1}{2}$ per cent, and the discount rate from $6\frac{1}{2}$ per cent to 7 per cent.

These measures all represent steps in the right direction, but their effects on inflation will be felt more likely in 1979 than in 1978. Wholesale prices of manufactures are expected to increase in 1978 by almost 2 per cent more in the United States than in other major industrial countries. The adverse impact of the inflation rate differential on the trade balance and the exchange rate, therefore, may partially offset the beneficial impact of the expected modest narrowing of the growth rate differentials.

REJECTED ALTERNATIVE POLICIES

The foregoing analysis shows that the US policy response to the record current account deficits has mainly been to develop an energy plan to slow the rise of oil imports and a policy to push exports either through direct incentives or through improved competitiveness. US policymakers have resisted pressures towards increased protectionism. Higher tariff barriers and quantitative restrictions probably could reduce US imports while maintaining the US growth rate in the short run. However, protectionism does not provide a long-run solution to structural problems in the United States. The solution to these problems is improving competitiveness at home and expanding markets abroad. Foreign competition is vital to maintaining efficiency in US industry and to the development of new products and production processes, and it is compatible both with higher real output growth and lower inflation over the long run. US trade policy, accordingly, has been directed at further liberalisation of the world's trading system in the Tokyo Round negotiations, rather than at resisting liberalisation.

At the same time, a number of developing countries, particularly those in the Far East, are concerned over rising protectionist sentiments in the industrial countries. They object to 'orderly marketing arrangements' aimed at limiting over the next three to four years US imports of products which have experienced especially rapid import growth, such as steel, textiles, clothing, shoes and colour televisions. On the whole, the United States, nevertheless, has supported the efforts of the developing countries to sustain high export growth and to restructure their exports away from over-reliance on primary products and towards increased emphasis on manufactures. It is recognised that high export growth is vital if these countries are to be able to repay their external obligations. Also, as these countries industrialise, they become excellent new export markets for the industrial countries.

The United States, furthermore, has rejected (against the advice of some European and US economists) the reimposition of controls on capital outflows for several reasons. First, as pointed out earlier, the heart of the US balance of payments problem is the current account deficit and not the magnitude of autonomous capital outflows, which narrowed from \$12½bn in 1975 to \$5½bn in 1976 and to \$1½bn in 1977. The sizable net capital outflows that did occur during the fall and winter of 1977 were of a short-term nature and were sensitive to confidence factors. Indeed, as soon as the US Government embarked on a convincing, anti-inflationary policy in the spring of 1977, the leads and lags were reversed and funds moved back into the United States and favourable interest rate differentials had their desired effect. During April and May 1978, perhaps half of the adverse leads and lags of the previous six months were reversed.

Secondly, capital controls in the past have been recommended as a 'bridging action' until more fundamental measures could yield results. Experience, however, suggests that such controls only postpone the adoption of more fundamental measures.

Thirdly, given the large number of channels through which funds can flow from money and capital markets in the United States, there is reason to question whether controls are likely to be effective. Our experience with controls in the 1960s and early 1970s suggests that they were effective in reducing particular types of outflows, but they also induced significant leakages through other channels, such as leads and lags and other channels not under surveillance. Furthermore, even if controls could be made more effective, it is unclear what the net effect could be on the balance of payments. A smaller volume of outflows on the capital account, for instance, would probably be offset to some extent by smaller trade and services inflows.

Finally, the United States has also rejected suggestions to trim the reserve currency role of the dollar. According to Treasury Secretary Blumenthal, this role is neither an 'exorbitant privilege' for the United States nor an 'exorbitant burden'. In the late 1960s and early 1970s, the United States was accused of running 'deficits without tears' as many European countries rapidly acquired dollar assets through foreign exchange market interventions, which were necessary to maintain fixed dollar parities. Under managed floating, however, foreign central banks are no longer obligated to acquire dollar assets and do so at their own discretion. As the 'privilege' aspect has been diminished, so has the 'burden' aspect since exchange rates can now move without tedious negotiations and international conferences. Nevertheless, the large stock of dollars in the hands of foreigners does impose constraints on US policy. While adjustments in the real effective dollar exchange rate are necessary and desirable, they also should occur in an environment of broad, general confidence so as to prevent large-scale shifting of reserves. Confidence in the dollar can best be maintained if policies promise a narrowing of the current account deficit and if interest rate differentials are sufficient to attract private capital inflows.

AN INTERDEPENDENT WORLD

It is now generally recognised that in this interdependent world the economic policies and trends of one country affect others and that any large-scale payments imbalance can only be corrected by cooperative action. It is also evident that as the substantial OPEC surplus was reduced to much smaller proportions, a new payments imbalance emerged that was centred around the United States, Japan, and, to a lesser extent, some other industrial countries.

What would be appropriate actions for countries with relatively large current account surpluses? First of all, they should accept the need, whenever appropriate, for changes in exchange rates that go well beyond offsetting inflation differentials. Too often, foreign monetary authorities only pay lip service to this desirable objective and real changes are either too small or too slow (see Table 4.3). For example, it is frequently pointed out that the US dollar should *not* be devalued in real terms in order to correct the trade deficit because the deficit is partly caused by high energy imports. To be sure, the United States must develop a policy of energy conservation and better exploit its domestic energy resources in order to moderate the increase in its oil imports. Beyond that, however, the secular decline in US energy self-sufficiency should be allowed to have an impact on the dollar exchange rate, particularly now that the OPEC surplus has narrowed sharply.

TABLE 4.3: Index of Effective Exchange Rates Adjusted for Inflation[a] (March 1973 = 100)

	1973	*1974*	*1975*	*1976*	*1977*	*June 1978*
United States	98.2	95.1	98.6	100.2	100.1	96.0
Canada	101.6	107.5	102.7	106.6	99.3	94.1
Japan	98.2	99.4	87.9	88.9	94.6	108.5
West Germany	104.3	105.1	100.6	101.6	103.0	99.2
France	101.2	94.5	102.9	100.6	96.8	99.6
Italy	100.2	105.6	98.9	93.8	97.0	95.7
United Kingdom	97.4	100.0	103.8	96.2	101.2	104.0

Note: [a] The index of effective exchange rates, adjusted for inflation, for each country is derived by multiplying a trade-weighted index of relative prices of manufactures times a trade-weighted index of exchange rates. A rise in the index indicates impairment of competitiveness because of changes in exchange rates and/or prices.

It is difficult to believe that the heavy foreign purchases of dollars – totaling more than $40bn in 1977 and the first quarter of 1978 – by the central banks of the industrial countries and the frequent calls on the United States to sell gold and to float foreign-currency-denominated bond issues in their capital markets were solely for the purpose of maintaining orderly exchange markets. Instead, these interventions appear to have had a protectionist bias, limiting the ability of the United States to correct its current account deficit. Furthermore, those interventions that supposedly have been for the purpose of maintaining orderly markets have been highly asymmetrical – heavy when foreign currencies appreciate against the dollar and light or absent when the movements are in the opposite direction. It is, therefore, desirable that the new Article IV Agreement of the IMF be given operational content in the form of a stronger surveillance role for the Fund, whereby it is empowered to examine the exchange rate policies of member countries.

Second, there is need for further trade liberalisation. While the Kennedy Round of trade negotiations in the early 1960s was successful in cutting tariffs on manufactured products by an average of 35 per cent, the remaining protection has shifted from tariffs to other forms of trade barriers and to barriers in agricultural trade. The United States, the world's largest exporter of agricultural products, has a strong interest in this area. The most significant agricultural protection is in Europe, where the EEC Common Agricultural Policy employs a system of 'variable levies' as part of a programme to maintain farm income, and in Japan, where quotas are used to restrict agricultural imports. Various studies made in recent years have concluded that liberalisation of the feed grains and livestock sector would cause a substantial increase in US agricultural exports.

On top of this, Japan has pursued policies over a number of years that discourage imports of manufactures. Thus, Japan's share of manufactures imports to total imports is only about 20 per cent, compared with more than 50 per cent for most other major industrial nations. Indeed, in 1977 the Japanese surplus on trade manufactures reached about \$65bn and its imports of manufactures were only \$15bn – about half as much as those of the Netherlands, with an economy one seventh of Japan's. Opening the Japanese market will not be an easy task in view of the difficult domestic distribution network, but Japanese authorities at least recognise the need to liberalise imports.

Third, just as a country with a large current account deficit such as the United States should welcome and encourage the import of autonomous capital from abroad, industrial countries whose current account balances are in surplus or near equilibrium should ease or remove their controls on private capital outflows. A number of countries have continued to limit such outflows long after there is any balance of payments justification. To the extent that other countries limit foreign access to their national capital markets, borrowers are diverted, directly or indirectly, to other countries that maintain open markets (such as the United States), thereby adding to the potential pressures on the dollar.

Japan, which has seen its current account surplus mushroom from less than $4bn in 1976 to more than $20bn in the first four months of 1978, at a seasonally adjusted annual rate, has been very slow to open its domestic capital markets to foreigners. Belatedly, Japanese authorities have allowed a considerable increase in the issuance of yen bonds by foreign borrowers from a total value of $230m in 1976 to nearly $1.3bn in 1977 and more than $2bn in the first half of 1978. But these amounts are still very modest in relation to the magnitude of Japan's current account surplus, and judging from the queue of willing borrowers, the volume of the foreign issue activity could be much higher if the authorities allowed it to be. Furthermore, a large portion of the foreign yen issues are purchased by foreign investors, so that the actual net export of Japanese savings is much smaller than suggested by the gross volume of new issues. Japanese banks also are limited in the amount of yen loans they are permitted to make to foreign borrowers. Meanwhile, Japanese banks and corporations continue to draw actively on overseas financial markets.

The United Kingdom is another country that has clung to capital controls much longer than necessary or justified by its current account performance. The United Kingdom, for example, heavily restricts foreign access to the domestic capital market either through the issuance of bonds or through sterling loans from UK banks. Moreover, UK direct and portfolio investors are required to pay a premium to purchase foreign currencies for overseas investment or to finance such investment by borrowing abroad. These capital controls were being maintained even when the country's current account moved into a small surplus.

It is also ironic that at the same time various foreign governments have been urging the US Treasury to issue foreign currency bonds abroad to help finance the US current account deficit, governments of several industrial countries have been taking advantage of the large and open US capital market, thereby tending to increase US capital outflows.

Fourth, while claims by proponents of the locomotive strategy were grossly exaggerated, there is, nevertheless, need for countries with large current account surpluses to pursue domestic policies that are compatible with moderate growth in the world economy. This is especially important if the US growth rate target is lowered over the next year or two. While no country can dictate domestic policy targets, Germany and Japan both should strive to achieve their 1978 target growth rates of $3\frac{1}{2}$ per cent and 7 per cent, respectively. These targets do not appear attainable to most observers with the policy measures presently in effect in these countries. It is important that surplus countries recognise that unless the growth gap between the United States and other industrial countries is narrowed, the adjustment of the US current account deficit will be more difficult.

The policy approach towards solving the large US payments imbalance described in this paper, which I believe also is similar to present US Government thinking, essentially is liberal and internationalistic and not protectionist and nationalistic. It recognises that major payments improvement can be achieved only through mutual, cooperative efforts. The issues of economic growth, inflation, exchange rates, international trade barriers and capital flows are all intertwined more than ever before. The United States has a major responsibility to tackle its problems of inflation, energy and exports, but other countries must not frustrate US efforts by protecting their exchange rates and their economic and financial markets. To be sure, the industrial nations have to work very hard to assure that the present liberal and international approach is successful in narrowing the economic growth gap, the inflation differentials, and also in bringing about structural improvements. If the present efforts fail and the major imbalance continues, the danger will increase that the world will move into controls over goods and capital flows.

5 Economic Nationalism and the Problem of the Weak Currency Countries: The Italian Example

Innocenzo Cipolletta

I have been asked to consider the weak currency countries, their position in the emerging tendency towards economic nationalism and the changes with which they are faced in this new context. The Italian example will serve as a background for the ideas which I propose to develop.

It is evident from the title of my paper that an implicit relationship is recognised between currency floating (in the absence of which it would be illogical to distinguish between 'weak' and 'strong' currencies) and the current tendency towards economic nationalism. Before dealing with the case of Italy, I would like briefly to illustrate my views regarding the way in which generalised currency floating acts on the evolution of various economic systems. Following this introduction, I propose to discuss the Italian case, as an example of a weak currency country confronted by external and internal pressures towards protectionism. In the last part of the paper, I shall briefly analyse the relationship between protectionism and floating exchange rates, considering the former as a response to the latter once all the other means to offset the consequences of floating have been exhausted.

SOME REFLECTIONS ON THE RECENT EXPERIENCE OF THE FLOATING EXCHANGE SYSTEM

The 1970s have witnessed the extension of a system of floating exchange rates, and it is therefore possible to draw some conclusions about its economic consequences. In my opinion, saying that this is not a true system of floating rates simply because the monetary authorities are not barred from intervening in the currency markets is like saying that free competition never existed because all the conditions required were never put together in any country at any given time. The latter statement may in fact be true but, nevertheless, certain countries have, for a long time, been considered to be 'market oriented economies', although everybody is fully aware that free competition is only an abstraction (whose actual existence would perhaps not be altogether desirable).

The shifts in exchange rates have involved a shift of purchasing power among countries. For the weak currency countries this has meant losing part of their real external purchasing power to strong currency countries.

In contrast with the exchange rate stability of the industrialised countries in the 1960s – despite the devaluation of the pound sterling in 1967 and of the French franc in 1969 – the 1970s have witnessed sharp changes. The Swiss franc and the German mark have gained on average 62 per cent and 43 per cent respectively in the seven years since 1971, while the Italian lira and the pound sterling have lost 41 per cent and 37 per cent.

Under such circumstances, in order to enable the international economic system as a whole to maintain the same growth rate as in the past, the strong currency countries should have accelerated their development so as to compensate for the lower growth of those countries experiencing a decline in their purchasing power. The transfer of resources would thus have taken place without causing a deceleration in growth rates and balance of payments disequilibria. (An econometric model could easily show which growth rates in the strong currency countries would have made possible the achievement of both the above-mentioned objectives.) Setting aside the influence of occasional factors, progress in this direction could have been expected by the end of a five-year period.

This, however, did not occur, as a comparison of the last decade (1960–70) with the first seven years of the present decade will show.

In the 1960s (Table 5.1), the growth rate of the six major industrialised countries (United States, Germany, Japan, France, the United Kingdom and Italy), while fluctuating considerably on an annual basis, reached an average of 4.9 per cent per annum, with a high of 10.8 per cent for Japan and a low of 2.8 per cent for the United Kingdom. During 1970–7, however, the growth rate of these countries dropped to an average of 3.3 per cent per annum; differences between countries also lessened (at least in absolute value), the lowest growth again taking place in the United Kingdom, at a rate of 1.7 per cent per annum, and the highest rate again in Japan, at 5.6 per cent per annum.

TABLE 5.1: Average Annual Percentage Change of Gross Domestic Product in Volume of Selected OECD Countries

	1960–70	*1970–7*
United States	+ 3.9	+3.1
Japan	+10.8	+5.6
Germany	+ 4.7	+2.6
France	+ 5.6	+3.8
United Kingdom	+ 2.8	+1.7
Italy	+ 5.5	+2.8
Total	+ 4.9	+3.3

In other words, weak currency countries actually reduced their rate of growth – having been forced to do so by their loss of purchasing power – but at the same time a corresponding increase in the growth rate of strong currency countries did not occur. While one would have expected the range of growth rates to widen, they have in fact narrowed towards the lower end of the scale.

The transfer of purchasing power from weak currency countries was actually 'sterilised' by the strong currency countries, which proved unable to increase their domestic demand as circumstances could have required.

As a matter of fact, many strong currency countries acted in the same way as some OPEC countries, which were unable to assimilate an increase in purchasing power arising from unilateral decisions. In fact, the explosion of oil prices can easily be equated – theoretically and practically – to a revaluation of the currencies of those countries whose sole or principal export is represented by oil. In both cases (currency revaluation and increase of oil prices) a substantial increase in purchasing power – expressed by a shift in the terms of trade – takes place. Moreover, both instances give rise to inflationary pressure, even though statistically this phenomenon is not perceived in its country of origin, owing to the above-mentioned change in the terms of trade.

It might, of course, be argued that the direction of causation should be reversed: currency floating could be the effect of a generalised slowdown in growth rates, (the cause of which must be looked for elsewhere). In turn, a more appropriate response to this slowdown would have been given by the strong currency countries, rather than by those with weak currencies. Such an explanation may have some validity, although it does not answer the question why the slowdown of growth was preceded by currency floating and not vice versa. However, the fact remains that strong currency countries have sterilized development capacity in weak currency countries.

Another generally held theoretical corollary of currency floating is that it should bring inflation rates back to equilibrium, so that if a source of inflation exists, it is internationally isolated until equilibrium is restored.

In this case too, disappointment of expectations (if any had been actually entertained) is manifest. In fact, if exchange rate alterations did balance inflationary differentials, this operation went *ultra petita*, i.e. well beyond what would have been necessary. In other words, inflation rates prevailing in different countries, when converted into a single currency, show an even greater variability than if expressed in the original currency, but their reciprocal position appears reversed (Table 5.2). When converted into dollars, the strongest inflation rates among the six above-mentioned industrialised countries occur in Japan and Germany with yearly increases of the order 13–14 per cent, while those of Italy and the United Kingdom are among the lowest at about 8 per cent per

TABLE 5.2: Average Rate of Change of Consumer prices

	In national currencies		*In US dollars*
	1960–70	*1970–7*	*1970–7*
United States	+2.6	+ 6.3	+ 6.3
Japan	+5.7	+10.0	+14.5
Germany	+3.0	+ 5.9	+13.1
France	+4.2	+ 9.0	+11.0
United Kingdom	+4.0	+13.3	+ 8.2
Italy	+3.9	+13.4	+ 8.0
Total	+3.3	+ 7.8	+ 8.6

annum. If inflation rates are expressed in national currencies, the position is of course the opposite, with the lowest inflation rate held by the United States.

Another consideration holds in this context: not only did currency fluctuations not reduce inflationary differentials, but they were also associated with an increase in the average rate of inflation. If related to a single currency (the US dollar), the rate of inflation of the six countries shifts from 3.3 per cent per annum in the 1960s, to 8.6 per cent per annum in the 1970s.

In this case as well, it is rather difficult to decide which of the two phenomena – currency floating and inflation – is the cause and which is the effect: it must, however, be emphasised once again that the outburst of inflation was preceded by strong variations in exchange rates.

Another 'benefit' expected from floating exchange rates is the alleged 'independence' of each nation to enact domestic economic policies appropriate to its specific structures and goals. It is evident that this expectation has not been fulfilled: industrialised countries have never been so mutually interdependent in their short-term development as in the 1970s: every attempt to follow a separate evolution has been thwarted. This is true not only for weak currency countries like Italy or Spain, but also for Germany, Japan, Switzerland and, to some extent, even the United States. Indeed, all industrialised countries experienced strong expansionary phases in 1972–3 (ending in 1973–4); this was followed by a deep recession that came to an end, with slight lags from country to country, between the spring and summer of 1975; finally there was a strong recovery between the autumn of 1975 and the spring of 1976. Subsequently, all these countries (with the exception of the United States) experienced a slowdown in the summer of 1976, a recovery in the following autumn and a further slowdown during 1977.

Under these circumstances, to what extent does it still make sense to speak of economic independence? Italy, which adopted restrictive policies starting in 1976, experienced a short-term evolution exactly similar to that of Japan and Germany, that is to say, countries which adopted a variety of measures to support domestic demand.

The industrial economies are, in fact, more and more closely linked with one another given the current economic situation: a single country is unable to deviate from the international cycle because the impulses it receives from abroad are amplified and accelerated by the floating currency system. Flattened growth rates in industrial countries, emphasising close cyclical concordance, have been accompanied by a wider dispersion of inflation rates, the consequence of which is currency floating.

In conclusion, whereas during the 1960s, relations among currencies were stable and individual economic systems fluctuated on the basis of accepted exchange rate variations, in the 1970s business cycles have become closely synchronised. The outcome has been highly destabilising: on average, growth has decreased , while inflation has increased.

The process of currency floating has thus shown such strong self-propagating characteristics that we are unable to interrupt it. The restoration of equilibrium is always postponed and that is why we are tempted to break this vicious circle by raising barriers at the borders – not only for trade but for currency movements as well.

On the other hand, currency floating cannot be compared with price fluctuations with their self-equilibrating effects due to demand–supply interaction. Even assuming that exchange variations depend on pre-existing structural differences among the various economies, they end up only apparently restoring the previous conditions from which such structural differences stemmed; in no case do they actually modify structures. The currency float is only a warning indicator of disequilibria, but it does not contribute to restore equilibrium. On the contrary, it hinders those structural changes whose absence is the very cause of such disequilibria.

When exchange rate variations do not arise from structural differences (as has so often been the case over the last few years), it still remains true that they determine such differences and thus find *ex post* the warrant they did not have *ex ante*. Who would doubt, nowadays, that the Italian rate of inflation is six to seven times the Swiss rate? But this was not the situation in the 1960s, before currency floating.

Clearly, the variations in exchange rates do not only involve differences in inflation rates. The entire production process becomes involved, since a country whose currency is revalued tends to redirect its production towards goods and services with a low price elasticity of demand (with a preference for physical or technological monopolistic production). In contrast, a country which is led to devalue its currency is increasingly driven towards products and services with a high price elasticity of demand (to take advantage of devaluation). This is another feature of the self-feeding mechanism of exchange variations, which tend to determine or reinforce dualistic patterns, accompanied by the implicit and imminent risk of further and deeper disequilibria not only at the economic level but at the social level as well.

THE CASE OF ITALY: A WEAK CURRENCY COUNTRY

In order to examine the case of Italy, it is appropriate to take a step backward and recall the equilibrium conditions of the Italian economy on the eve of the floating process that has involved all currencies, including the lira, since the beginning of 1973.

Despite the destabilising impact of the sharp salary increases that followed tense wage negotiations in the autumn of 1969 (which came to be known as the 'hot autumn'), in mid-1970 the current account showed only a slight deficit which was readily absorbed in the year's average. Thus, the year 1970 ended with a current account surplus of over $1 bn. In 1971, due also to a slight recession, the surplus was about $2 bn and remained at the same level in 1972. During that period, Italy was still described as being unable to develop sufficient domestic demand, and thus having to find investment outlets abroad. A few months was all that was needed to change this image of Italy to one of a country living above its means.

Italy's balance of payments felt no strain up to the end of 1972. The pace of inflation was also relatively satisfactory. The increase of consumer prices in Italy throughout 1972 was the same as that in Germany, slightly lower than that in France and Japan and definitely lower than that in the United Kingdom; Italy's inflation rate was higher only than that of the United States.

Table 5.3 shows the ratios between consumer price indices in Italy and in five industrialised countries for the years 1970–2 and for each quarter of 1972. The mean has been calculated by weighing each national index with its relative weight on the world market, taking into account the competitive importance of each country compared to Italy.

Summing up, until the end of 1972 the Italian inflation rate was of the same order of magnitude as that in other countries and the balance of payments was firmly in surplus. These brief remarks on the equilibrium conditions of the Italian economy are not, of course,

TABLE 5.3: Ratios Between Index of Consumer Prices in Italy and in Five Industrialised Countries (1970 = 100)

	1970	1971	1972	1972			
				Q1	Q2	Q3	Q4
Italy/United States	100.0	100.5	102.9	101.6	102.1	103.0	104.9
Italy/Japan	100.0	98.8	99.9	99.6	99.0	99.9	101.2
Italy/Germany	100.0	99.5	99.7	99.1	99.4	99.8	100.9
Italy/France	100.0	99.5	99.2	99.2	99.2	99.0	99.6
Italy/United Kingdom	100.0	95.8	94.5	94.8	94.4	94.4	94.7
Italy/Average Five Countries[a]	100.0	99.1	99.6	99.2	99.3	99.6	100.8

Note: [a] Weighted with the relative share of Italian competitors in world markets.

sufficient to deny the overvaluation of the Italian currency. Many other considerations have to be kept in mind, such as those concerning the overall production structure and those regarding expectations (in 1973, labour contract renewals were preceded and accompanied by serious controversies). The fact remains however, that even today in Italy, these two variables, inflation and balance of payments, are treated as if they were a cause of lira devaluation, rather than an effect.

I believe Italy provides clear proof of the view that the floating exchange system, far from facilitating a return to equilibrium or structural evolution, requires, on the contrary, much stronger efforts than a fixed exchange system in order to obtain these two results.

Italy, in fact, reacted to devaluation in the 'classical' manner by giving up domestic growth, reducing real imports and developing exports, in relative terms. Between 1972 and 1977, real GDP increased at an annual rate of 3 per cent, against an average annual increase of over 5 per cent during the 1960s. Imports increased at an annual rate of 4 per cent in volume terms, that is to say, one third the average rate of the 1960s; moreover, their GDP elasticity was 1.5 or much lower than in the 1960s when it had been about 2. Exports, on the contrary, increased twice as fast as imports during the same period; the annual volume rate of growth of exports was 8 per cent, or two thirds of their growth rate during the 1960s.

The lira devaluation thus depressed both imports and the growth of internal demand, but 're-equilibrium' in real terms was permanently outweighed by the performance of the same variables in monetary terms. Imports at current prices almost quadrupled, equalling the increase in export values and thus cancelling, in balance of payments terms, the advantages of this transfer of income to the rest of the world. Moreover, owing to the fact that this performance was not linear, but involved in the first years a faster increase in import than in export values, Italy accumulated – between 1973 and 1977 – a current account deficit of about $8 bn. Its debt towards foreign institutions amounted to some $18 bn by the first half of 1978.

This divergent evolution of the same variables in real and monetary terms is reflected, of course, in higher price increases for imports than for exports; in fact, the terms of trade deteriorated by about twenty points between 1972 and 1977 as a consequence of both higher oil prices and, above all, the devaluation of the lira.

The aforesaid transfer of real resources, which took place through the squeeze of domestic demand and the development of exports, has thus become a necessary compensation for the loss of external purchasing power.

The loss of purchasing power has, in turn, led the Italian, as well as other economies, to a lesser propensity to save in order to maintain a certain rate of growth of consumption. Investment has declined sharply during the past five years, while consumption growth merely slowed down. Both development potential and employment growth were thus jeopardised. Therefore, the process started by the lira devaluation turns into a continuing devaluation through the lack of new investment: this is a vicious circle which cannot be interrupted by mere short-term intervention.

The restoration of equilibrium in the Italian balance of payments in 1977 cannot in fact be considered as having resorbed the lira devaluation and the increase in oil price, and the earlier development of the economy cannot be resumed, beginning from today, on the basis of a new order.

This is so, not because the Italian economy did not respond 'correctly' to its loss of purchasing power (we have already mentioned its 'classical' response), but rather because highly unstable exchange markets and the pursuit of national goals in fighting inflation generate constantly destabilising impulses. In fact – as we have already seen for 1973 – the turmoil in exchange rates is not justified by the different pace of inflation among the various industrialised countries. On the contrary, the present lower inflation rates in countries such as Germany or Switzerland originate essentially in the appreciation of their respective currencies and therefore – through a transition process – in the higher inflation rates of weak currency countries. Consequently, the most effective way to keep inflation under control in strong currency countries is to maintain a strong currency, and this obviously entails further devaluation and a higher rate of inflation for other countries.

We must then acknowledge that the industrialised economic system is going through an inflationary phase which cannot be considered as the sum of national inflations, but derives from an alteration in the terms of trade with respect to the rest of the world. Every individual attempt, within industrialised countries, to reduce their own inflation rate only amounts to a transfer of inflation to other countries – through currency floating. The resulting destabilising processes delay – if they do not prevent – the restoration of a more balanced development. That is why any stabilisation of exchange rates will necessarily entail a higher inflation rate for strong currency countries.

This will be the arithmetical result of the compression of inflation in weak currency countries. Thus would come to an end the absurd competion – conducted essentially by means of monetary instruments – which sees the industrial countries involved in an effort to restrain the progression of domestic prices while pushing them up externally. In fact, how can Switzerland and Germany possibly be referred to as countries with the lowest inflation rate when prices for their products on world markets have grown more than, or as much as, those of other countries?

Coming back to the Italian case, the restoration of balance of payments equilibrium, which took place in 1977 and which has been maintained in the early part of 1978, cannot warrant exchange stability, just as it could not warrant it in 1973. But since then, the situation has worsened: the re-equilibrium attained in 1977 is based on a substantial slackening of import growth arising from a sharp slowdown in economic expansion. Recession is therefore a necessary consequence of devaluation, even if the immediate effect of the latter (a 'perverse' effect to use the prevailing terminology) consists, to a certain extent, in the recovery of demand. It thus follows that domestic demand must be continuously kept under control in order to avoid further destabilising increases in imports.

In 1977, the slowdown in imports was also accompanied by a reduction in import elasticity with regard to GDP. However, this phenomenon – which was favoured by the variation in the terms of trade – cannot be extended beyond certain limits, in the short and medium term, because import substitution (beyond the 'step' recorded after the oil crisis) requires important restructuring of the overall production system. This, in turn, implies circumstances and factors generally absent from weak currency countries. Therefore, the reduction of imports – on which the re-equilibrium of the Italian balance of payments is largely based – appears to be inconsistent with a durable recovery of the economy and thus represents a built-in element of potential equilibrium.

The structure of Italian foreign trade also points to the precariousness of the recently attained equilibrium. As a typical response to terms of trade changes, the re-equilibrium of the Italian balance of payments was not obtained through a reduction of imbalances in the usual deficit items, but resulted mainly from a considerable improvement of those traditionally in surplus.

In fact, the deterioration of the terms of trade was at the root of two parallel trends. First, expenditure rose for essential imports, such as oil, raw materials and food products. Second, strong domestic inflation occurred and was transferred to export prices for manufactured goods (which were later re-introduced on the international market, owing to devaluation), while recession reduced imports of manufactures. As a result, within five years, the surplus on manufactured goods fully compensated for the growing deficit caused by oil, raw materials and food products.

The Italian balance of payments thus suffers from a strong dualism between surplus and deficit items: this phenomenon increases the vulnerability of the Italian economy, since the magnitude of sectoral disequilibria makes the Italian balance of payments more sensitive to external events (rises in food or raw material prices, recession in the industrialised countries, etc.).

A further indication of such vulnerability is demonstrated by the relative weight of import–export movements in the Italian economy. By a considerable acceleration of a tendency already present in the 1950s and 1960s, the ratio of imports and exports to current GDP shifted from 45.7 in 1972 to 61.3 per cent in 1977. At such levels and at such a rate of change, the Italian economy is influenced to a greater extent than in previous years by the international context – hence the constant need to adapt the domestic short-term evolution of Italy to that of other countries. If this adjustment fails to occur, a further devaluation of the lira can hardly be avoided; this may provide some respite in the short run, but in the longer term, would again bring about the above-described constraint, with even more serious repercussions.

TABLE 5.4: Italian Balance of Trade, by sector (lira bn)

	1970	*1971*	*1972*	*1973*	*1974*	*1975*	*1976*	*1977*
Oil products	− 910	−1156	−1205	−1534	−5459	−5206	−7348	−8014
Raw materials	− 845	− 758	− 850	−1335	−2187	−1814	−2941	−3135
Food products	−1055	−1314	−1557	−2565	−2949	−2885	−3788	−4204
Other products	+1708	+2688	+3197	+2179	+3706	+7572	+8513	+13132
Total	−1102	− 540	− 415	−3255	−6889	−2333	−5564	−2221

If we now turn from the conditions of external equilibrium to those of internal equilibrium, we will see that in this case too, the improvement of the last few months might prove to be short-lived. In fact the self-perpetuating mechanisms of the devaluation process are to be found in the explicit or implicit indexation of incomes received by factors of production.

This mechanism is evident in Italy, given the explicit indexation of wages, with a virtually complete coverage even today. Econometric evaluations show that in Italy the advantages of devaluation are practically resorbed by domestic price increases within a period of about eight quarters; well over 50 per cent of such advantages are absorbed within the first four quarters.[1]

Wage indexation, however, is not the only problem. Other revenues are also linked to an indexation process which through subsequent steps amplifies inflation. In 1977 dependent workers in Italy accounted for 70 per cent of total employment, compared with much higher percentages in other countries: this testifies to the continuing importance of self-employed workers in the Italian economy.

Thus, no wage-earner will accept that his spending power be reduced when an external event – such as devaluation – intervenes to alter a given price–income relationship, nor can such a reduction be imposed authoritatively. The interaction of mutual catching-up processes, occurring through an increase of remuneration per product unit, causes prices to rise to a level above the one which would have been implicitly justified by the initial impact of devaluation. This 'reaction' could be broken, in a way, by the 1972–73 (ending in 1973–74); this was followed by a deep recession phenomenon and warrant an even distribution of burdens.

Italy has, however, witnessed the failure of this function, since the public sector – in the broad sense, that is to say, including public corporations – is the only one not to have completely 'indexed' its revenues. If, in fact, taxation has increased in line with the increase in income, the same has not occurred for prices of public services and goods, which are seriously lagging behind their respective production costs. The burden of devaluation has thus been passed onto some sectors (transport, electric power production, public health, etc.) which have been immunised from 'market laws'. In fact, a correct functioning of market laws would have imposed a drastic reduction in expenditures, as well as a downward adjustment in the quality of public services (in conformity with 'sticky' price adjustment).

Extensive public borrowing resulted from the above phenomenon, contributing to inflation through an ample creation of money (accompanied by capital outflows from Italy in the expectation – which obviously materialised – of subsequent devaluations). Its effect will weigh heavily in the near future because every price adjustment in the public sector (whether effected through increases in public tariffs or direct/indirect taxation) will again trigger a process of reciprocal adjustments tending to amplify price increases.

In conclusion, from the standpoint of the Italian economy, the past few years' experience appears to demonstrate that devaluation processes – essentially connected with the business cycle – cannot find valuable correctives in short-term adjustments: the Italian economy has achieved a modest growth rate in line with its reduced spending power abroad. It has re-equilibrated (at first in 'physical' and subsequently also in 'monetary' terms) its balance of payments, but the lira still remains in the area of weak currencies. Meanwhile, the overall production system has deteriorated, because economic recession and inflation have imposed a 'stop–go' policy with negative effect on investment. Therefore, the large public spending deficit casts a shadow on future prospects. In the first place, should the deficit be resorbed too swiftly, it will have a generally destabilising effect. Furthermore, if additional resources are not readily put to use in some realistic form of planning for public expenditure, progressive deterioration will occur in all the public services.

EXCHANGE RATE FLOATING AND PROTECTIONISM

We have seen how in recent years, exchange rate flexibility has started self-perpetuating 'vicious' or 'virtuous' circles tending to widen differences among countries and, therefore, to exacerbate conflicts of interest. No country, however, has passively accepted these changes in its position, since this would have implied painful restructuring, both for strong currency countries, whose weak sectors would have been overtaken by foreign competition, and for weak currency countries, for which devaluation would entail drastic losses in purchasing power and thus, more expensive supplies from abroad. The impossibility of accepting these burdens has resulted in a general search for protective measures. Among these, fiscal policy seems to have acquired some popularity within the industrialised countries.

For many years, wide support has been given to the theory of social (and also economic) preference for direct taxation on incomes, while indirect taxation was considered almost as a necessary evil to attain an adequate level of taxation, or at best, as a tool to direct consumer demand. The preference for direct taxation derives from the desire to impose an equitable burden on taxpayers. Short-term considerations are also taken into account, and in fact, direct taxation is recognised to have a smaller inflationary effect than indirect taxation, which has an immediate impact on final prices.

The analysis of theories underlying the choices of different countries as to fiscal policy is beyond the scope of this paper. It should, however, be emphasised that in industrialised countries the general preference is shifting, covertly or openly, from direct to indirect taxation. There have been many such examples in the recent past; from a more theoretical point of view, a group of experts in the United Kingdom, headed by Professor James Meade, has recently advocated total replacement of direct by indirect taxation, particularly on consumer expenditure.

The arguments in favour of indirect taxation are certainly not lacking in foundation and apply particularly to those countries – such as Italy – where production is not sufficiently controlled and is consequently only partially taxed. It must, however, be emphasised that a shift from direct to indirect taxation results, to some extent, in a shift of taxation from domestically produced goods, to imported ones. This occurs not only because imports are more sensitive to tax rate differentials under a system of indirect taxation, but also because a shift takes place from taxation on national value added to taxation on goods or services with a specific import content.

Three cases can be quoted as examples. Immediately after the German mark revaluations, German taxpayers, especially farmers, requested a reduction of direct taxation, to be compensated, in terms of fiscal revenue, by an increase in indirect taxation. Other things being equal, this manoeuvre would have allowed German producers to reduce their prices, thus offsetting indirect taxation increases on the domestic market which would have additionally burdened only imported products.

In Italy, only a partial 'fiscalisation' of social charges has been carried out (for example, social security taxes paid by the firm have been reduced) and the lower receipts of social security agencies have been recovered through an increase in indirect taxation. In this case as well, domestic producers have been favoured (both on foreign and domestic markets) to the detriment of foreign producers.

In the United Kingdom, a Temporary Employment Subsidy was recently introduced for enterprises with redundant labour. In the United Kingdom, as well, measures such as this are financed by means of an increase in indirect taxation. Often in this country, the various 'pay guidelines' have been essentially based on wage restraint, accompanied by relief on direct taxation; this has been compensated, in turn, by a progressive increase of indirect taxation.

In other words, in all three cases tax relief on internal production has been partially compensated by taxation of imports. Even though all countries have admittedly resorted to this practice, the strong currency countries undoubtedly stand to benefit the most from it.

In the first place, the budget policy of a strong currency country is bound to be less restrictive, owing to fewer balance of payments constraints; such a country is also in a better position to manoeuvre tax rates. Secondly, as we have already seen, a country that revalues also manages, in this way, to restrict price increases: it can consequently increase indirect taxation with greater ease, without setting in motion an inflationary spiral. Thus, even with respect to the negative consequences of exchange floating, strong currency countries have an advantage over weak currency countries. This lack of symmetry helps also to explain why floating spontaneously tends towards equilibrium.

From what has been said above, it follows that the only way to offset or stop exchange rate alterations is to resort to external, authoritarian interventions: if, in the long run, reorientation of production is the only viable response, then in the short period, such interventions may only amount to a recourse to protectionism (in its various aspects).

Protectionism evidently concerns not only reciprocal relationships among industrialised countries, but also, and most importantly, affects relations with developing countries. In this respect, the position of weak currency countries is particularly delicate: exchange depreciation allows their technologically less advanced products to enter temporarily the international markets. But these goods are not competing with similar goods produced by countries which have revalued or, more generally, by industrialised countries: competition takes place against developing countries whose production costs are inevitably lower than in the industrialised countries, including weak currency countries.

The latter are therefore experiencing an evident contradiction: on the one hand, depreciation drives them back towards the production of goods which either have a low technological content or are characterised by a mature technology; on the other hand, the pressure exercised by developing countries cuts them off from this market and pushes them towards the market of advanced technology production. Their production costs, however, will never drop to the level of the developing countries because notwithstanding currency floating, it is still true that the factors of production market – and in particular the labour market – is highly integrated today among the industrialised countries, especially in Europe. This is so, not because large movements of workers are to be expected from low-wage to high-wage regions (labour mobility tends on the contrary to diminish everywhere), but because labour conditions tend to become alike everywhere, thus imposing the same costs.

This is a constraint which it would be useless, or detrimental, to refuse to acknowledge. For this reason as well, pressures towards protectionism are becoming increasingly strong, affecting various social and political components in industrialised countries.

After five years of notable modifications in reciprocal exchange rates, it would be pointless and dangerous to ignore them and call for, beginning from 'tomorrow', a situation of fixed exchange and free trade. Some aberrant modifications in exchange rates should however, be corrected. Others should be 'assimilated' and structural modifications reflecting the present exchange rates must therefore be favoured. We probably even need to accept – for a limited period of time and under sufficient control – a certain amount of protectionism. This should, however, be aimed at creating the preconditions for those structural changes which would subsequently render even safeguard measures unnecessary.

By way of conclusion, I would like to stress that the restoration of exchange stability and free international trade must be deliberately programmed and actively desired, as it cannot result spontaneously from free market forces and can only be the outcome of a deliberate action of the international community.

NOTE

1. Cf C. M. Pierucci and C. Tresoldi, 'Il settore dei prezzi interni: aspetti istituzionali di riferimento e verifica empirica', *Banca d'Italia*, December 1976.

6 Financial Markets and Economic Nationalism

Nicolas Krul

Money and finance are an essential part of power. Financial markets had become subject to government management well before Keynes' famous statement in the 'End of Laissez-Faire':

> My second example relates to savings and investment. *I believe that some coordinated act of intelligent judgement is required as to the scale on which it is desirable that the community as a whole should save, the scale on which these savings should go abroad in the form of foreign investments and whether the present organisation of the investment market distributes savings along the most nationally productive channels.* I do not think that these matters should be left entirely to the chances of private judgement and private profits, as they are at present.

However, it was only when growth and stability became matters of specific national policies, and technological progress made for interrelated financial markets, that systematic financial nationalism emerged. It is this systematic effort to police private financial transactions in view of collective national targets, and the evaluation of its repercussions, mainly in Europe, to which I shall address myself in this paper.

I

The effort to police the savings – investment process in abstraction from its international context is habitually studied as part of the welfare economics of controls on international capital movements, by analogy with the trade model. According to the assumption of efficient allocation in competitive markets, this theory focuses on the restriction of capital movements as a tool of intervention affecting world real income. In my view, this is too narrow an approach as in fact the fragmentation of world finance is rooted in two different categories of intervention: internal interventions aiming at the establishment of a privileged relationship between domestic savings and domestic investment, especially those favoured by the public sector; and capital movement controls aiming at the isolation of that domestic savings–investment process from its international context, especially in times of volatile capital flows.

The first category is composed of a bewildering variety of institutional, interest rate, fiscal and regulatory interventions within a strictly domestic framework. Thus, in many countries, a large part of financial savings is collected by savings banks, insurance and provident institutions or specialised banks whose active operations are restricted to certain types of domestic placements or investments (government debt and housing in particular). Often, the interventions on active operations are strengthened by selective or discriminatory state guarantees, tax privileges and subsidies in order to enhance the attractiveness of the passive services offered by these intermediaries. Domestic intermediation is privileged or protected by special interest rate regulations (contractual savings in Germany, Regulation Q in the United States), the selective fiscal treatment of interest or dividend income on national financial claims, discriminatory treatment of new issues, the restrictive quotation of bonds and shares and artificial limits to capital market transactions. Many more instances of intervention with regard to institutions and instruments could be quoted but suffice it to state that in almost all cases, national intermediation is privileged over foreign intermediation and that this fact, associated with the extensive public participation and control, reduces – in practically all countries – the financial market's capacity to respond efficiently to changing domestic or international conditions.

The second category, direct or indirect controls of cross-border flow, has become a universal component of packages to deal with balance of payments or exchange rate disturbances. Measures on short-term movements, mostly directed at banks' behaviour (reserve requirements, access to central bank facilities, foreign currency swaps and the financing of foreign trade), their external capacity (limits on foreign financial assets and participations, foreign liabilities and foreign currency positions) or at foreign investors' attitudes (limits on interest payments, negative interest rates, new accounts, import of bank notes, etc.) and may go as far as total exchange controls or split exchange or two-tier markets. Non-banks have been subject to regulations on the timing of trade receipts and payments and reserve requirements or through limits on foreign assets and liabilities. Further instruments include moral suasion, special informal 'understandings', interest equalisation taxes, restrictions on foreign lending or foreign direct investment and the purchase or sale of debt instruments, equity and real estate. The generalised floating exchange rate regime exerts, since 1973, an obvious direct impact on both bank and non-bank financial behaviour.

Partly as a result of these long standing efforts to constrain the spontaneous trend to a one market – one price system, a third, and more subtle form of financial nationalism has made its appearance: the persistent proclivity of private sectors to forgo the benefits of multinational allocation of financial resources. Charles Kindleberger once labelled this 'private discrimination'. Private savers thus react with a 'second best' choice because of the confusion produced by the amazing variety of financial instruments, which is induced by the regulations; these differ with regard to the basic nature of the contract, maturity, marketability, security, yield, callability, transparency and, of course, currency. That this heterogeneity, compounded by the efforts of distance and language, is a direct factor of inhibition is readily visible in the United States for instance.

In the last few years American institutional and private investors were abundantly informed about financial investment possibilities in Europe and Japan, and they were in theory well aware of the substantial net gains to be made, both in terms of currency appreciation and risk diversification. Yet, American acquisition of European and Japanese financial claims remained extremely modest, demonstrating the existence of a nationalistic bias affecting the willingness to hold foreign financial assets within the overall objective of maximising income and wealth.

And the same reluctance is to be found on the debtor side. Potential issuers, in addition to their reluctance to abandon the comfort and security of well-established relations with domestic banks, are impeded by the variety of ways regulations define, and more often than not obscure, disclosure obligations, the organisation of issuance and trade, accounting practices, legal procedure in instances of conflict or default, etc. Also, corporations and institutions are well aware that national laws and customs confer very different rights and duties upon the various legal entities such as corporations, banks, brokers or other intermediaries, lenders and borrowers. Lastly, no internationally active agent can ignore the fact that the administration of the law remains in itself one of the principal attributes of national sovereignty. In practice, therefore, there is a matching, often irrational nationalistic bias of savers and borrowers.

II

The array of interventions and attitudes contained in these three categories suggests an all-pervasive financial nationalism, and the high cost of these inhibitions to the development of competitive, adaptable financial markets.

In my view, however, such a broad generalisation would be misleading, even if, in many cases, intervention has patently contributed to the lack of depth, breadth and resiliency and many markets are clearly operating at too high levels of interest rates and transaction costs. The problem, at this point, is that we have as yet no agreed framework of analysis with regard to the financial markets' contribution to welfare and that, in addition, the study of the real cost of existing or newly introduced controls or constraints, is rudimentary. The effort of a balanced appraisal thus raises important methodological issues.

The first issue, the financial markets' contribution to welfare, has been debated by Goldsmith (1969), McKinnon (1973) and Shaw (1973) among others, but until now, to quote Goldsmith:

> We have not yet succeeded in developing reliable methods to measure the extent and the results of the facilitating function of finance, to determine the optimal size of the financial superstructure in relation to the real infrastructure of the economy, and to distinguish effectively the contribution of different forms of financial structure to economic growth.[1]

The absence of a reliable method to measure the contributing function of finance, hence to compare national systems, makes it difficult, if not impossible, to distinguish efficient intervention from ill-inspired, inefficient controls and constraints.

In practice, the trend which emerged after the period of external inconvertibility and of *clear-cut reconstruction finance priorities* favoured more openness and competitiveness. This is clear from the 1963 Dillon Report,[2] from the 1965–6 OECD Capital Market Study[3] and from the European Community's Segre Report.[4] But the official papers are devoid of a specific theoretical underpinning, and the proposals for reform are mostly subjective or intermingled with the effects of the substantial technological changes which dominated the financial sector and of the novel aims of monetary and fiscal policy pursued by governments at that time. Moreover, neither theory nor pragmatic studies investigated the considerable differences among the national polices as to the optimal distribution of private and social returns from financial intermediation which could result from more openness and increased competitiveness. In short, we cannot define an efficient financial market in today's international context.

The second issue, the measurement of the real cost of intervention, is similarly still uncertain. The cost effects of existing regulations (or cartels) often go unnoticed because they result in the preservation of cost–benefit conditions which without intervention would have been different. Evidence of existing costs is not found in statistics or in econometric models but in evasions or circumventions, and in the attempts of agencies and pressure groups to prevent change. And the advance of communications technology or the application of a new range of controls and constraints as means to combat the malfunctioning of economic and monetary variables – in other words welfare losses – elsewhere in the system have confused the recent efficiency discussion on changes in financial intermediation to such an extent that we are, in fact, retreating to the basics of methodology. Thus, there is a body of thought, which, by virtue of a revived concept of instantaneous adjustment to new information as measured by covariance of interest rates in the existing structure, concludes that private market integration is now such as to eliminate the cost of official controls; that is to say, that controls and regulation can be dismissed as inefficient. On the other hand, those who assume a real cost continue to discuss the various measuring techniques by means of the law of one price, of transferability or substitutability. Since the very existence of that controversy is crucial to the whole issue of financial nationalism, it is perhaps useful to spend some time on these two opposing views.

Perhaps the best recent example of the instantaneous adjustment approach – the first body of thought – is to be found in Logue, Salant and Sweeney who applied the covariation analysis to quarterly long-term interest rates in seven major countries and concluded that coordinated movements in interest rates occurred without international capital flows.[5] In the words of Logue, Salant and Sweeney:

> The interest rate approach to integration is considerably more straightforward than the alternative approaches. Whereas alternative approaches focus on the flow of capital, this concept of integration ignores flows and concentrates on prices, specifically on interest rates. This concept involves, in essence, a notion of market efficiency which suggests that the prices of financial assets adjust instantaneously to new information, perhaps even in the absence of international capital flows.

Though the authors admit some doubts ('perhaps even in the absence of international capital flows'), they come very close to implying competitive efficiency in the allocation of financial resources and, by extension, the absence of any real cost in today's interference with the functioning of capital markets.

Generally, those who assume a real cost of fragmentation, approach the problem via the law of one price: two or more markets are reputed to be integrated when prices are the same and behave like one. The cost of fragmentation in this second type of approach is measured by means of deviations from market prices to more sophisticated indices of conveyance or dispersion.[6] More recently, other methods, yielding similar results, have measured integration by the transferability of assets – responsiveness or unresponsiveness of asset prices to asset transfers[7] – or by substitutability, either direct or indirect.[8] Thus Allen measures the degree of integration between two or more securities markets 'by the degree of substitutability between those securities', and notes in addition: 'Two markets can be integrated indirectly, if each of the two securities is regarded as a substitute for a third security.' The latter notion introduces the additional variable of endogenous changes (innovation) in the supply (production) – and therefore in the opportunities to increase efficiency of allocation – of financial assets.

The intellectual ingenuity of these analytical efforts is often admirable. The results, however, remain disappointing for those actively engaged in the practice of international finance. First, as already stated, the measuring technique by covariance of interest rates as advanced by Logue, Salant and Sweeney (or other similar work with respect to domestic markets), is too narowly based on the existing structure and the established functioning of the institutional (or wholesale) financial market. Actually, in that market, identical access to information, as well as typical reactions to price changes lead to covariation because if at a given price, and within a given structure, two assets have an identical present and expected return, the two will be regarded as substitutes and investors will have no yield or risk reason to hold both assets simultaneously. But in turn, this implies that it is insufficient to measure market efficiency by means of the covariation approach in isolation from an appraisal of the *existing* structure of regulation and behaviour. As to the cost-assuming techniques of measurement, the law of one price ignores the astonishing non-price heterogeneity of financial assets, a point which has been stressed by Viner, Cairncross and Bloomfield notably. The method can thus eventually only be of help in highly developed, well-informed market systems – such as in the United States – where individual or institutional savers and investors are able to derive the community's collective time and risk preferences from prices. It is, however, irrelevant in underdeveloped, tightly regulated or fragmented financial systems. And as to transferability or substitutability, it may be that they effectively exist and are supported by an unbiased willingness to transfer or to swap. But the test is whether or not these characteristics are matched by the holders' ability to do so. In other words, transferability and substitutability are a necessary, but not sufficient, part of efficiency measurement.[9]

In general, therefore, we can conclude that there is no objective method with which to define the frontier between constructive intervention and opportunistic misuse of the financial system; that is to say, an optimum mix of private and social returns. Similarly, there is no agreed method to measure the real cost of a change in that mix and little prospect of such a measure becoming available over the short or medium run.

III

As usual, the handicap of theoretical uncertainty has not paralysed policy. In complete agreement with practitioners' opinion, the Dillon

Report, the OECD and EEC studies and the various national reports have now generalised the assumption that, as the Dillon Report already stated, European markets 'taken as a whole, are not as efficient and as effective as they might be, and as they will need to be, to play the role in the financing of European economic growth of which they are potentially capable'. And because of the need to act, these studies, and the academic work they generated, tend to propose a set of principles which roughly divide constructive and abusive regulation, namely interventions and constraints which impair productivity, distort demand and supply and raise the price of capital. Although the line is admittedly normative, it is based on three theoretical considerations supported by considerable pragmatic evidence. The first consideration is that financial markets, as composed by institutions active in risk-absorption for a wide variety of unequally endowed and informed firms or households, hence extremely sensitive to variations in confidence, should be regulated in order to protect savers and investors. The second consideration postulates that since smoothly functioning markets are conducive to lower risk and liquidity premiums, market oriented intervention to safeguard the stability of flows must be considered a normal part of policy. And thirdly, in the same framework of a more global optimality objective, temporary measures to stem erratic fluctuations of capital flows (assuming an erratic divergence of social and private returns to capital) are to be considered legitimate.

The gradual emergence of these considerations has led to some measure of consensus on regulatory matters, particularly since the late sixties.

Thus, governments tend more and more to standardise domestic regulation so as to eliminate the confusing differences among financial charters, asset and liability regulations, fiscal status, deposit rules, etc. The effort to create more uniformity aims at the elimination of artificial boundaries among otherwise comparable institutions (or groups of institutions) so that, within the limits of general rules of solvency, security and economic balance, the money and capital markets become the open, competitive mechanism through which the full range of public and private financing needs is brought into correspondence with, and accommodated to, the amount and composition of funds provided by households and institutions. The application of this principle automatically indicts a number of unduly narrow or discriminatory customary and legal rules which influence the flow of savings and investment and inhibit the development of competitive, adaptable markets.

In the same way, governments recognise the necessity of promoting the harmonisation of pro-competitive change in the general rules of solvency, security and economic balance in and among the industrial countries. Of course, such a harmonisation cannot lead, and need not lead, to complete uniformity. However, it is important that at least the measures aiming at pro-competitive revision of national systems (or the revision of regulations with regard to the need to safeguard confidence and security) should converge rather than diverge, as is still often the case. Such a pragmatic convergence seems especially important given the OECD and EEC objectives of a progressive interpenetration of national financial markets and the permanent temptation to enshrine doctrines and ambitions of a particular period into detailed plans. Convergence is, of course, essential to the EEC currency project as now discussed under the heading of a 'European Monetary System'. The principle of pragmatic, gradual convergence indicts measures geared to the conservation or strengthening of a peculiar local financial environment.

Finally, there is the case of capital controls motivated by the need to dovetail national financial objectives with still underdeveloped local financial mechanisms, to avoid the cyclical and structural consequences of involuntary pegging of exchange rates (in the dollar zone) or to prevent the emergence of sudden, massive shifts in asset preferences to countries where offsetting monetary policy measures, exchange adjustment or reserve shifts are unavoidable or inoperative (Switzerland).[10] Governments tend to agree with A. Cairncross that in such cases capital controls offer a less costly solution than revising domestic demand management or restricting imports of goods (because the national savings rate can be policed by fiscal and monetary measures whereas goods imports do not have perfect substitutes). But beyond that intention of principle, governments also tend increasingly to agree on reservations with regard to dual exchange markets and on the operational use of flexible exchange rates, interest rate differentials, external financing and, if unavoidable, of administrative controls of capital movements.

All this being said, the effective results of the official admission of financial market inefficiency, or of the need of a harmonised attack on abusive regulation, remain extremely modest. In fact, after a period of progress during the late sixties, the seventies became decidedly a phase of regression. First of all, the generalised floating of exchange rates has exerted an important fragmenting and cost effect on cross-border operations, the latter under at least four headings: an increased demand for exchange risk cover, higher unit costs of forward cover, larger currency exchange spreads and higher financial management costs; that is to say, higher expenses associated with information gathering, processing, control and decision making. More generally, flexibility means that the crucial capital market concept of future returns – whether from enterprise or from the accumulation of financial claims – can no longer be expressed as a mathematical expectation. In that respect, I fully share the view that the structural deterioration of capital markets observed in the last ten years – their decreasing contribution to risk capital, the greater volatility of flows, the shortening of maturities and the split of expectations between demand and supply – is also due to excessive exchange flexibility. Let us not forget Keynes' warning against the effects of uncertainty: 'The individualistic capitalism of today, precisely because it entrusts saving to the individual investor and production to the individual employer, presumes a stable measuring rod of value, and cannot be efficient – perhaps not survive – without one.'

Secondly, there has been a substantial increase in distortive interventions on cross-border flows. As stated before, some of the new measures did not lack justification. However, interventions have often spread, have been escalated or remain in effect for reasons unrelated with destabilising flows or the protection of infant markets. I suspect that in many cases governments are simply attracted by the mercantilist underpinning of policy autonomy which is given by a controlled and inward-oriented financial system as a complement to a growth oriented, floating rate system. In fact, what we have been witnessing for a number of years is a reversal of the trend toward international allocative efficiency and a return to the conflict between the economic attractiveness of a one market – one price system for private entrepreneurs and the political preference for a multi-market – multi-price configuration divided by sovereignty lines. Today, direct private arbitrage can fulfill its function in only a handful of countries.

Thirdly, the trend towards competitive equality in domestic markets has been arrested, if not reversed. Governments are again strengthening the network of 'captive' savings–collecting institutions, as is evident in the revised regulations for government savings banks, provident funds or housing finance establishments, and in particular in the extension of tax or interest rate privileges enjoyed by these institutions or by national interest and dividend earners. In most of Europe this phenomenon is a simple return to traditional preferences, but it is new in the United States. In the US, thrift institutions are now allowed to issue six-month consumer certificates of deposit pegged to the Treasury bill rate, thus effectively freeing them from the threat of disintermediation. The objective is not more competition but a greater protection for the housing industry, as became evident when at the same time the Administration narrowed rather than broadened the investment powers of thrift institutions. In the words of Saul Klaman, President of the United States Mutual Savings Banks' Association: 'It soon became apparent, however, that the Washington climate had shifted dramatically. The primary concern now was that savings banks remain committed to housing finance, not that they achieve broadened flexibility to cope with an increasingly competitive environment.'[11] Also in the United States, the security provisions of ERISA (Employment Retirement Insurance Security Act) applicable to provident funds, or of rule FASB8, concerning the accountancy rules of foreign assets and liabilities, have enlarged the effective constraints on the foreign deployment of assets. In other countries, special interest regulations are spreading. Thus Germany has introduced a dividend taxation which is clearly discriminatory with regard to foreign holders of German equity; France has strengthened its tax-credit system and in a number of cases in some other countries withholding taxes have been increased and the conditionality of double taxation claims have been accentuated. Finally, governments have abstained from promoting the international cross-quotation of securities advocated by the OECD and the EEC. The resulting persistent thinness of international secondary markets is not only a limiting element in investment selection, it is also an important impediment to the expansion of the new-issues market for foreign and international securities.

The events of the last few years make it difficult to give an adequate answer to the question whether or not, and to what degree, governments have been successful in preventing a closer integration in and among financial markets. But in cautiously examining the domestic markets, using pragmatic observation of volumes and yield differentials to trace short-term changes as a guide to changes in wealth holders' ability to minimise risk and to maximise return, I have failed to find evidence of a growing willingness to shift claims efficiently. And, partly as a result of the persistent fragmentation, even a superficial study of European continental capital markets seem to confirm today what Kurt Richebächer found ten years ago:

> The countries of Continental Europe, and particularly the EEC member countries have grown in financial and economic strength since the war. They have achieved an overriding importance in world trade, but the financial markets even of the major countries still appear underdeveloped by American or British standards . . . these markets obviously lack depth, breadth and resiliency.[12]

Since at the same time fiscal, legal and regulatory impediments to efficient adaptation have grown in the United States and in Great Britain, whereas nascent capital markets (with the exception of the Arab Peninsula) invariably show highly nationalistic characteristics, it is safe to assume an overall regression in openness and competitiveness on the domestic capital markets of the world. This conclusion concurs with the findings of economists who have come to the conclusion that despite the growth of capital movements and the development of large international capital markets, the world-wide process of financial integration has slowed down in recent years. Argy and Hodgera find that 'there is a noticeable drop in dispersion (of short-term interest rates) between 1961–2 and 1964–6 but no evidence of any continuing decline in later years'.[13] Indeed, since then, markets have registered a very sharp increase of dispersion, up to a record degree at present. The same is true inside the EEC since 1972, when Hawkins noted that 'while there is some observed tendency for differentials between interest rates of EEC members to narrow, that tendency was not strong, irreversible, or even sustained over the period of integration'.[14]

IV

How can we at present summarise the trend and the cost of financial nationalism? Obviously, the trend is in the wrong direction, despite the European Community's, the OECD's and private efforts. And every day we witness the short-run repercussions of interference. Yet looking beyond the short term, I would hesitate to consider this in itself as damaging as arguments conducted in terms of traditional market definitions and general principles tend to assume.

First of all, the recent developments have made for induced endogenous changes in demand and supply which, though hardly emphasised in the theoretical literature, have become an important factor in the attenuation of the effects of financial nationalism. On the demand side, savers have become sensitive to the sophisticated retail services offered by the institutional financial market – such as international investment funds or multinational bond funds – managing assets by means of investment techniques based on a broad access to markets and an efficient input of world-wide information. The increase in the share of institutional saving implies that opportunities to maximise return are better exploited and direct or indirect competition for savings has substantially increased. An even more striking development has occurred in the corporate sector. Before the period 1971–3, financial officers of multinationals or exporting and importing firms mostly handled their assets–liabilities exposure to exchange rate risks on the back of an envelope. Today, all the subtleties of analysing risk in an uncertain economic and monetary environment are integrated and extend to alternative after-tax exposure models in accounting terms, cash terms or both. Strategies are simulated and, of course, so are protection alternatives, also with respect to borrowing and lending. Overall demand for such services has become such that while it is true that financial intermediaries are usually ready to comply with the official standards engendered by financial nationalism, they also look for loop-holes and novel solutions under the pressure of increasing competition.

Secondly, the development of financial nationalism encounters strong and effective resistence from the growth of non-national markets such as Euromarkets and off-shore banking. The growth of Euromarkets raises a number of awkward monetary policy questions. But there is no doubt that its contribution to financial innovation – especially on the short-term side – has substantially increased substitutability and transferability, up to a point where Charles Kindleberger has been able to raise the root question 'whether European monetary integration is to be achieved through direct connections between European capital and money markets, or whether it is to be accomplished through third markets: the Eurobond and Eurodollar markets in capital . . . .'[15] The growth of the Eurobond and Eurocurrency markets, both in volume and in the supply of wide range of asset and liability services, leaves the question still wide open. A similar development in the Arab Peninsula confirms Kindleberger's view on the impact of indirect linkage, as Bahrain's off-shore banking units are rapidly forming a regional centre; this has been generated by the dichotomy between official practice and commercial needs in some of the neighbouring countries. It is significant to note that 'the Bahrain off-shore banking units have more or less become an extension of the Saudi banking system, beyond the direct control of SAMA (Saudi-Arabian Monetary Agency) but taking an ever-increasing share of the Saudi banking market.'[16]

Finally, the objective of financial insulation is increasingly subordinated to the search for currency protection by means of currency areas. Incidental evidence in Logue, Salant and Sweeney: 'we found traces of a 'Germanic' factor which further linked interest rates in the Netherlands, Switzerland and Germany and an 'Atlantic' factor tying interest rates in France, the United Kingdom and the United States together . . .'[17] already suggested a trend toward the formation of a poly-centric monetary and financial system before 1976. Since then, the pressure to create areas with tendentially fixed inside exchange rates and a joint float against outside currencies has been intensified in the EEC (the July 1978 decision to re-establish a zone of currency stability) and in the Arab Peninsula (negotiations between the Gulf countries, Saudi-Arabia and Iraq), while at the same time the volatility of inter-area exchange rates has made for more spontaneous regional integration. Especially since the end of 1976, the intra-European flows show more of a pattern commensurate with what one would expect from an objective appraisal of real yield differentials; that is to say, interest rates adjusted to exchange and inflation rate differentials.

The longer-term adaptive trend on domestic markets, the development of non-national financial services and the gradual formation of currency areas tend to confirm the historical findings of Goldsmith and Kindleberger that, *in the long run*, the global structure of the financial system's supply and demand is little affected by interference. But financial nationalism is beyond any doubt a causal factor in the prolongation and aggravation of the cost trend discovered by Goldsmith – 'there has been no long-term downward trend (in the cost of financing) since the mid-nineteenth century in the developed countries of Europe, North America, and the British Commonwealth'[18] – and since then constantly confirmed by pragmatic evidence. The recent developments in financing and financial management costs are partly obscured by inflation and exchange rate volatility, and in part related to the substantial qualitative improvement of the financial product. But there is a variety of cost factors which we can relate without hesitation to financial nationalism.

The first and most obvious cost resides in the important residual barriers to the efficient international allocation of financial resources, in terms of the flows of current saving and the distribution of the stock of capital as well as in terms of gains that accrue to individual wealth holders when they can maximise the return on, and minimise the risks of, their financial assets. Though the statement is to be adapted in most specific cases, it is still generally true that the higher the degree of integration, the more reduced the discrepancies between private and social rates of return, removing disincentives to saving and fostering a better inter-temporal allocation of resources. In other words, the gains-from-trade principle is generally applicable but presently not satisfied. With the qualifications stressed by Johnson in particular, this allocative efficiency can be extended to the facility offered to monetary policy when capital is mobile.[19] When financial markets are integrated, monetary policy can be used to regulate the balance of payments, freeing other instruments of a lesser comparative advantage in the quest for external balance, for the pursuit of domestic objectives according to Mundell's principle of 'effective market classification'.[20] Also this potential gain is not materialising today.

The measures aiming at wealth holders' ability and willingness to acquire and deal in claims on foreigners also entail frequent and serious distorsions of the overall and allocative efficiency of the domestic capital market. On the one hand, and although it is hardly possible to conclude that interference has led to a lower volume of aggregate saving, it is evident that lack of alternatives and interest rate manipulation behind the walls of protective controls has led to a sub-optimal division between financial savings and other forms of asset accumulation and to an excessive preference for liquidity. The phenomenon is well known in some European and in developing countries, but it is emerging more and more in other countries, including the United States. On the other hand, the measures have contributed to a compartmentalised market, in which some borrowers – especially the Treasury, nationalised enterprises and houseowners – receive a subsidy whereas other borrowers can compete only for those savings which are left over – and pay a higher price for them. In some countries the effort of insulation has induced such a complexity of structure that the loss of productivity in the financial sector and elsewhere is evident. Thus in France, the system of monetary and financial controls is such that the allocation of savings and the flexibility of portfolio management is severely reduced:

> Ceiling rates of credit expansion freeze the relative size of financial firms, and protect inefficient firms from the competition of more efficient firms thus tending to prevent cost reduction in the financial industry. Administrative controls, coupled with interest rate ceilings force lenders to choose among borrowers on grounds other than price and usually result in discrimination against smaller and new customers.[21]

Another macroeconomic cost is found in the fact that financial nationalism may entail costs of excessive structural diversity or increase the cost of adjustment to exogenous disturbances, especially by increasing the speed and size of the change in income required by a disturbance. In the monetary chaos of today, the former is by now well established. As Despres, Kindleberger and Salant pointed out in 1966, European structures were already largely responsible for the excessive liquidity preference of European savers and institutions, and, with short-term rates relatively low in Europe and long-term rates relatively low in the United States, the same structural feature has induced the intermediation function of the United States capital market.[22] As is well known, the American capital supply excesses led first to European resistance and later to an implicit but no less destructive erosion of confidence in the dollar. It is interesting to note that this destructive interaction was already mentioned in Kurt Richebächer's introduction to the OECD Capital Markets Study:

> It is now generally agreed that the strengthening of the international monetary system required not only an improvement in liquidity arrangements but also in market mechanisms. Most observers hold the view that if European capital markets were improved this would constitute one step in this direction.

The facts are established, but despite the efforts of Kenen,

Whitman, Fieleke and others, research as yet provides no definite model to evaluate its cost. This is not only because a useful analysis of intervention of the type we are concerned with is immediately entangled in the intricacies of 'second best' pursuits of balance in a complex cyclical–structural interplay, but also because in most cases of excessive diversity and capital controls – monetary policy, the pragmatic evidence is mixed, or rather mixed-up with other issues such as the competition between public and private borrowing and the timing of exchange rate changes. Nevertheless, it can be safely assumed that the European official tolerance of what Kindleberger calls the 'oligopoly' structure of European financial intermediation, or the interventions which on both sides of the Atlantic impeded efficient linkages between productive resources and legitimate demand, have largely contributed to the emergence, and subsequently to the increasing cost, of the adjustment mechanism.

Finally, interference with the market mechanism entails an evident microeconomic cost of information, administration, circumvention and control. The avoidance network, which stretches from the Bahamas to Chiasso and from the Far East to Panama and may be attractive to travel-hungry young bankers, in economic terms severely reduces economies of scale, adds to overheads and increases the risk premium on transactions. Bankers, and, I dare say, asset holders, would be happy to pay higher transaction costs if it were simply a matter of financing the transition to a competitive and transparent financial world. Unfortunately, what we witness is a persistent trend of policymakers skirmishing with practitioners, and consequently the persistence, often the increase, of the costs associated with superfluous complexity of financial transactions, and a global reach on which the sun never sets.

Let me conclude with the remark that, against the backdrop of volatile exchange markets, the unusual nature of the disappointing and uneven recovery of the industrial world, the extensive changes in international competitiveness, the persistent imbalances of external accounts and the sharpening dilemmas of domestic policies, financial nationalism has been surprisingly well contained. The seventies obviously represent a drawback as compared with what we hoped and expected in the sixties, when the Dillon Report, the OECD and the EEC came to the unanimous conclusion to which I referred earlier. But the damage is as yet limited and certainly has not killed the Darwinian evolution started in the late fifties. In a certain sense, the drawback compels bankers and asset holders to adjust further, and as such, financial nationalism continues to be both a toxic and a tonic.

NOTES

1. R. W. Goldsmith, *Financial Structure and Development* (New Haven: Yale University Press, 1969), p. 401.
2. Paper No. 3, *Economic Policies and Practices. A Description and Analysis of Certain European Capital Markets*, Joint Economic Committee, 88th Congress (Washington DC: US Government Printing Office, 1964).
3. OECD, *Capital Markets Study* (Paris: 1965 and 1966).
4. EEC, *The Establishment of a European Capital Market* (Brussels: 1966).
5. D. E. Logue, M. A. Salant and R. J. Sweeney, 'International Integration of Financial Markets: Survey, Synthesis and Results', pp. 91–137, in *Eurocurrencies and the International Monetary System* (Washington DC: American Enterprise Institute, 1976).
6. Thus Kindleberger and Krause. Krause for instance, compared spreads in a number of countries and concludes 'that there is no time trend toward a reduction of spreads, which would indicate that domestic banking is not becoming more competitive'. (Lawrence B. Krause, 'Implications for Private Capital Markets' in *European Monetary Unification and its Meaning for the United States*, Washington: Brookings Institution, 1973, p. 126).
7. T. Scitovsky, *Money and the Balance of Payments* (New Haven: Yale University Press, 1969).
8. P. R. Allen, *Organization and Adminstration of a Monetary Union*, Princeton Studies No. 38 (Princeton: 1976).
9. Thus Marina Whitman states that 'the efficiency gains from market integration are maximized by ignoring the boundaries of the nation-state; for private transactions in goods and factors of production, the optimum size of the integrated area is the world. By implication, the economic justification for the nation-state must lie in the existence of public or collective goods – including stabilization targets, the distribution of income, and the regulatory climate – and of differences in national consumption preferences for such goods'. (Marina V. N. Whitman, *Sustaining the International Economic System*, Essays in International Finance No. 121, Princeton, N.J.: Princeton University, International Finance Section, 1977, p. 3). Cooper also puts the case for regional policy in terms of public goods (Richard N. Cooper, *Economic Mobility and National Economic Policy*, Wicksell Lectures, Stockholm: Almquist and Wicksell, 1974).
10. Examining insulation and capital flows, Tower and Willett state: 'This conclusion of greater insulation under flexible rates is rather widely accepted and we believe it to be generally correct.' (Edward Tower and Thomas D. Willett, *The Theory of Optimum Currency Areas and Exchange Rate Flexibility*, Special Papers in International Economics, No. 11, Princeton University, International Finance Section, 1976, p. 52).
11. Dr Saul B. Klaman, commentary before the 58th Annual Conference,

National Association of Mutual Savings Banks, Pittsburgh, 9 May 1978.
12. Kurt Richebächer, Introduction to Volume III of the OECD Capital Markets Study: *Functioning of Capital Markets* (Paris: OECD, 1968), p. 11.
13. V. Argy, and Z. Hodgera, *Financial Integration and Interest Rate Linkages in the Industrial Countries*, IMF Staff Papers, vol XX, March 1973, pp. 1–77.
14. R. G. Hawkings, 'Intra-EEC Capital Movements and Domestic Financial Markets', in F. Machlup (ed.), *Economic Integration, Worldwide, Regional, Sectoral* (London: Macmillan, 1976).
15. Charles P. Kindleberger, Comments on 'European Monetary Unification: Implications for Private Capital Markets', by Lawrence B. Krause, in *European Monetary Unification and Its Meaning for the United States*, L. B. Krause and W. S. Salant (ed.), The Brookings Institution, Washington, 1973, p. 151.
16. David Shirreff, 'Saudi Arabia: Tight Controls', in 'Arab Banking and Finance', *Financial Times*, 24 July 1978.
17. Logue, Salant, and Sweeney, op. cit., p. 98.
18. Goldsmith, op. cit., p. 47.
19. Harry G. Johnson in Richard N. Cooper (ed.), *International Finance* (Baltimore: Penguin Books, 1969). Johnson rightly argues that when interest rates are fixed according to balances of payments criteria: 'The resulting pattern of international capital movements obviously need not be anything like an efficient one, since there is no reason to expect that the real return on investment in countries with current account deficits is higher than that on investments in countries with current account surpluses; it may on the contrary involve a serious distortion of the allocation of new investment resources, and a consequent welfare loss for the countries concerned and the world economy.'
20. R. A. Mundell, 'The Appropriate Use of Monetary and Fiscal Policy for Internal and External Stability', IMF, *Staff Papers*, vol. IX, March 1962, pp. 70–9.
21. Donald R. Hodgman, 'The French System of Monetary and Financial Controls,' Banca Nazionale del Lavoro *Quarterly Review*, December 1971, p. 350.
22. Emile Despres, Charles P. Kindleberger, Walter S. Salant: 'The Dollar and World Liquidity. A Minority View', *The Economist*, 5 February 1966, pp. 526–9.

Part II: The Trade Policy Environment

7 Reluctance to Adjust and Economic Nationalism

Richard Blackhurst[1]

INTRODUCTION

It does not require great insight to recognise that we live in a constantly changing world. Demographic developments, technological innovations and a variety of other factors constantly create pressure for changes in patterns of production and trade. Moreover, the fact that the timing and intensity of these developments vary among countries is itself an independent source of pressure for change. An obvious corollary is that an economy's prosperity is crucially dependent on its capacity to adjust its pattern of production and trade in response to these pressures for change. Smooth and continuous adjustment allows a country to use its labour, capital and land efficiently and stimulates economic growth. Lack of adjustment, in contrast, breeds cumulative inefficiency and reduces the country's material well-being.

The thesis of this paper is that a majority of the domestic and international economic problems which have plagued the world economy in recent years can be traced to an inadequate pace of adjustment in the industrial countries. The inadequate adjustment is not an inherent and mysterious condition of the industrial economies, but rather a result of a conscious resistance to change on the part of labour and capital – a resistance which, moreover, often appears in the guise of economic nationalism. The problems caused by the resistance have been compounded by various investment-depressing developments, in particular the dramatic increase in recent years in the degree of uncertainty facing potential investors (a development to which the aforementioned resistance to change contributes).

Before turning to the main analysis, it will be helpful to define the two terms in the title of the paper. 'Reluctance to adjust' refers to the degree of willingness to adjust patterns of production and trade, with an emphasis on the adaptability of specific industries via the reallocation of labour and capital between industries. As such, there is little or no mention of the related issue of balance of payments adjustment.

It is not easy to give a simple, analytically useful definition of 'economic nationalism'.[2] The task is made easier, however, by the fact that the paper is concerned with only one aspect of relations between countries – the exchange of goods and services. Within this context, three possible definitions of economic nationalism come to mind:

a. The pursuit of national economic interests which involves a genuine, broadly based consensus among a country's citizens that it is worthwhile to sacrifice some national income in order to achieve certain national goals. An example would be a decision to subsidise a major sector of the economy in order to increase its size relative to what it would be in the absence of government support.
b. The pursuit of economic interests which are often labelled 'national' in an attempt to give the impression that they come under the first definition, but which in reality involve one or more special interest groups gaining at the expense of other domestic groups. This definition is distinguished from the first by the lack of a general concensus, and by the efforts of the beneficiary groups to obscure both the fact that their gains come at the expense of their fellow citizens and the fact that the economy as a whole winds up a net loser. Always present to some extent, this type of economic nationalism has been increasingly evident in the industrial countries in recent years.
c. The pursuit of national economic interests whose achievement is necessarily at the expense of other countries. In this instance, it is important to distinguish between the long run and the short run. In the long run, a country can gain at the expense of foreigners in the trade area only if it has permanent monopolistic or monopsonistic power in world markets – that is, if variations in the amount it sells or buys in the world market can have a non-transitory effect on its terms of trade. Outside of a few producers of certain primary products, this does not seem to be an important factor in the current resurgence of economic nationalism. However, because adjustment

to economic disturbances is not instantaneous – information costs, contractual commitments and short-run immobility of labour and capital all introduce some lags into the adjustment process – it may be possible for a country which lacks long-run market power to gain certain short-run advantages at the expense of its trading partners. This is the second type of economic nationalism which we see increasingly in the industrial countries.

A common trait of the two types of economic nationalism which are important in the current situation is the absence of any possible long-run gain for the country as a whole. Indeed, as I argue below, not only is there no hope of long-run gain, there is a real danger of substantial short-run and long-run losses.

(I) SOURCES OF PRESSURE FOR CHANGE

Although the existence of change is obvious enough, the nature and magnitude of the various factors at work are less well known. The purpose of this section is to provide a brief look at five of those factors:

a. *Demographic trends* can create pressure for change on both the demand and supply sides of markets. Consumption patterns vary among different age groups, which means that changes in the age structure of the population affect the pattern of national demand. Moreover, changes in population growth rates affect aggregate (as opposed to per capita) demand for products. These two considerations are important because the industrial countries are facing a period of slower population growth, combined with progressively older populations. On the supply side the effect is via labour force growth rates. In North America and Japan the growth of the labour force has already begun slowing from the high rates of the late 1960s, and (allowing for participation rates) this trend is expected to continue through the 1980s. In Western Europe the labour force is expected to grow faster during 1975–90 relative to the very slow growth for the period 1960–75.

b. *Technological change* creates pressure for changes in production and trade in several ways. Advances in transportation and communications reduce the costs of exchanging goods and services between countries, and innovations leading to a diversification of products create opportunities for increased specialisation. The spread of technological innovation to new countries via direct investment, licensing agreements, and imitation stimulates trade by altering the pattern of competitive advantage.

c. *Changes in the relative prices of key commodities* is a third source of pressure for change. Developments in the petroleum market offer an important example. The sharp price increase stimulated production of alternative types of energy, of energy-saving capital equipment and consumer products, and of products desired by the oil-exporting countries, while at the same time depressing the production of many energy-intensive products. On a more aggregate level, the higher price worsened the pattern of current account imbalances, itself a development that created pressure for adjustment.

d. *Environmental policies* introduced for the purpose of cleaning up the natural environment affect production patterns in three ways. First, aggregate demand for conventional final consumer goods and services declines (relatively) as people increase their consumption of 'environmental cleanliness'; for example, in 1976 the per capita expenditure on pollution abatement and control in the United States was $162, or $648 for a family of four;[3] this represents money not spent on conventional goods and services. Second, production of pollution control equipment and of 'pollution-free' products rises, while consumption of pollution-intensive products declines in importance. Third, trade patterns are affected by these first two developments, as well as by the relocation of polluting production processes from areas with strict environmental standards to those with less strict standards.[4]

e. *Trends in developing countries* qualify as a fifth entry on the list from the viewpoint of the industrial countries. During the period 1964–74, population in the developing countries was increasing at an average annual rate of 2.6 per cent; the comparable figure for North America and Japan was around 1 per cent, and for Western Europe 0.6 per cent.[5] In addition to the (differing) demographic trends, there is the on-going industrialisation process in many developing countries which increases their capacity to participate in the international division of labour. Between 1960 and 1973, for example, employment in manufacturing grew at an average annual rate of 4.2 per cent (with the rate rising over time) in the developing countries; the comparable figure for the industrial countries was 1.3 per cent (with the rate falling over time).

It is important to keep in mind, however, that the developing countries still supply only a small share of imports of manufactured goods into the industrial countries. They accounted for only 10 per cent of the increment in the industrial countries' imports of manufactures between 1963 and 1973 (during the same period, they purchased 21 per cent of the increment in the industrial countries' exports of manufactures).[6] As for consumption, in 1975 the developing countries supplied approximately 2 per cent of the consumption of manufactured goods in the industrial countries; among the major sub-categories, the largest share was 8.6 per cent for clothing.[7]

This completes the brief look at five sources of pressure for change in the industrial countries' patterns of production and trade. Although the list is by no means exhaustive, it helps to clarify the 'pressures for change' argument. And, with the possible exception of the 'change in a key relative price', each entry on the list can be expected to continue to exert pressure for change in the foreseeable future.

(II) RELUCTANCE TO ADJUST: LABOUR MARKET DEVELOPMENTS

Smooth and continuous adjustment to pressure for change requires an adequate amount of occupational and geographic mobility, as well as enough flexibility in the wage structure to permit changes in relative wages to signal the emergence of labour shortages or surpluses in particular occupations or industries. There is considerable evidence that labour markets in the industrial countries are becoming more rigid in both respects.[8]

Current high levels of unemployment constitute direct evidence that labour markets in the developed countries are functioning poorly. It is true that part of the increase is the result of the widespread emphasis on using cautious monetary and fiscal policies in the fight against inflation, but the story cannot stop there. For example, unemployment was rising relatively fast during 1969–71, well before the appearance of very restrictive macroeconomic policies in 1974. Indeed, a plausible explanation for the very rapid monetary expansion in developed countries during 1971–2 – made possible by the tremendous growth of international monetary reserves during 1970–1 – is that governments were attempting to stimulate aggregate demand in order to reverse the rise in unemployment associated with increased labour market rigidity in the late 1960s. If this interpretation is correct, then labour market rigidity is not only directly responsible for part of the current unemployment, but also indirectly responsible for a good part of the 'deficient demand unemployment' caused by the policies introduced in response to the 1972–3 inflationary boom.

Recent developments in the United States, where the recovery from the 1974–5 recession has been the strongest, offer supporting evidence of inadequate occupational and geographic mobility. While unemployment remains high by post-war standards, labour shortages are emerging in several occupations, and similar reports are beginning to appear in the United Kingdom.[9]

Labour market rigidities generally are most apparent in situations in which an industry's relative importance is declining. The problems are less severe, however, when the market for the product is growing reasonably fast, because a decline in the relative importance of the domestic industry often takes the form of reduced or stagnant growth, rather than an absolute decline in employment and output. In such cases, few if any workers become involuntarily unemployed.[10] Alternatively, if aggregate demand for the product is stagnant or growing very slowly, the relative decline in the importance of the domestic industry is much more likely to require absolute declines in output and employment, with the latter often involving a high proportion of transitional involuntary unemployment.

This brings to mind the 'lubrication' argument for a mild inflation. Just as a 2–3 per cent a year inflation may permit adjustments in relative wages and prices without the need for absolute declines, an expanding market for a product would often make it possible to achieve a reduction in the relative importance of a domestic industry without the need for absolute declines in employment or output.

We may draw two conclusions from this, one encouraging and one not so encouraging. First, it is clear that adjustment in the pattern of production is much more difficult under depressed economic conditions than it is when the economy is healthy and expanding. Thus some of the current adjustment problems are likely to 'go away' once the pace of the recovery picks up. This must be qualified, however, to the extent that the structural imbalances which need correcting, as well as policies which have been introduced for the purpose of blocking the needed changes (such as increased restrictions on imports), are standing in the way of a more vigorous recovery.[11]

The less encouraging conclusion stems from the projections of reduced population and labour force growth in North America and Japan. Under these conditions, aggregate economic growth is likely to slow down even if per capita income continues at its high post-war rate. It seems probable, therefore, that these two areas face a future in which an increasing proportion of the adjustments in the pattern of production will require absolute declines in the less competitive industries.[12] If this is correct, then there is an even greater urgency to find acceptable solutions to the problems responsible for the increasingly inadequate degree of labour market flexibility.

(III) RELUCTANCE TO ADJUST: INVESTMENT BEHAVIOUR

The generally disappointing nature of recent trends in investment is well known. Among the major industrial countries, except Canada,[13] the level of real non-residential fixed investment (primarily plant and equipment) in 1977 was below the 1973 level. If we take instead the share of real gross domestic product which is spent on investment in plant and equipment, the 1977 figure is not only below the 1973 figure, but also below the 1970 figure.[14] If the investment is disaggregated into the plant component and the equipment component, another interesting trend appears. In five of the six countries (data for Japan are not available) there has been a perceptible decline, at least since 1970, in the share of non-residential investment spend on plant, and a commensurate increase in the share going to equipment. Only in the United Kingdom was the reverse true. This disappointing behaviour of business investment is both a cause and a result of the inadequate pace of adjustment.

Below average profits generally signal declining demand for the industry's product or an increase in the competitiveness of foreign suppliers – the only exception being temporary declines during recessions. Leaving aside the latter case for a moment, the decline in total profits will lead either to a decline in the rate of return on the original book values of plant and equipment, or to a decline in the firms' book values. The two effects are equivalent, and they act to divert investment away from less competitive industries and into the expanding efficient industries.

Long-run adjustments of the pattern of investment in plant and equipment in the predominantly private enterprise economies do, in fact, occur along these 'textbook' lines. It is also true, however, that the owners and managers in the less competitive industries often are very unhappy about being exposed to this adjustment process, and it is not surprising that they seek (with the active support of their workers) ways to avoid the necessary adjustment. That search always ends up in the same place, for there is only one way to avoid the adjustment, and that is to obtain a subsidy from the rest of the community either in the form of direct subsidies from the national treasury or in the form of artificially high prices made possible by increasing restrictions on imports that compete with the domestic industry's output.

Seen in this light, it is reasonable to interpret the escalating demands for government subsidies and increased restrictions on imports as evidence that industries are increasing their resistance to adjustment. Several possible explanations for this resistance come to mind, including the following:

a. In principle, it should be relatively painless for an industry to adjust by simply investing its depreciation funds in the expanding industries, rather than reinvesting them in the declining industry. This suggests that firms resist adjustment only in situations involving capital losses – that is, situations in which there is pressure to reduce the book value of the capital stock in an industry at a rate in excess of the depreciation rate. However, I suspect that this contributes only a small part of the resistance, and that in most instances in which it is an important factor, the situation has been created by the industry itself through a prolonged resistance to pressures for adjustment (after all, trade in cotton textiles has been subject to special restrictions for 18 years – more than enough time for the plant and equipment in existence in 1961 to have been fully written-off).[15]

b. Industrial managers are often in the same position as the industry's general work force – for example, having skills specific to the threatened industry, a desire to remain in the same geographic area, and so forth. The only difference is that they are able to influence investment decisions, whereas the production workers generally are not.

The two reasons just mentioned are always at work, regardless of the state of the economy. In contrast, the remaining two entries are, in one way or another, likely to be much more important in periods of inflation and depressed economic activity.

c. Above average levels of uncertainty have two kinds of negative effects on business investment. The overall level of investment is depressed, and the increased risk premiums bias the remaining investment toward projects with a short-run payoff.[16] Both effects are especially worrisome because adjustment to the pressures for change outlined at the beginning of the paper nearly always involves long-term investment.

Two developments explain much of the increase in uncertainty since the beginning of the decade. The key factor is the high and variable rates of inflation, which increase the degree of uncertainty surrounding business decisions by increasing the variability of the prices of a firm's inputs and output, and by raising the prospect that the government might resort to restrictive monetary and fiscal policies just as the contemplated investment project would begin producing. High rates of inflation also discourage investment through their impact on after-tax rates of return on corporate investment and individual savings.[17]

The second important source of increased uncertainty is the resurgence of protectionism in recent years and the intensified pressure for new (additional) subsidies. A considerable amount of post-war business investment took the form of outward looking long-term investments – as is evidenced, for example, by the fact that world trade expanded at a faster rate than world production throughout the post-war period (with the exception of two recession years, 1958 and 1975).[18] This was stimulated in large part by the establishment of rules delineating permissible monetary and trade behaviour. Protectionist developments in recent years have progressively undermined that stability of expectations, and it is impossible that the resulting increase in uncertainty has not had a depressing effect on the level of business investment.

d. Recessions increase resistance to change in two ways – one specific and one general. First, the depressed state of aggregate demand increases the likelihood that a decline in the relative importance of a particular industry will require an absolute decline in output. Second, the increased uncertainty and widespread idle capacity depress investment and reduce the alternative investment opportunities facing asset owners in uncompetitive industries.

The issue of 'excess capacity' raises a number of interesting questions – in particular, how it should be measured, and what (if anything) should be done about it – which would easily take me beyond the scope of this paper.[19] I would, however, like to mention two points which are related to the problem of adjustment in the pattern of investment in plant and equipment.

The concept of capacity which is easiest to grasp is 'engineering' or 'technical' capacity – for example, a steel plant may have a physical capacity of 100 tons per day. Unfortunately this concept of capacity is virtually useless because it tells us nothing about the efficiency of the operation. Thus if that plant produces steel at a cost of $400 per ton at its most efficient level of operation, whereas the world price of steel (set by more efficient firms) is $350 per ton, the plant has an economic capacity of zero. The difficulty in a recession lies in distinguishing between physical capacity which is only temporarily idle, and physical capacity whose economic value has been permanently destroyed – for example, by the establishment of newer and more efficient plants elsewhere.[20] When firms are resisting adjustment, it is not surprising that they often exaggerate the proportion of the excess physical capacity which is estimated to be only temporarily idle.

In addition to demands for subsidies and higher trade barriers, a third form of resistance to adjustment in the face of excess capacity has reappeared in the last year or two – pressure for special exemption from competition (anti-cartel) regulations.[21] This raises a number of problems. The higher cartel price requires increased restrictions on imports. If the product is an intermediate good – as is generally the case – the reduced domestic supply and higher price have a negative impact on employment and output in every industry which uses that product as an input. Because excess capacity is a major reason for creating the cartel, the agreement is likely to include restrictions on expanding existing capacity; this virtually precludes productivity-increasing innovation, which means that the threat posed by increased competition from abroad is likely to worsen. And so on.

As I mentioned above, the latter two explanations of the resistance to adjustment on the part of business firms are especially important during periods of inflation and recession. This is often interpreted to mean that once the industrial countries return to reasonable price stability and reasonably full employment, much of the resistance to adjustment (including the protectionist pressures) will disappear. This is true enough, but as I noted in making a similar remark about the labour market, it overlooks the extent to which existing maladjustments, and the 'temporary' policies introduced to protect firms from having to make the needed adjustments, are blocking the hoped for recovery.

(IV) ECONOMIC NATIONALISM AND THE FALSE DICHOTOMY BETWEEN DOMESTIC AND INTERNATIONAL INTERESTS

I would like to begin this concluding section by recalling the two types of economic nationalism which are contributing heavily to the protectionist trends which have increasingly affected international economic relations in recent years. One involves a country attempting to take advantage of the short-run stickiness of the adjustment process to gain something (such as a decline in unemployment) at the expense of other countries. The second involves the pursuit of economic interests which are labelled 'national' but which in reality involve one domestic group gaining at the expense of the others.

In the course of reviewing evidence in support of the 'reluctance to adjust' view of labour and capital markets in the industrial countries, I mentioned certain developments which reflected one or the other (or both) types of economic nationalism. For example:

– Implicit in much of the material I reviewed was the presumption that increased restrictions on imports provide employment for people who would otherwise be unemployed, and therefore that higher import restrictions increase both employment and national income; this amounts to exporting unemployment or, as it was

alled in the 1930s, a beggar-thy-neighbour policy. This is an example of the first type of nationalism which is bound to turn into the second type sooner or later, depending on whether the foreigners engage in overt retaliation or simply cut back on imports as their foreign exchange earnings decline.
– Efforts to protect profits and book values in uncompetitive industries rely on direct (for example government cash grants) or indirect (for example higher trade barriers) income transfers from the rest of the community:

Neither type of nationalism holds any hope for long-run gains. Under the first type, the foreigners always 'get even', either directly or indirectly, while the second type simply redistributes income among various domestic groups. In addition to the absence of any gain, nationalist policies of this type are certain to reduce national income by blocking efficiency-increasing changes in the pattern of production.

This is particularly apparent when we consider the ways in which protectionism spreads from industry to industry, and from country to country. These include: (i) the creation of political precedents ('If them, why not us?'); (ii) higher protection for intermediate goods stimulates demands for protection from industries using those inputs; (iii) imposing restrictions on the importation of good *y* causes the exporting country to shift labour and capital into the production of *z*, which in turn often stimulates demands for new restrictions on imports of *z*; (iv) country B raises import barriers in response to imports deflected from A because of A's new restrictions; (v) when the protection is discriminatory – as with orderly marketing arrangements – other countries often emerge as new low-cost suppliers, and therefore must be added to the OMA; and (vi) simple, old-fashioned retaliation. This kind of chain reaction is very difficult to stop.

The False Dichotomy

Economic nationalism, defined loosely as a belief that there are situations in which a country's domestic economic interests come in conflict with, and therefore should take precedence over, the economic interests of other countries, almost certainly has been with us since the establishment of the nation-state. We saw a particularly virulent form of it in the 1930s. It subsided during the quarter century following World War II, only to begin increasing once again around the beginning of this decade. About that time articles and books began to appear which stressed a viewpoint whose flavour is captured by the following brief quotation: 'Economic interdependence is a two-edged sword . . . it involves costs as well as benefits.'[22] As far as trade is concerned, this is nothing more than ageless economic nationalism dressed up in modern words.

I would like to explain very briefly why I believe that the dichotomy or juxtaposition between domestic and foreign interests is false.[23] My remarks apply only to economic nationalism at the level of trade in goods and services, although I suspect that the argument applies as well to most other kinds of nationalism.

The viewpoint quoted above suggests that interdependence is costly because certain legitimate national objectives may have to be sacrificed to the discipline of the international order. Since participation in the international order – for example, through membership in GATT and the IMF – is voluntary, this implies that each country has certain goals whose achievement depends on the existence of international rules of behaviour, but at the same time it may have a second set of goals whose attainment is impeded by those rules. Put this way, the latest version of economic nationalist thinking begins to look suspicious.

The suspicion is well-founded, for the view in question contains one mistake of fact and one fallacy of reasoning. The factual error is the presumption that behavioural rules in the trade area prescribe specific national goals for an economy. What the rules do is regulate the policies which governments use in pursuit of their national goals. While it is true that during the post-war period GATT members have participated in several rounds of negotiations designed to liberalise trade, GATT rules do not require that a member country liberalise its trade, but only that it observe certain rules in regulating its trade. The OECD's 'polluter-pays-principle' says nothing about the level of pollution standards which a nation should adopt – it asks only that the costs incurred by the adoption of whatever standard a country chooses be allocated in a way that does not distort trade patterns. Many similar examples could be given.

Moreover, the rules governing policies in the trade area generally ask countries to use the most efficient of the available policies. For example, the General Agreement expresses a preference for tariffs over other kinds of barriers to trade, as well as an implicit preference for relying on policies other than trade estrictions for the achievement of national goals – in other words, all policies which are broadly consistent with the recommendations of the modern theory of commercial policy.[24]

The fallacy in the domestic/foreign interest dichotomy is the assumption that goals whose achievement requires a violation of existing rules can be pursued without seriously reducing the likelihood of achieving the other goals whose attainment depends on a well-functioning international order. This clearly is impossible because it requires that other countries continue to observe the international rules while the country in question violates them whenever they appear to restrict the achievement of a particular national goal. It is obvious that things just do not work that way. Any violation of an international rule creates a precedent which encourages other countries to engage in similar violations, as well as encouraging other domestic groups whose special interests would be served by violations of the rules to pressure the government to violate the rules in question. In the 1930s we saw the end product of that process. It was the destruction of the international order whose existence is crucial to the achievement of what presumably is the primary economic goal of most countries – the improvement of its citizens' material standard of living.[25]

What Should We Do?

There are no easy solutions to the problems which underlie the inadequate pace of adjustment in the industrial countries. The argument for change rests instead on the fact that a failure to increase substantially the pace of adjustment must eventually create problems for society as a whole which are far more serious than those which confront inefficient industries exposed to world market competition. Against this background, several recommendations come to mind, including the following:

a. There is a great need for more familiarity with the facts concerning such things as the relative importance of imports as a source of job displacement and the export performance of the industrial countries' efficient industries. Many studies indicate, for example, that technological innovation is a much more important factor in job displacement than are imports.[26] Or consider the near hysteria in some quarters over imports from the developing countries at a time when (i) they are supplying an average of 2 per cent of the domestic consumption of manufactures in the industrial countries, and (ii) they are buying on average an additional $2 worth of the industrial countries' exports of manufactures for every additional $1 worth of manufactured exports sold to the industrial countries. Between 1963 and 1976, the industrial countries increased their export surplus in manufactures trade with the developing countries from $16bn to $93bn (their surplus in manufactures trade with the oil-importing developing countries alone increased from $11bn to $37bn).[27] In short, there are many efficient firms and industries, but their success makes the headlines much less often than the problems faced by the small number of threatened inefficient industries.

b. As a balance to the widespread talk about the 'costs of adjustment', there is a need for more emphasis in public discussions on the 'costs of not adjusting'. It is true that progressively higher trade restrictions make life easier for workers and owners in certain import-competing industries. But what about the rest of the society – the vastly greater number of people who work in efficient industries, who are retired, and so forth (not to speak of the workers and owners in the exporting countries)? As I have already stressed, the *only* way to forestall adjustment is to transfer income in one way or another from the rest of the community to the inefficient industries (with low-income groups often bearing a disproportionately large share of the burden, as when inexpensive clothing and shoes are subjected to increased trade barriers). Increased protection in the industrial countries also means that fewer job openings are available in the more efficient and productive export sector; this in turn depresses the rate of return on the acquisition of skills, an effect which is not lost on young people about to enter the labour force. On a broader level, spreading protectionist measures are very costly in terms of their impact on relations among countries.

c. We need to learn to focus more on long-run interests. Too often people advocating and making policies seem to be concerned only with the next 18 months. There is no way in which a series of expedient short-run policies can add up to a decent long-run policy. A related improvement would involve a better perception of what is in each of our own individual interests. A retreat into a trading system of the kind experienced in the 1930s would harm a great many people who have, thus far in the current upsurge in protectionism, sat silently on the side lines.

d. There is an urgent need to reaffirm and strengthen the rules which helped to bring us a quarter century of unprecedented prosperity. The current Tokyo Round of trade negotiations offers just such an opportunity.[28]

e. To end on a more general note, we need to search hard for policies that will allow us to satisfy the desire for a reasonable degree of order and stability in our individual economic lives without simultaneously introducing rigidities into the economy which are certain to frustrate eventually that desire.

NOTES

1. Any opinions, conclusions or recommendations expressed herein are my own and are not intended to reflect the views of GATT. The paper draws on two recent studies, dealing with trade relations and adjustment, which I co-authored with Nicolas Marian and Jan Tumlir (see below). Whatever shortcomings and errors that remain are my responsibility.
2. A limited survey of the literature turned up a variety of definitions which, in most instances, did not seem to have a well-defined common thread. See, for example, H. G. Johnson, 'A Theoretical Model of Economic Nationalism in New and Developing States', A. Kahan, 'Nineteenth-Century European Experience With Policies of Economic Nationalism', and R. W. Weiss, 'Economic Nationalism in Britain in the Nineteenth Century' all in H. G. Johnson (ed.), *Economic Nationalism in Old and New States* (London: Allen and Unwin, 1968).
3. F. W. Segel and F. J. Dreiling, 'Pollution Abatement and Control Expenditures, 1972–76', *Survey of Current Business* (Washington, DC: US Department of Commerce, February 1978).
4. See General Agreement on Tariffs and Trade, *Industrial Pollution Control and International Trade* (Geneva: GATT Studies in International Trade No. 1, July 1971), and R. Blackhurst, 'International Trade and Domestic Environmental Policies in a Growing World Economy', in *International Relations in a Changing World* (Geneva: Graduate Institute of International Studies, 1977).
5. Data in this part are taken from the United Nations, *Statistical Yearbook* and the OECD, *Labour Force Statistics, 1964–1975*.
6. Table 18 in R. Blackhurst, N. Marian and J. Tumlir, *Adjustment, Trade and Growth in Developed and Developing Countries* (Geneva: GATT Studies in International Trade Number 6, 1978).
7. Ibid., Table 19.
8. See, for example, P. McCracken, et al., *Towards Full Employment and Price Stability* (Paris: OECD, June 1977), especially pp. 145, 222–3, and Chapter

III; and OECD, *A Medium Term Strategy for Employment and Manpower Policies*, (Paris: OECD, 1978), especially pp. 30–1 and 88).

9. See, for example, *Business Week* (10 October 1977, pp. 34–5 and 5 June 1978, pp. 48–9), and the *Economist* (24 June 1978, pp. 115–16).
10. Another situation in which involuntary unemployment is avoided (or at least minimised) is one in which natural attrition of the industry's labour force (principally retirements and voluntary quits) is utilised to affect the necessary reduction in employment. See, for example, C. Hsieh, 'Measuring the Effects of Trade Expansion on Employment: A Review of Some Research', *International Labour Review*, January–June (1973); and W. S. Salant, *The Effects of Increases in Imports on Domestic Employment: a Clarification of Concepts*, Special Report No. 18, National Commission for Manpower Policy (Washington, DC: January 1978).
11. For example, the decision in several industrial countries to take both trade and domestic measures to raise the domestic price of steel – a key input for a variety of large industries – by restricting its availability is hardly the kind of policy that contributes to the goal of speeding up the economic recovery.
12. 'In these circumstances [of slow growth of manufacturing employment] a contraction (or a further contraction) of unskilled labour-intensive branches appears inevitable and, in a medium- and long-term perspective, a condition for permitting a vigorous growth of the technologically more advanced branches.'; United Nations, Economic Commission for Europe, *Structure and Change in European Industry* (New York: 1977), p. 79.
13. The United States, Canada, Japan, the Federal Republic of Germany, France, Italy and the United Kingdom.
14. It should be added, however, that the 1977 share was above the average share for the 1950s in each of the seven countries except Italy and Canada. It would be possible, therefore, to interpret the recent trends as a return to more 'normal' long-run rates of investment in plant and equipment, rather than as being unusually low.
15. A good way of testing the view that the speed of the adjustment is the only problem is to pose the following question: Assuming that the maximum write-off period for a plant or piece of equipment is 20 years, assuming that we continue to have a 'safeguard' mechanism for dealing with temporary surges in imports, and keeping in mind the option of relying on retirements and voluntary quits to reduce the size of a firm's labour force, what is the likelihood of getting the industrial countries to agree on a plan to phase out *all* trade barriers by reducing them in equal instalments on 1 January of each year from 1980 to 1999?
16. See, for example, A. Greenspan, 'Investment Risk: the New Dimension of Policy', *The Economist*, 6 August 1977.
17. See Blackhurst, Marian and Tumlir, op. cit., Chapter II, and the references cited therein.
18. See R. Blackhurst, N. Marian and J. Tumlir, *Trade Liberalization, Protectionism and Interdependence* (Geneva: GATT Studies in International Trade Number 5, 1977), pp. 7–8.
19. See G. C. Winston, 'Capacity: an Integrated Micro and Macro Analysis', *Papers and Proceedings*, American Economic Association, February 1977.
20. Examples of other developments which can reduce or destroy the economic

capacity of existing plant and equipment include pollution control regulations and the higher cost of energy.

21. See J. Tumlir, 'The New Protectionism, Cartels and the International Order' in R. Ammacher (ed.), *Challenges to Liberal Economic Order* (forthcoming).
22. L. E. Krause and J. S. Nye, 'Reflections on the Economics and Politics of International Economic Organizations' in C. F. Bergsten and L. E. Krause (eds.), *World Politics and International Economics* (Washington, DC: The Brookings Institution, 1975), p. 334. References to other examples of this line of thinking are cited in Blackhurst, Marian and Tumlir, op. cit., 1977, pp. 2–3, and Tumlir, op. cit.; my discussion in this section is based on these two references, particularly the latter.
23. The one possible exception is the monopoly power or terms of trade argument. Considering the possibilities for retaliation and other forms of deterioration in international relations which can result from the use of such market power, it is not clear how much of an exception this really is.
24. See H. G. Johnson, 'Optimal Trade Intervention in the Presence of Domestic Distortions', in R. Baldwin et al. (eds.), *Trade, Growth and the Balance of Payments: Essays in Honor of Gottfried Haberler* (Chicago: Rand-McNally, 1965 [reprinted in H. G. Johnson, *Aspects of the Theory of Tariffs*, (London: G. Allen and Unwin, 1971)]; J. N. Bhagwati, 'The Generalized Theory of Distortions and Welfare' in J. Bhagwati et al. (eds.), *Trade, Balance of Payments and Growth* (Amsterdam and London: North–Holland, 1971); and, W. M. Corden, *Trade Policy and Economic Welfare* (Oxford: Clarendon Press, 1974).
25. From 1913–48 world per capita income increased at an average annual rate of approximately one per cent; during this same period the volume of world trade grew at an average annual rate of one-half of one per cent. From 1948–78, world per capita income and the volume of world trade grew at average annual rates of 3 per cent and 7 per cent, respectively.
26. See Hsieh, op. cit., and Blackhurst, Marian and Tumlir, op. cit. (1978), Chapter II.
27. Blackhurst, Marian and Tumlir, op. cit. (1978), Chapter I.
28. See O. Long, 'International Trade Under Threat: a Constructive Response', *The World Economy*, June 1978.

8 The Multi-Tier GATT System

Gerard and Victoria Curzon

The current round of trade negotiations in Geneva is drawing to an end set by the expiration of the US trade legislation in January 1980. Should it succeed, its contents will be hailed as yet another – alas, perhaps the last! – milestone on the road to trade liberalisation and orderly commercial relations among civilised nations. Our statesmen will congratulate themselves – and expect us to congratulate them too – that they succeeded against all odds, not only in withstanding the rising tide of protectionism, but in actually reducing barriers to international trade in such adverse circumstances. Mixed metaphors (which the tariff question inevitably attracts) will abound. A 30–40 per cent cut in industrial tariffs is, after all, a considerable achievement at the best of times, and is quite remarkable in the depths of an economic recession.

If the negotiations in Geneva succeed, trade in industrial goods among developed countries will bear lighter duties than ever before. To all intents and purposes, bar a few items in the textiles, steel and chemical sectors, the North Atlantic Zone will be a vast free trade area. Tariffs will not only be low, but almost all 'bound'. This adds to the North Atlantic trade zone the crucial element of predictability which is said to be one of the most important features of a permanent integration scheme. It will, of course, be flexible and pragmatic; and as such scarcely recognisable. Some of its members already belong to a customs union, others to various free trade arrangements, and still others to an interesting experiment in integrating the automobile sector. All have now and will continue to have, highly individualistic policies towards developing countries, Eastern Europe and the Far East.

A skeptic might remark that the painstaking needlework of tariff reduction is, however, constantly being undone, like Penelope's knitting, by hordes of non-tariff barriers: formal and informal restraints to trade abound. There are strict quotas on textiles from some developing to most of the developed countries;[1] countries exporting steel to the EEC have agreed to respect minimum prices (on pain of paying offsetting variable duties on entry),[2] while the United States' 'trigger price' mechanism levies especially high duties on especially low-priced steel imports;[3] 'orderly marketing' arrangements with respect to *inter alia*, shoes, automobiles, television sets, cutlery and other 'sensitive' items abound, but information in this respect is limited to what can be gleaned from the press. In the EEC a 'crisis cartel' has been created in the steel sector to reduce supply and raise prices, and another for man-made fibres was created but ruled out by the anti-trust division of the EEC Commission before it went into operation.[4] In many countries, subsidies to unprofitable enterprises in the name of 'industrial policy' further contribute to the impression that all is not well with the liberal trade system.

It is nevertheless highly significant that most of the recent non-tariff barriers, especially orderly marketing arrangements, are aimed at imports from outside the North Atlantic Zone. Free trade among developed countries with similar price structures is almost untouched by encroaching protectionism.

The GATT trade negotiators would hasten to point out, however, that although the Tokyo Round tariff cuts may hit the headlines, really solid progress has been made precisely in the field of non-tariff barriers, and that the era of erosion of tariff liberalisation by their proliferation may be drawing to an end. Indeed, the final package will doubtless allude to several 'codes' relating to such important non-tariff barriers to trade as government procurement, technical norms and standards, customs valuation, subsidies and countervailing duties and escape clause action.

Some of these non-tariff barrier (NTB) codes have been in the pipeline for years. Madariaga once said of disarmament conferences that the function of delegate should be made hereditary, and the same could be said of trade negotiators. Of the freeing of trade there is no end!

The oldest code is perhaps the one relating to government procurement. Talks on this started in the OECD shortly after 1960,[5] but never got anywhere because no one was prepared to fight for it: the United States was handicapped by its own 'Buy American' act, which made embarrassingly clear what other countries did without broadcasting the fact. Most countries use 'administrative guidance' to encourage government agencies to 'buy national'. This provides implicit support for certain sectors of industry without going to the legislative branch for an explicit subsidy – a step which might involve misplaced public concern for such irrelevant issues as to whether there were alternative uses to which the taxpayers' money might have been put, or whether the same ends could have been achieved by different means. Despite the undoubted attractions of being free to offer implicit subsidies to promote domestic industry, governments have drawn up a code which (if they sign it) will oblige them to allow the nationals of co-signatories to tender for public contracts (outside reserved sectors, such as telecommunications) and to award the contracts on commercial grounds only. If this code is really to be found in the final Multinational Trade Negotiations (MTNs) package, it will be quite astonishing.

Different national technical norms and standards are another venerable NTB issue. They are fully recognised as important and largely involuntary non-tariff barriers to trade, but they are singularly intractable. The Secretary-General of the International Organization for Standardization has estimated that an advanced industrial economy needs some 20,000 standards,[6] and new ones are being established daily. Efforts to draw up internationally accepted standards are condemned to lag perpetually behind the changing reality with which they are trying to cope. For instance, even within as tightly-knit a group as the nine-member EEC, efforts to harmonise certain food standards, which had lasted over a decade, were finally abandoned last year because they had been taken over by events. The solution adopted in the MTNs, pioneered by EFTA in the 1960s,[7] consists of drawing up codes not for the harmonisation of standards, but for the prior notification of new ones to an examining body, and for the mutual recognition of each other's certification procedures. The practical impact of such a code would presumably be positive, but small. It is not clear whether it would apply to all GATT members on a most-favoured-nation basis, or only as between signataries.

Another hardy perennial is the code on customs valuation, a subject which has also been with us for more than a decade and which, behind its deceptively bland title, hides a number of prickly issues. We all remember the American Selling Price dispute, but how many of us recall the *cif-fob* debate? The United States takes the *export* value of goods without counting transport costs, as a basis for customs valuation, while European countries take the *import* value of goods and include the cost of insurance and freight. A minor difference, one might think, and indeed, the *cif* method probably adds no more than one-tenth to European tariff rates relative to US ones.[8] But there are unexpected consequences. Thus the European system is said to discriminate both country- and product-wise: it penalises distant countries like the United States and Japan, and it works against goods with a low weight/value ratio, like those from developing countries. The American system, on the other hand, is said to be neutral in these two respects. However, the *cif* method of valuation recognises that services such as transport and insurance are as much a part of the value of goods as labour, raw materials and technology.

An international code which resolves some of these issues to the mutual satisfaction of the principal protagonists would be of undoubted value. It would help to simplify the sometimes quite discouraging diversity of administrative regulations affecting trade and besides being of interest to traders the world over, it would, incidentally, help to improve the uniformity of customs administration in the EEC.

A draft code on subsidies and countervailing duties is absorbing a considerable amount of diplomatic energy. It is intended to complement the already existing anti-dumping code. The latter was negotiated during the Kennedy Round; it clarified the law and established an international surveillance mechanism which has proved moderately successful. Whereas the anti-dumping code lays down the conditions under which an importing country may raise an exceptional tariff on dumped goods, the subsidies and countervailing duty code would establish uniform criteria for the levying of exceptional duties to offset foreign government subsidies.

The GATT prohibits export subsidies and a number of developed countries have agreed to be bound by this provision. However, it does not prohibit general production subsidies. In either case, an importing country which considers that its local industry is suffering 'material' injury as a result of a foreign government subsidy is entitled to levy a countervailing duty.

This self-policing system, however, falls down on interpretation. What is a subsidy? There is room for considerable disagreement on this point. How much 'suffering' is required before a countervailing duty can be legally levied? Should the duty cancel the subsidy or the suffering? If the subsidy (as is the law under GATT at present), how should one calculate it? (Some subsidies are far from transparent.) Would it not be simpler to get to the root of the problem, and outlaw harmful subsidies? This is the US position: it is based on the idea that if something is bad, like drunken driving, it should be outlawed all the time, and not just when it causes an accident. The EEC, on the other hand, takes the view that governments should have the right to subsidise if they please and only if injury occurs should offsetting action be taken. According to this view subsidies can be compared with smoking, in which one person's pleasure may cause another person's discomfort. However, the answer is not to outlaw smoking, but to protect the interests of smokers and non-smokers alike.

One could debate these intricate and fascinating questions at leisure were it not for the fact that US law allows for the imposition of countervailing duties on imports bearing any 'bounty or grant', even if a US producer is not suffering from 'material injury'. This provision has been temporarily waived until January 1979, after which date, since European governments at present offer a wide variety of investment subsidies, a large number of European exports are liable to legal action by US citizens to impose countervailing duties: a gold mine for lawyers, and a potential non-tariff barrier against European exports of massive dimensions.

Hence the EEC's interest in a subsidies and countervailing duty code under which the United States would accept a 'material injury' criterion, while all signatories would agree to the prior notification of subsidies and to an international surveillance mechanism to judge the damage they do to others. The United States suggested that subsidies, like toxic substances, should be classified into groups, according to which some would be totally outlawed (for example direct export subsidies), others would be tolerated under surveillance (for example regional investment grants), while a final category of subsidies would be permitted (for example general aids available to all enterprises). This proposal did not lead anywhere, and the present approach concentrates on clarifying Article XVI of GATT so as to strengthen the prohibition of export subsidies and make governments more alert to the harm they do to others in the pursuit of national industrial policies. Only if the United States accepts an 'injury' clause will the other delegations sign the code. This is still in considerable doubt because it would imply a change of US law. Adding to the complexity of the situation, developing countries are asking for the right to subsidise their exports *a volonté* without running the risk of being countervailed. Quite how all these positions are to be reconciled remains, at the time of writing, a mystery.

Finally, we have what is perhaps the most far-reaching and complex NTB problem of all: safeguards. The GATT permits members to raise emergency tariffs to protect local producers threatened with 'serious injury' by low-cost imports, but only after offering compensation in the form of a lower tariff on another product. The purpose of this provision is not so much to protect the interests of the exporting countries, as to discourage importers from taking such a drastic step. Indeed, Article XIX is very expensive to use. Furthermore, emergency measures taken under it are frequently likened to using a canon ball to kill a fly. Thus, emergency tariffs, if introduced, have to apply to all contracting parties, even if the 'problem' is caused by only one of them. It is argued very persuasively that if a direct causal link is discovered between 'serious injury' and men's shirts from Hong Kong, why should the emergency duty apply to men's shirts coming from everywhere else? The reason is respect for the most-favoured-nation clause. Yet it is most inconvenient. In practice, 'serious injury' can often be traced back to a relative new-comer on the world trade scene, who does not take many of one's exports in return; by gate-crashing the party he not only upsets the host, but his long-established friends as well. It is much more soothing to stop him coming to the party than to offend everyone by calling it off altogether.

This is in fact what happens. Article XIX is hardly ever invoked at all, and countries infinitely prefer to negotiate informal 'orderly marketing agreements' (OMAs) with all potential gate-crashers.[9] OMAs have proliferated in the 1970s and the root cause is not only the rapid economic development of some countries, but also the over-strict terms of Article XIX, especially with regards to compensation. A rule as consistently ignored as Article XIX clearly needs amending.

The objective of amending Article XIX would be to stop the spread of OMAs and to replace them by internationally acceptable forms of adjustment assistance. It is also argued that a better escape clause would encourage tariff-cutting: governments are by nature risk-averters. They cut tariffs where adjustment costs are estimated to be low, relative price differences small and the gains from freer trade minimal, and an improved safeguard clause is necessary to persuade them to take greater risks.

For both these reasons, a reform of Article XIX of GATT is desirable, but the implications of the current proposals are alarming. According to one proposal countries would have the right to introduce *selective* emergency restrictions and would not have to offer compensation as long as they could show proof of a genuine attempt to restructure the injured industry. An international surveillance body would supervise the application of the new rules. This, however, went too far, and the negotiators were once more obliged to fall back on a reinterpretation of the existing article, with more elaborate surveillance and reporting procedures. In a July 1978 press release the GATT Secretariat reported that 'the question, of how and under what circumstances and conditions a selective application of safeguard measures would be provided for in the code, is still a subject of intensive negotiations'.

While a good case can be made for alleviating the burden of offering tariff compensation and for better international surveillance, it is not possible to justify the use of selective protection in economic terms. What it amounts to is an internationally sanctioned system of guaranteed market shares, where the most efficient world producer would have the smallest share and would be able to expand it only at a 'reasonable pace'. However, of the 'Big Three' both the EEC and the United States favour selectivity, and only Japan is holding out for a non-discriminatory safeguard system.

THE MULTI-TIER SYSTEM

It is clearly important to tackle matters such as these. GATT was drawn up thirty years ago. The world has changed, *ergo* GATT must change. But GATT started out with 23 contracting parties. It now has 83. They are incapable of agreeing unanimously to change even a comma in the original agreement.

How, then, is GATT to change? The answer is to draw up codes, of the type briefly discussed, based for the most part on existing GATT articles, and to create a network of new rights and obligations among the countries which accept them. GATT, as one wit has put it, must give birth to Gittens. This will have the inevitable effect of creating a multi-tier GATT system. Not that GATT has been a one-tier system for a very long time: the myth of universality died many deaths at the hands of such venerable institutions as the OEEC, EEC, EFTA, GSP and the like. But if five new NTB codes are now adopted, there will be a quantum jump in the non-universality of trade law. Progress in international trade law can perhaps only be made crab-wise in this fashion, now that the sheer number of sovereign states and the complexity of inter-governmental decision-making render universal agreements on general principles unattainable.

The danger lies in the fact that the *principle* of discriminatory treatment, through the conditional most-favoured-nation (MFN) clause, will become an accepted way of dealing with non-tariff barriers. From there it is but a short step to applying the conditional MFN clause to tariff bargaining. The conditional MFN clause as applied to tariffs can only be considered a retrograde step, because it leads directly to the jungle of tariff discrimination, where only the largest and strongest can survive.

So far one has talked of 'selective' measures only in relation to the reform of the safeguard clause. Other proposed NTB codes merely imply discriminatory treatment between signatories and non-signatories: under the government procurement code, only nationals of co-signatories would be given the right to non-discrimination in public tenders; under the norms and standards code, only co-signatories would benefit from the mutual recognition of certificates of conformity; under the subsidies and countervailing duties code, only co-signatories could protest against the arbitrary levy of a countervailing tariff; only the customs valuation code at first sight appears to have no obvious discriminatory impact.

Perhaps the advantages of joining these codes will be such that they will quickly attract sufficient signatories for these fears to be unfounded. Nevertheless, while hailing the progress made in the non-tariff barrier field, one must continually bear in mind that the codes are of a 'second best' and imperfect nature.

OUTLOOK

Whether one is a pessimist or an optimist depends partly on one's time horizon: for instance, one can be a pessimist in the short term, an optimist in the medium term and a pessimist again in the long term, without necessarily contradicting oneself. It is not too difficult to be a short-term pessimist with regard to trade matters. The Tokyo Round, if it succeeds, will be considered to have made a significant contribution to liberal trade, all the more impressive by virtue of the circumstances in which it was negotiated. But it will apply mainly to industrial trade among developed countries. Fair enough, one might say, since developing countries have not offered much in return (we are aware that it has been agreed in the Tokyo Round that developed countries do not expect to receive, and developing countries are not expected to give, reciprocity, but we venture to doubt the practical value of this approach to trade negotiations).

In fact, if one group of countries liberalises trade among its members, while erecting emergency tariffs and non-tariff barriers towards another group of countries it is, in effect, creating a preferential trade zone. This, in itself, could be good or bad for world welfare: customs union theory tells us to take a hard look at the specific circumstances, for the answer is unclear from theory alone.

The specific circumstances are as follows: for 30 years a group of countries in the North Atlantic area have cut tariffs on each others' products, and, because of the MFN clause in GATT, have passed on the benefits of these tariff cuts to a large number of non-participants. Before claiming exceptional virtue for this period of GATT's history, one must remember that this was a relatively costless, and therefore relatively worthless, gift: the countries which were given a 'free ride' were not then competitors of the central area. Now they are. The gift of relatively free access to the North Atlantic markets has suddenly become valuable, but, by the same token, the donors show every sign of wishing to withdraw it for revaluation purposes.

In the short run, and from an economic welfare viewpoint, this is likely to reduce world income. Trade liberalisation among the members of the North Atlantic Zone (NAZ) has probably already passed Meade's point of diminishing returns to preferential tariff cuts. Relative price differences are now minimal, so further gains from trade are likely to be small. On the other hand, the volume of trade thus affected is very great, since industrial countries' intra-area trade in manufactures amounts to a staggering 89 per cent of their total non-primary exports.[10] On this count, further small, but relatively painless gains from trade and specialisation can doubtless be made.

Looking now at NAZ trade with the rest of the non-oil producing, developing world, we note that although it used to be complementary, it is now increasingly competitive, especially with regards to Third World-type goods which the NAZ group tends to protect. Furthermore, relative prices in this competitive range of goods are very different. Thus the loss per unit of trade from trade diversion will tend to be very high. On the other hand, the volume of trade thus affected is still comparatively low (some 7 per cent of NAZ countries' manufactures imports), so the overall loss from trade diversion might not be considered important.

However, the phenomenon of a low volume of trade at very different relative prices is clearly a dynamic situation: one would expect the volume of trade to grow rapidly until relative price differences were reduced. Thus the *potential* loss from preventing this from occurring is likely to be very great indeed, and almost certainly greater than the limited trade creation gains described above. The same would be true of the consumer loss/gain situation.

Why are countries so eager to form trade-diverting customs unions, and to subject themselves willingly to the costs of protection? The answer has been given many times but bears repeating. While the burden of adjustment is concentrated on a few identifiable producers, whose problems can easily be raised to the level of a national disaster, the benefits of freer trade, which are *truly* of a national dimension, are enjoyed by such large numbers and are thus so thinly spread, that people remain largely ignorant of them. If domestic protectionist forces were not offset by industrial export interests, democracies would have a built-in bias towards protectionism. As it is in times of economic adversity import-competing industries tend to outweigh export-oriented interests and liberal trade is very much a fairweather policy.

In the longer term, however, one can afford to be a cautious optimist. One can view the formation of NAZ as only a step in the gradual integration of the entire world into a free trade system. Countries outside NAZ have been left with high tariffs because they did not participate actively in GATT rounds to date, and were busy industrialising behind protectionist walls. NAZ countries themselves have little reason to initiate a further round of GATT tariff negotiations. They are so close to free trade among themselves that there is simply no point in tying up scarce, skilled negotiators in Geneva for five years at a time any more. Instead, they will probably appoint a standing committee to supervise the day-to-day management of the present level of tariff liberalisation and will work diligently at various nontariff barrier codes, making real though slow and unspectacular progress. So where will the next step come from?

By raising barriers to trade with third countries, NAZ is putting itself in a negotiating position which it would not have had if it had remained free-trading. One could argue that this preliminary phase is needed to persuade emerging industrial powers to reduce their tariffs, because unilateral free trade is politically impractical for them. In due course, when trade between NAZ and the rest of the world has been sufficiently restricted so that the gains from liberalising it become self-evident, the gradual process of trade liberalisation can begin again. Perhaps by the year 2000?

NOTES

1. See for instance, *Official Journal of the European Communities*, Vol. 21, 11 February 1978, No. L42.
2. Bulletin of the European Communities, No. 3, 1978, pp. 34–5 and pp. 76–7.
3. *Daily Bulletin*, No. 244, U.S. Mission, Geneva, December 8, 1977, pp. 1–5.
4. *Financial Times*, 18 May 1978, p. 20.
5. Gerard and Victoria Curzon, *Hidden Barriers to International Trade* (London: Trade Policy Research Centre, 1970), p. 16.
6. Olle Sturen, 'Towards Global Acceptance of International Standards' (New York: American National Standards Institute, 1972), p. 3.
7. Gerard and Victoria Curzon, 'EFTA's Experience with Non-Tariff Barriers', in Corbet and Robertson (eds.), *Europe's Free Trade Area Experiment* (Oxford: Pergamon Press, 1970), pp. 129–45.
8. Ernest H. Preeg, *Traders and Diplomats* (Washington: The Brookings Institution, 1970), p. 131.
9. Gerard and Victoria Curzon, 'The Management of Trade Relations in the GATT' in Shonfield (ed.), *International Economic Relations of the Western World 1959–1971*, Vol. I (London: Royal Institute of International Affairs, Oxford University Press, 1976), pp. 246–52.
10. GATT, *International Trade*, 1976–1977, Geneva, 1977, Table 7, pp. 26–7. Japan, though geographically not in the North Atlantic, is becoming part of the zone we are referring to. The Japanese trade surplus within NAZ can be considered as the first phase of this process. The next phase will be characterised by greater trade equilibrium and closer relative price structures.

9 Escape Clauses and the Multi-Fibre Agreement

Jacques A. L'Huillier

Those responsible for the liberalisation of international trade, which has made impressive progress since World War II, were well aware of the necessity of establishing an equilibrium between two contradictory constraints. On the one hand, in order to take full advantage of the liberalisation measures, the competitive producer had to have a reasonable guarantee that the possible abrogation of the liberalisation measures from which they were benefiting would not condemn, prior to depreciation, the investments which they were undertaking in order to increase their exports. This view placed emphasis on making the liberalisation procedures as irreversible as possible. On the other hand, if governments are aware that all commitment to liberalisation on their part is irrevocable, then they will show themselves to be exceedingly cautious in granting tariff concessions. The compromise between these two positions consisted in providing the liberalisation rules with escape clauses. These clauses, however, should be temporary and should not alter the nature of the fundamental rules of trade liberalisation.

Article XIX of the General Agreement on Tariffs and Trade (GATT) is a particularly important example of such a compromise.

The GATT attempts to give stability to tariff cuts which are consolidated for a three year period. At the end of this period, however, a government – let us say A – may hesitate to revoke the concession because it fears subsequent retaliatory measures. Indeed, it is not only the principal exporting country of the product concerned which may revoke a concession in retaliation, but also less important exporters who had benefited from A's concession through the most-favoured-nation clause.

Thus the irreversibility of concessions in fact constitutes the norm.

But Article XIX of the GATT introduced an escape clause which allows a country temporarily to reduce, or actually revoke a concession, even during a triennal consolidation period. However, recourse to this clause is subject to the fulfilment of a number of conditions.

First of all, it is not sufficient for the imports of the product, or products, under concession, simply to have increased sharply. The increase of the imported product must: (i) be the result of the granting of the concession; (ii) have been unforeseeable at the time when the concession was granted; and (iii) severely injure the rival domestic industry.

Secondly, supposing that all of these conditions are fulfilled, then the state wishing to revoke the concession must consult with the GATT members who actually benefited from it: not only with the major supplier, but also with the secondary suppliers. Article XIX expects such negotiations to terminate in an agreement, which implies that the state wishing to revoke the concession must offer compensation in the form of additional concessions on one or more products. If an agreement is not reached, the state wishing to revoke the concession may do so, but in so doing, it exposes itself to retaliatory measures. Whether agreement is reached or not, the concession must be revoked *erga omnes*; this embodies one of the fundamental GATT principles, that of non-discrimination.

Finally, Article XIX stipulates that the revocation of the concession should not last any longer than the period of injury to the domestic industry.

In this paper, we shall attempt, first of all, in the light of past experience, to evaluate the grievances which have been put forward concerning Article XIX. Secondly, we shall examine a new kind of safeguard measure that has appeared, outside of the GATT, in the form of bilateral agreements on voluntary export restraints. Finally, we shall see how the GATT came to recognise these new safeguard measures, in the hope of being able to control them.

THE APPLICATION OF ARTICLE XIX

Looking back, it appears that governments have rarely made use of the terms of Article XIX. Even its main user, the American Government, employed it with relative moderation. But this discretion on the part of states cannot be entirely attributed to their fidelity to trade liberalism. In the first place, it is clear that, up to about 1973, a highly expansive economic situation countered tendencies towards protectionism.

Furthermore, numerous countries, both developed and developing, were able, either permanently or for long periods of time, to delay the concessions which they had made, by utilising clauses other than those of Article XIX. The clauses included the special provisions of Article XVIII for the developing countries, and the safeguard clauses opened by both the IMF and the GATT for countries experiencing balance of payment difficulties.

The fact that numerous countries were able to make use of facilities outside of Article XIX explains, in part, why the United States was the chief culprit with respect to Article XIX. But for reasons which we shall indicate further on, from the beginning of the 1960s the United States made increasingly less use of Article XIX.

So although actual examples of the application of Article XIX are rather rare, it is useful nevertheless to examine the various lines of criticism which have been voiced against it.

The users of the escape clause tend to criticise Article XIX for being too formalistic in its approach of the safeguard. What is essential, they claim, is to protect the vital interest of an industry threatened by a rapid increase in imports. By requiring proof that this increase in imports is the result of the prior granting of a concession, Article XIX needlessly complicates the situation. In practice, it may be very difficult to evaluate the influence of the concession, compared with that of other factors, on the relative competitiveness of national producers and foreign exporters.

A second line of criticism claims that the withdrawal of the concession may be an insufficient safeguard. This criticism is linked with the first in the sense that if the increase in imports does not stem from the granting of the concession, then there is no reason for which the withdrawal of the concession would constitute the appropriate remedy. The principal objective should be to stop the growth of exports, and here only a quantitative restriction is capable of providing the necessary guarantees.

Another point of view is expressed by those injured by the withdrawing of the concession, who criticise the illusory nature of the precautions taken by Article XIX to defend their interests. The only means of pressure which this article has conferred upon them – namely, the threat of retaliatory measures – is too dangerous to be actually implemented. For every government, (even that which is the least conscious of its responsibilities), is well aware that the 'snowball effect' of retaliatory measures could progressively destroy the whole network of tariff concessions so laboriously worked out by the GATT. Rather than to try in vain to prevent a state from temporarily protecting one of its industries, it would be wiser simply to control this increased protection. But on this point Article XIX is very vague. It sets neither a 'floor' for the volume of imports nor a time-limit for the implementation of protection.

One can observe, moreover, on the side of both the users and the victims of the clause of Article XIX, some irritation concerning the non-discriminatory character of the escape clauses. Past experience has shown that, most frequently, the substantial growth of the import of a product in one country does not correspond to a more or less even increase, proportionately, in the sales of all the countries exporting that product. Rather, it is the sales of just one or two of these exporters which have shot upwards. Since the origin of the 'offense' can thus be pin-pointed, both the importing countries, as well as the exporters who behaved 'reasonably', wonder why the innocent should be punished at the same time as the guilty.

THE BILATERAL AGREEMENTS ON VOLUNTARY EXPORT RESTRAINTS

Up to 1962, the President of the United States, on the advice of the Tariff Commission, was obliged to make use of the escape clause in order to come to the rescue of a national industry threatened by imports. The Trade Expansion Act of 1962 opened two alternative lines of action: either to conclude a voluntary export restraint agreement with the country, or countries, whose exports constituted a danger, or to obtain financial aid for the recycling of the business and workers in the threatened industry. We propose to examine the first alternative here.

The United States does not seem to have experienced much difficulty in concluding this kind of bilateral agreement with various countries, particularly with Japan. It is true that these agreements foresaw the stabilisation of the exports of the countries concerned within a very recent time period, as well as the promise of a progressive raising of this ceiling. This kind of quantitative restriction may appear more attractive to the exporting country concerned than the revoking of a tariff concession.

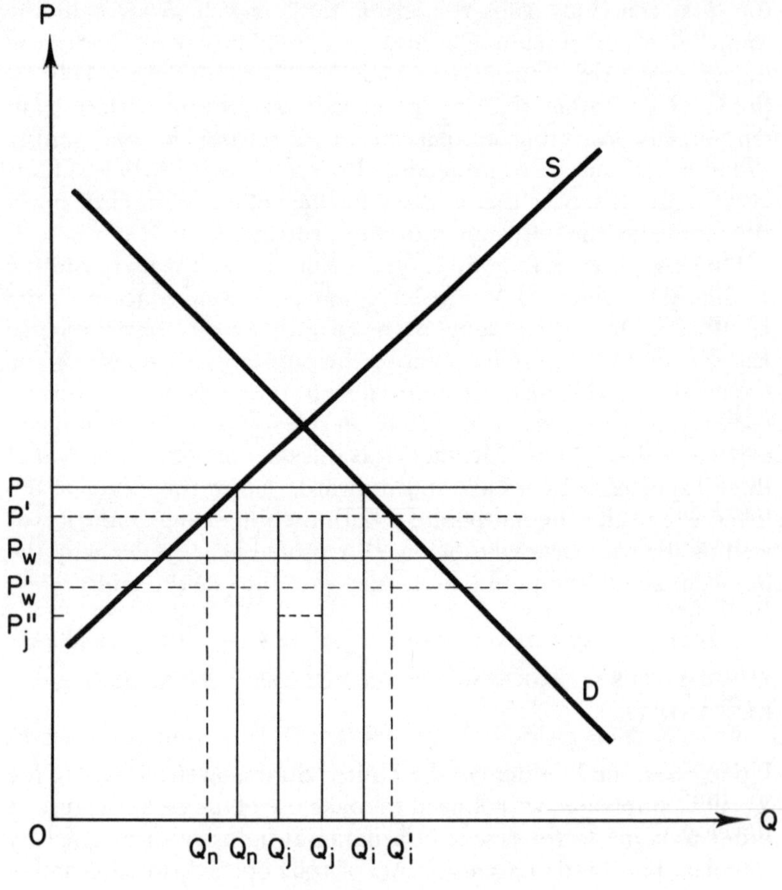

FIGURE 9.1 The Impact of Voluntary Export Restraints

Figure 9.1 illustrates this situation. With customs duties taking account of the concession, a world price (P_w) corresponding to the price of the most competitive exporters and given supply and demand curves in the importing country, the quantity Q_nQ_i of the product was imported. The price on the domestic market of the importing country was P (P_w+the customs duty).

Let us imagine that the world price goes down (P'_w) through the competitive effort of an exporting country. The quantity imported goes up: $Q'_nQ'_i$, due both to the increase in demand and to the suppression of domestic production in the importing country, brought about by the lowering of the market price from P to P'.

The agreement on voluntary export restraints blocks the volume of exports of the most competitive country (J) at the current level, let us say $Q_j Q_j$, which we can insert, *in abscissa*, anywhere in the imported quantity $Q'_n\ Q'_i$. Let us say that the export price of country J continues to fall (P''_j). The total import volume remains unchanged and the distribution of the equivalent exports among the exporting countries has no reason to alter. But the importers of J's products benefit from a rent, since their cost is the price of the product P''_j plus the customs-duty $P'_w P'$, while they in turn sell the product at price P'. They thus have a revenue equal to $P''_j P'_w$, multiplied by the quantity $Q_j\ Q_j$.

But if the exporters of country J can reach an agreement among themselves, they can then appropriate this revenue by offering their product not at price P''_j, but at price P'_w. This possibility is all the more plausible, since voluntary export restraints, by their very nature, imply close contact between the exporters, directly or under the aegis of the government. If the industry is fairly concentrated, then the conditions are favourable for an agreement among the exporters. Understandably, the attractiveness of this revenue can, at times, transform those who are the target of an export restraint agreement into consenting victims.

First 'launched' by the United States, the voluntary export restraint tactic spread quickly, particularly in the textile sector, due to the breakthrough of various developing countries on the developed world market.

THE GATT ARRANGEMENT REGARDING INTERNATIONAL TRADE IN TEXTILES

The first GATT arrangement on cotton textiles dates from 1962. The defensive reactions on the part of the developed countries in response to the penetration of their markets by a few developing countries constituted a real challenge to the rules of international trade policy as laid down by GATT. The United States, as we have already noted, was preparing to extend the network of its bilateral agreements on voluntary export restraints. At the same time, numerous Western European countries were meeting the flood of

Asian cotton exports coming into their markets, with quantitative restrictions, pure and simple.

The guiding principle of this arrangement was to confer a certain legitimacy, through GATT recognition, to the concept of market disruption, in a particular sector of international trade. The concept of market disruption overlaps with two criteria already stipulated in Article XIX of the GATT, namely, the rapid growth of imports and the damage caused to the rival domestic industry. But it is no longer necessary to prove a direct link between these phenomena and the previous granting of a tariff concession.

The safeguard measures which can be adopted by the importing country with a disorganised market consist of quantitative restrictions; these restrictions, however, are not left up to the discretion of the country applying them. One of the most praiseworthy aspects of the arrangement has been to require those European countries using the ordinary provisions, to accept the principle of progressively enlarging them, until the total disappearance of their restrictive effects can be attained.

The government of a country with a disorganised market must consult with the exporting country or countries which are to blame for the disorganisation, in order to establish a ceiling for their exports. Modelling itself after the American agreements, the arrangement establishes a minimum level for this ceiling, based on the imports of the year preceding its introduction; the arrangement also stipulates an automatic lifting of the ceiling by 5 per cent a year.

The limitation is highly selective, with respect to not only the exporting countries, as we have just seen, but also the producers. What is involved here are perfectly individualised products, rather than customs positions, which are sometimes very heterogeneous.

Theoretically, the restraints form the subject of an agreement between the importing country and the exporting countries concerned. In actual fact, the exporting countries cannot refuse their consent. To the extent that these bilateral agreements are concluded within the framework of the international arrangement, the latter countries benefit from the guarantees which we have already mentioned. If they appear too reticent, they run the risk of having the developed importing countries question the international arrangement itself.

All the same, in the event that the exporting countries fail to reach an agreement, the arrangement allows the importing country to take unilateral safeguard measures analogous to those which would have resulted from an agreement.

The 1962 arrangement was renewed in 1967 and in 1970, without any changes. Its renewal in late 1973, however, was accompanied by some important innovations. The arrangement was extended to all categories of textiles – hence the name 'Multi-Fibre Arrangement', by which it has been known ever since. This extension was motivated by the fact that the remarkable competitivity of certain developing countries, first demonstrated in the cotton sector, later spread to other kinds of textiles, particularly synthetics. In return for the extension of the area covered by the arrangement, satisfaction was given to the exporting countries through the creation of the Textiles Surveillance Body which receives notification of all restrictions, makes them publicly known and tries to help to settle disputes which arise in the application of the arrangement. Furthermore, the average rate of the annual raising of the export ceiling was moved from 5 to 6 per cent.

This Multi-Fibre Arrangement expired at the end of 1977. Its renewal appeared to be in danger up to the last minute, because of the hesitation of the European Community. While the United States had promptly passed restraint agreements for all textile products and with all exporting countries posing a 'serious threat' to the US market, the EEC lost much time due to the complexity of its trade negotiation mechanism.

Imports of certain 'sensitive' products had increased sharply over the years and the EEC felt that, having been unable to control this development, it should be permitted to stabilise these imports at their 1976 level.

In order to avoid renegotiation, which would have brought into question the very existence of the arrangement, the GATT made the following concession: it decided that in the restraint agreements which the EEC would conclude after the renewal of the arrangement, the EEC could – within reasonable limits and with respect to precise points – bypass the provisions of the arrangement on a temporary basis.

Benefiting from this derogation within a system which already constituted an exception with respect to the normal GATT rules, the EEC finally signed the renewal of the Multi-Fibre Arrangement without any changes. This arrangement will remain in effect until late 1981.

CONCLUSIONS

In addition to its own intrinsic importance, the Multi-Fibre Arrangement is significant as a potential model for a new escape clause in the GATT, which would replace that contained in Article XIX.

A new safeguard system such as this contains both advantages and disadvantages.

On the positive side, the decision not to require proof of a direct link between the granting of a tariff concession on the one hand, and market disruption on the other hand, would seem to testify to an attitude of healthy realism. Past experience has shown that if market disruption exists, it is impossible, in most cases, to stop the government of the importing country from resorting to safeguard measures. As far as the GATT is concerned, it is far better to be able to control these measures, than to see its authority flouted.

Furthermore, regarding the actual safeguard measures, the raising of the customs duty would appear preferable, at first glance, to a quantitative restriction, since tariff protection does not interfere directly with the functioning of the market, but interferes indirectly, through prices. However, we are dealing here with safeguard measures. From this point of view, it is clear that quantitative restrictions such as the Multi-Fibre Arrangement have a double advantage. First, they make it possible to confine the restriction to a selected product, whereas the removal of customs duty normally affects all the products covered by a customs position. Secondly, and more importantly, the restriction is formulated so as to give specific guarantees simultaneously to the importing country and to the exporting countries. The former country knows that the growth of its imports is restricted so long as the market remains disrupted. The latter are assured that the volume of trade will not fall, and that it will even continue to grow over time.

From the negative point of view, it is regrettable – although this is a minor point – that the restraint ultimately creates a rent, although it is immaterial whether this revenue goes to the importers or to the exporters. It would be preferable, of course, for this rent to be appropriated by the government of the importing country and to be used in the recycling of workers whose jobs are threatened by imports.

In the second place, the special facilities accorded the EEC during the last renewal of the Multi-Fibre Arrangement would appear to be undesirable. They constitute an unfortunate precedent which, if repeated, would be detrimental to the guarantee given to competitive exporters that their sales will not decrease.

In the third place, although surrounded by an aura of justice, the principle of the selectivity of the restraints, according to country, conceals covert discrimination. In fact, it results in the granting of protection not only to the local producers in the importing country, but also to the less competitive exporting countries over the more competitive exporters. Generalising the restriction so that it would apply to all the exporting countries would have the advantage of emphasising the conservational character of the safeguard measures by fixing the relative positions of the different exporting countries. This remark leads to a last point of criticism.

The term 'conservational' must be interpreted in the sense of provisional, since the purpose of the safeguard measure is to give the threatened industry time to adapt. If the validity of the safeguard measures is not given a precise time-limit, then there is the risk that the industry will altogether slacken its efforts at adaptation.

Part III:
New Trends and Policies and the International Economy

10 International Trade and Economic Growth: the Outlook for the 1980s

Emilio Fontela

BACKGROUND

Often in the past, economists have analysed the relation between international trade and national economic growth. For the market economies they have usually concluded that international trade makes a more efficient use of national resources possible and that it generates several multiplicative effects (via incomes and prices of products and production factors) which are likely to enhance economic growth. There are economists who will be inclined to identify in the rapid growth of the recent post-war period the application of many of the theoretical mechanisms of the positive enhancing relation between trade and growth. However, as always happens in the social sciences, various other factors stimulating economic growth have been at play during this period: conscious growth policies of governments, for one; also, the more subtle effect of psychological attitudes in production agents and the population at large, continuously favourable to so-called 'material' economic growth. Furthermore, economic growth has had an effect on international trade, facilitating structural readjustments, making possible and accommodating rapid shifts in the relative prices of commodities.

The growth of trade and output appears to be openly complementary in market economies. Empirical observations show that up to the energy crisis, international trade at world level was growing much faster than output. Table 10.1 shows, however, that this difference in growth rates was only characteristic of the OECD

TABLE 10.1: Trade and Output, 1965–73 Average Compound Annual Rates (computed at constant prices)

World output	5.6
World trade	8.1
OECD output	5.1
OECD trade	9.0
Rest of world output	6.6
Rest of world trade	6.8

Source: Battelle, Explor-Multitrade Data Bank

countries. For the rest of the world, trade closely followed production outputs.

What emerges from this observation is that the growth in trade has been taking place mainly within a group of industrialised countries that have accepted during this period a continuous process of liberalisation and consequent integration; it has taken place within a community of countries which broadly share some basic principles of political philosophy and moral values, a community working towards the creation of a supra-national institutional framework; a community that had accepted, not always without reticence, that the wealth of individual nations is gained through the wealth of the community.

There can be no doubt that international trade has played a major role in the moral, social and political integration of the OECD community.

As shown in Table 10.2, it is in the area of manufactured products and equipment goods that the growth of trade has been particularly remarkable. During the post-war period, interdependence in the manufacturing sector has therefore increased; the technology embodied in equipment goods has been transferred, as well as the

TABLE 10.2: Intra-OECD Trade 1965–73, Average Compound Annual Rates (computed at constant prices)

Agricultural products	5.6
Raw materials	5.0
Basic products	5.4
Equipment goods	12.8
Manufactured products	10.5

Source: Battelle, Explor-Multitrade Data Bank

consumption habits embodied in the final manufactured products.

The increase in economic interdependence was not limited to the effects of international trade. Massive movements of capital and labour also took place, together with movements of management capabilities and technological know-how. In overemphasising all these evolutions, one could perhaps say that up to 1973 the community was involved in a long-term process towards becoming an economic supra-nation.

The consequences of this growing economic interdependence are a quicker transfer of cyclical fluctuations, a greater need for coordination of policy measures and a certain loss of national economic independence.

For many socio-cultural reasons, the community started to suffer a crisis in the late sixties and the long-term process of integration was severely affected by it. The international monetary crisis emerged from national conflicts of interests and a lack of common views as to the role of the community in the future of the world. Short-term interpretations of national interests often prevailed. But the economic production machine was still proving its robustness.

An unexpected event was, however, finally to strike at the community's Achille's heel: the sudden increase of petroleum prices. Since then, conferences on 'risk and uncertainty' have gained momentum. Many have begun to have serious doubts. Should the process of economic integration of the community be stopped? Should protectionism and nationalism become the means of fighting the economic crisis?

Since 1973, the OECD countries are in a transition process. The outlook for trade and growth for the 1980s is being determined by the outcome of this process.

TRADE AND GROWTH IN THE ADVANCED INDUSTRIALISED COUNTRIES (AICS)

The development of trade within the AICs has been accompanied by a process of profound structural change. The more efficient use of production factors in the manufacturing sector has made possible a transfer of labour to the service sector, a reduction of working time and a transfer of capital and technology to the rest of the world. These changes took place during a period of growth of consumption by the population of the world which probably has no historical precedent.

In an attempt to describe the patterns of economic growth in industrialised nations, a few broad generalisations can be made.

First, it seems that during the 1950s and 1960s, thanks to a long-term decline of the real prices of energy and raw materials and also to fast increases in productivity (rapid diffusion of technological innovations), the prices of manufactured goods relative to those of services have been continuously declining. In some ways, this evolution has facilitated the replacement of human services by manufactured products; it has also induced a reduction of the costs of acquisition versus the costs of maintenance and has tended to favour products with short life spans.

Second, the growth of manufacturing activities with great productivity gains permitted fast increases of wages and salaries without substantially modifying the distribution of income between labour and capital. Investments in the manufacturing sector were enhanced by continuous high capital returns.

Finally, the relative size of the public sector was slowly increasing, but the emphasis in this development was put on the creation of infrastructures (required for the development of manufacturing activities) rather than on the supply of services for collective consumption.

There are reasons to believe that this very simple growth process, centred around capital accumulation in manufacturing activities, had been seriously shaken towards the end of the 1960s and in the early 1970s, when as a result of social tensions and growing discontent, disruptive protests started to take shape. Since then, in practically all industrialised countries, social pressures have modified substantially income distributions in favour of labour and have also increased demands for collective services. The result of these greater pressures on the economic system has been a new form of generalised inflation and a reduction of investments which has practically put an end to the dynamic 'exponential' growth process.

Also in the early 1970s, the awakening of the OPEC countries to the advantages of the capitalistic game has suddenly changed the relative price of energy, a fact which, when coupled with the already mentioned success of labour has reversed the long-term declining trend of the prices of manufactured goods.

When looking at the dimensions of the changes that have taken place in this very short 1969–74 period, what is surprising is not the generalised stagnation that has followed, but rather the solidity of the socio-economic structures of the industrialised countries that have managed (with a few exceptions) to avoid a major crisis.

In many economic circles it is customary to place the post-1973 recession in a historical context of other short post-war recessions, and therefore to assume that a recovery will bring the economies back to their previous growth process. Although this hypothesis is far from unrealistic (the fear of a crisis and unemployment may reduce social pressures, readjust capital returns and once more encourage investments, technology and productivity), there are a number of deep societal evolutions that point to a sizable long-term change of the growth process.

The industrialised societies are in search of life-styles that would help to reduce the psychological tensions generated by the post-war growth of material consumption.

The business community itself is increasingly convinced that a major change in values is taking place. Democratic practices are taking shape in the decision-making process of industrial firms; participation by workers is starting to favour decentralisation, autonomy, discontinuities, thus reducing the intrinsic cost advantages of the large production centers.

In the public sector also, decentralisation and citizen participation in decision making is reducing potentially the cost advantages of national governments.

All these evolutions point to an increasing need for capital in the services sector (both private and public) and a decrease in the productivity of capital (the inverse of the capital–output ratio).

The causes for the possible reduction of the overall productivity of capital are found in the manufacturing sector itself (see the requirements for better working conditions and also those derived from other societal constraints, like environmental control) and in the increased need of capital for collective services that are known to be more capital intensive than manufactured goods. It is important to note that the rate of growth of capital productivity in Northern and Western Europe has been declining progressively since the early sixties and has been negative since 1966, as shown by recent studies of the UN Economic Commission for Europe.

Should this evolution continue (and the sociological considerations made above tend to confirm this view) with high requirements of capital accumulations and savings and lower capital productivity, economic growth in the industrialised countries would be much smaller than in the post-war period.

In this prospective, the growth rate should be mainly determined by the capacity of not only technology and innovation to increase capital productivity in the services sector, but also the entire economic system to adapt to major changes in the structures of relative prices and productive activities.

If we accept as an hypothesis this new framework for the world, with lower growth in the AICs, what is the possible consequence for trade?

Explorations made with a world trade model by Battelle (Explor-Multitrade) show that a reduction of the growth of intra-AICs trade should be expected: while during the high growth period foreign producers could easily obtain a large share of the increase of a given market, if markets grow less rapidly, they will have to fight for a larger share of the market itself and not only of its increase; if they do succeed, the adjustment problems in the importing country will be accentuated.

The projections prepared by many national agencies reveal, however, expectations for a continuation of the fast growth of exports and imports. If they do materialise in the future, it is reasonable to assume, in the framework of our hypothesis of lower economic growth in the AICs, that they will be due to a faster growth of trade with the rest of the world.

TRADE AND GROWTH IN THE REST OF THE WORLD

If we consider the 'long term' a point in the future relatively free of the constraints of existing structures, then to call the year 2000 'long term' is already optimistic; 2000 remains, however, a reasonable horizon to explore 'theoretical' courses of action which could really have longer-term effects. This is the case for the UN study of the world economy, which uses the Leontief world model with a set of scenarios of different degrees of plausibility.[1] This study was done with the idea of exploring world development in relation to environmental questions.

In general, the following can be derived from the UN study: on the basis of existing technological knowledge, the constraints of environmental decay, exhaustion of mineral resources and insufficient food production should not substantially inhibit future economic growth, and in particular a strong acceleration of economic growth in the Less Developed Countries (LDCs).[2]

Furthermore, neither the Centrally Planned Economies (CPEs) nor the LDCs are affected by the socio-economic factors that tend to reduce the growth rate of the AICs, as their levels of material consumption are still very low. As far as the LDCs are concerned, the situation is very different in each country and any effort of synthesis is bound to oversimplify the nature of the problems. Nevertheless, several sub-groups have to be identified of which at least three seem very different in terms of assets and problems:

– LDCs 3: the very poor developing countries, with very low incomes per capita, strong demographic pressures, insufficient agricultural capacity, reduced availability of raw materials and energy. These countries, which cover large areas of Asia and Africa, are permanently menaced by famines and endemic diseases;
– LDCs 2: a group of developing countries that have started a process of industrialisation but remain mostly exporters of raw materials and agricultural products; they suffer from the instability of their export receipts due to the fluctuations of prices;
– LDCs 1: the OPEC countries and a number of rapidly industrialising countries (like Brazil, Mexico or South Korea) with large export receipts and an internal capacity to develop their industrialisation process. These countries could become very rapidly new manufacturing 'growth poles', trading with neighbouring countries; the logical sequence includes their integration into a broader 'industrialised world' together with today's OECD countries and eventually some of the CPEs of the Eastern European block. This enlarged area of AICs could well pursue the pattern of development of trade based on the reduction of protectionist barriers and multilateralism which has characterised the OECD zone since the 1950s.

The short- and medium-term future is strongly constrained by the present structure and policies. This structure and its underlying mechanisms, these policies and the forces that support them, are the object of continuous observation by numerous analysts. Our body of knowledge is nevertheless insufficient for adequate forecasting of future developments; we have therefore to rely on opinions that are more or less rationalised insights into the structure of the social phenomena being considered. The development of methods for gathering coherent sets of these opinions about the future constitutes an interesting aspect of research in the social sciences.

Using one of these methods,[3] Battelle–Geneva conducted (in late 1975 and early 1976) a survey among 35 planners, modellers, forecasters and policy makers (in national and international organisations in Europe and North America) interested in the future of world trade.

As a result of this survey, a set of scenarios of world development during the next ten years was established.

For the South, the most probable scenario for the 1975–85 period can be briefly described as follows:

– Both OPEC and LDCs 1 follow a rapid industrialization process, and some of them become regional growth poles, activating economic development in neighbouring countries. Capital markets in the OECD and OPEC are open for financing industrial investments in the area, which progressively becomes part of an Extended OECD zone. For LDCs 2 the needs of technology, equipment goods and energy as soon as they start industrialisation can be met by a long-term process of improvement of the prices of their exports.

– LDCs 3 suffer food shortages, develop little export capacity and virtually no possibility for direct access to foreign capital markets. International aid is reduced in real terms. During the 1980s strong autarchic policies are adopted and agriculturally based development processes are established.

Indeed the central idea that seems to emerge from this survey of *opinions* is that the geographic make-up of the North–South dichotomy is to follow an evolutionary process by which additional countries would join the 'privileged' industrialised North and the gap with the rest of the South would widen progressively.

If this scenario (of which we are not going to explore the political implications) materialises, then international trade could, as in the post-war period, continue to be a major, fast-growing vehicle of international integration in a broader geographic area than in the past.

STRUCTURAL PROBLEMS OF THE INDUSTRIALISED NATIONS

The enlargement of the industrialised world to include other countries, in which the manufacturing sector is the key to the development process, will raise structural problems in what is today the OECD area.

It is interesting to remember that a rather similar situation existed during the 1950s and 1960s between the USA and the other industrialised countries of Europe and Japan; the USA had advanced more rapidly into a 'human resources era' of white-collar and service employment, while the other OECD countries were mostly driven by the dynamics of the manufacturing activities. Despite occasional protectionist reactions, the US economy has managed to face this international challenge, and indeed seems to have emerged from it substantially reinforced even in the manufacturing sector and in its competitivity.

The enlargement of the industrialised world should create a progressive transfer of capital and technology to the upcoming countries in the area of manufacturing; it is reasonable to expect that this transfer would take place mainly for basic and intermediate industries (petro-chemicals, textiles, metals, glass, etc.) and for durable products; it does not seem realistic, however, to suppose that this transfer will imply a substantial and dangerous reduction of the output of these industries in the present OECD countries and a replacement by imports. The American example shows that despite increased competition from Europe and Japan, the manufacturing sector has not been seriously damaged; also the increased Franco-German competition within the Common Market has not had the negative effects that some expected in the late 1950s. Increases in the level of international competition are a necessary incentive to technological innovation.

There appear to be areas in which the speed of technological innovation is at times insufficient to keep costs at a competitive level with those of the new producers (which should benefit in principle from lower labour costs and from the advantages of internal fast-growing demand).[4]

The necessary restructuring of the production activities in the AICs should be essentially a function of changes in consumption structures and of the direction and intensity of technological change.

As pointed out earlier, consumption patterns should evolve progressively towards a relative increase of quality versus quantity, durability versus disposability, services versus goods; this evolution, which is mainly a result of sociological trends and changes in life-styles, could be encouraged by a major change in relative prices.

It is likely that the recent change in the trends of relative prices, which has taken place within the short period of double-digit inflation of the last few years, will continue into the future; that is, that contrary to what happened in the 1950s and 1960s, the prices of manufactured goods will now increase faster than the average price index taken as a whole, or at least will stop their long-term decline. This evolution would be the economically coherent counterpart of the underlying sociological trend. In terms of output and employment, this evolution of relative prices and consumption patterns should create a transfer from manufacturing to services, reinforcing the trend of the last decade and following the path already visible in the USA.

It is really in terms of technology and innovation, however, that we should consider the restructuring of the industrialised countries.

During the last two decades, all manufacturing sectors have increased their efficiency by the introduction of new processes and the development of new products; innovation has been greatly encouraged by the high rate of economic growth. Today it has become increasingly difficult to identify new areas for technological research and innovation.

It is highly probable that the presently industrialised countries will keep their technological leadership. At least, it is difficult to conceive of a change in this situation for the technology intensive sectors (like aero-space, computers and control equipment, robotics, fine chemicals, etc.). Technology in these areas is developed by the governments or by the large multinational corporations based in these countries. For less technology intensive industries, innovation has largely benefited from fall-outs of the larger public research and development programs and from the general progress of the state of the art.

The new growth process, with its emphasis on the development of the services sector, and the relative reduction of the use of primary materials and energy, requires a partial reorientation of technological research. New products with longer durability, new processes for recovery and recycling, new techniques for repair and maintenance, and, above all, new methods and processes to increase the productivity of the services sector (private and collective) are required.

The main condition for the entrance of the industrialised world in a new long-term growth process is for technology to succeed in re-establishing a process of growth of overall productivity of the system, without calling upon unduly high levels of investment and saving and by staying within the constraints of the new relative prices and consumption structures.

TOWARDS A NEW INTERNATIONAL ECONOMIC ORDER

The idea of a new International Economic Order includes some form of a redistribution of the international division of labour. In many cases it is viewed as a transfer of some manufacturing activities, technology and capital to the developing countries. We have seen that it is very probable that this transfer will effectively take place and even that it will be concentrated in some new *growth poles*, not benefiting the more underdeveloped zones of the world. This probability will tend to be reinforced by the evolution of the arms industry and the constitution of strong regional military powers.

All the economic forces of the industrialised countries are favourable to this development: the geographic extension of the AICs area offers a unique opportunity to continue developing international trade and capital movements, and to open new large markets at a moment when there are saturation signs in many sectors of the industrialised economies. Indeed, the change in relative prices which may result from this evolution – a change less favourable to material goods – should help to bring about a desired evolution in these countries towards more 'quality' and better services.

As far as the arms industry is concerned, the revival of colbertism is also a strong driving force for the organisation of a world order including a set of regional sub-powers in the South.

The consideration of existing trends leads us to the conclusion that the geographic extension of the AICs zone, going beyond an Atlantic – Pacific community, is a necessity that will become a reality before the end of the century. This extension could solve the long-term economic growth problem of the advanced industrialised countries of today, and allow them to perform their own sociopolitical evolution towards more participative forms of democracy. It will not, however, solve, or even start solving, the North–South problem, viewed as a rich–poor relation; and from this schematic exploration of the outlook for the 1980s, one may end with the question: how just, how equitable, how good, how generous is this emerging new International Economic Order?

NOTES

1. United Nations, *The Future of the World Economy* (New York: 1976).
2. This conclusion is valid even with yearly average growth rates of per capita income, up to the year 2000, of 3.3 per cent in the developed world and 4.9 per cent in developing countries. These growth rates are extremely high by historical standards: Kuznets has computed long-term rates of growth per capita obtaining a maximum 2.9 per cent per year for Japan (from 1869–74 to 1963–7), 2.6 per cent for Sweden (from 1861–9 to 1963–7) and less than 2 per cent for the remaining countries in Europe and North America. (S. Kuznets, *Economic Growth of Nations, Total Output and Production Structure*, Cambridge, Mass., The Belknap Press of Harvard University Press, 1971).
3. The method used, a special version of cross–impact analysis, was reported in E. Sallin-Kornberg and E. Fontela, 'The Explor-Multitrade 85 Model' (Brussels: Third International Conference of Applied Econometrics, February 1976).

   For a review of different Cross–Impact approaches see A. Duval, E. Fontela and A. Gabus, 'A Handbook on Concepts and Applications' in Portraits of Complexity, Battelle Monograph 9 Columbus: Battelle Memorial Institute, June 75.

   For a discussion of the interface between (X-I) analysis and economic modelling see E. Fontela and A. Gabus, 'Events and Economic forecasting models' in *Futures*, London, August 1974.
4. The situation is particularly difficult for those industrial sectors that depend on others for their technological innovation; this is the case for the textile sector. An analysis of this sector will show that its technology is essentially developed by the chemical industry (new fibres) and by the engineering and electronics industry (new machines and control equipment); the textile industry itself has a very low level of research and development expenditures (equal to approximately 0.5 per cent of turnover); for internal strategic reasons the chemical industry is concentrating its research effort only on improving the technical properties of existing man-made fibres and its production investment is extending outside of the existing AICs; the engineering industries are finding more promising markets for textile machines also outside the OECD. These factors are favourable to the development of a highly competitive sector in some non-OECD countries, using advanced technologies while still benefiting from low labour costs.

11 Europe and the Advanced Developing Countries

Lawrence B. Krause[1]

INTRODUCTION

The oil crisis of 1973–4 was a watershed for the world. Economic trends and relationships that existed before were profoundly altered by the crisis. The most obvious change was a shift of relative economic power from the advanced industrial countries which rely on imported petroleum to the OPEC countries which supply those imports. In 1973 the OPEC countries exported \$39.2bn of goods which was only 7.5 per cent of world exports. By 1977, OPEC exports were valued at \$144bn which was 14.1 per cent of world trade. OPEC not only doubled its share of world trade, it did so just by raising prices since the volume of oil exports was not appreciably different in the two years. The remarkable improvement of the OPEC terms of trade supported rapid growth and made them the fastest growing group of countries in the world. Moreover since a large gap existed between OPEC exports and imports, they amassed a large amount of financial claims on the rest of the world including about \$50bn of official reserves and \$130bn of other assets. While the extraordinary OPEC current account surplus is being reduced rapidly, some further accumulation of financial assets will occur before the unusual surplus is eliminated in the early 1980s.

Another change, much less obvious but possibly more enduring than that of OPEC, was the rise of relative power of the advanced developing countries (ADCs) relative to the advanced industrial countries. This development was not anticipated at the time of the oil crisis. Most analysts expected that the non-oil less developed countries (LDCs) would suffer the worst fate. Part of the error came from the failure to distinguish the really poor developing countries, which indeed had few options, from the advanced developing countries which already had considerable economic flexibility as a result of their rapid development. Another part of the error came from an underestimate of the adaptability of all developing countries to external challenges. Thus the industrial countries lost ground relative to both OPEC and the ADCs.

The success of the ADCs can be appreciated by examining their record of economic growth before and after 1973. To sharpen distinctions, only the ADCs in East Asia, ASEAN and Latin America will be considered.[2]

TABLE 11.1: Growth Rates of Real GNP and GNP Deflators (compound annual rates)

	GNP		*Deflators*	
	1967–73	*1973–6*	*1967–73*	*1973–6*
East Asia				
Hong Kong	7.3	7.6	n.a.	n.a.
Republic of Korea	11.6	10.8	12.7	22.2
Taiwan	10.6	4.8	6.4	14.2
ASEAN				
Indonesia	8.7	6.5	30.0	23.8
Malaysia	6.3	6.5	4.2	7.7
Philippines	6.1	6.2	10.7	15.2
Singapore	13.1	5.7	4.8	7.0
Thailand	7.6	7.1	4.3	7.1
Latin America				
Argentina[a]	5.1	1.0	28.8	86.9
Bolivia[a]	5.7	6.8	9.4	32.7
Brazil[a]	11.3	7.7	24.2	32.1
Chile	2.2	0.3	77.3	402.2
Colombia[a]	6.6	5.3	12.2	24.6
Dominican Republic	9.4	6.3	3.5	11.6
Ecuador[a]	6.2	9.1	9.9	17.9
Guatemala	6.5	5.3	3.3	13.3
Mexico	6.6	4.0	5.8	20.5
Peru	4.9	4.4	9.5	23.5
Uruguay[a]	1.4	3.3	54.8	74.2
All industrial countries	4.8	1.5	4.6	10.3
United Kingdom	3.0	0.1	7.3	10.3

Note: [a] 1973–5.

There are three ADCs in East Asia (Hong Kong, the Republic of Korea and the Republic of China), five ASEAN countries (Indonesia, Malaysia, Philippines, Singapore and Thailand), and 11 countries in Latin America (Argentina, Bolivia, Brazil, Chile, Colombia, Dominican Republic, Ecuador, Guatemala, Mexico, Peru and Uruguay). As can be seen in Table 11.1, even in the 1967–73 period, 17 of the 19 ADCs had higher growth rates than the average of all industrial countries. However, before 1973, the higher level of GNP in the industrial countries meant that, even with a lower growth rate, the absolute gap of wealth between them and the ADCs was increasing. After 1973, the growth rate of 14 of the ADCs was moderated somewhat, but five experienced increases. By way of contrast, the growth rate of industrial countries dropped to about one-third of the previous level. Still, 17 of the ADCs exceeded the industrial country average, but after 1973 the ADC growth was so much greater that they began closing the gap in absolute GNP.

One should not get the impression that the ADCs have no economic difficulties, or that the oil crisis was not a problem for them. Indeed these countries have difficulties, not the least of which is a severe problem of inflation (Table 11.1). During 1967–73 14 of the ADCs had inflation rates (measured by GNP deflators) above the average of industrial countries and five of them had hyper-inflation (that is, above 20 per cent a year). After 1973, inflation accelerated in the ADCs, 15 having rates above the industrial country average of which 10 were in the hyper-inflation range. What is remarkable is how they managed to sustain economic progress despite their inflations. Somehow, these countries have learned to deal with the problems affecting their economies better than have the industrial countries in recent years.

Some of the success of the ADCs since the oil crisis has been achieved in international trade, as seen in Table 11.2. During 1967–73, seven ADCs had larger export growth (measured in current US dollars) than the average for the industrial countries; 11 had slower export growth (Hong Kong data not included).[3] Since 1973, 14 experienced larger export growth, and only four slower growth, than the average for industrial countries. In the aggregate, ADC exports were less than 10 per cent of those of industrial countries in 1973, but over 15 per cent in 1977. The notable success of the ADCs in exporting manufactured goods to industrial countries, particularly labour-intensive manufacturers, has drawn considerable attention to this aspect of their relations with industrial

TABLE 11.2: Growth of Export Value
(measured in current US dollars and expressed in compound annual rates)

	1967–73	1973–7
East Asia		
Hong Kong	n.a.	n.a.
Republic of Korea	47.0	32.9
Taiwan	37.7	20.9
ASEAN		
Indonesia[a]	29.6	40.8
Malaysia	16.5	18.9
Philippines	14.3	14.1
Singapore	21.5	22.4
Thailand	14.9	22.2
Latin America		
Argentina	14.3	15.4
Bolivia[a]	9.7	28.8
Brazil	24.6	18.3
Chile	6.4	15.5
Colombia[a]	15.2	16.5
Dominican Republic[a]	19.0	17.4
Ecuador	19.3	22.1
Guatemala[a]	14.3	20.7
Mexico	12.2	16.5
Peru[a]	11.6	5.8
Uruguay[a]	12.5	19.2
Industrial countries	18.2	15.8
United Kingdom	13.3	17.4

Note: [a] 1973–6.

countries. However their export success is not confined to these products or just to the markets of industrial countries. With only a couple of exceptions, the growth of exports (measured in local currency) of ADCs is greater than the growth of national incomes (similarly measured), indicating that international trade is now playing a strategic role in their economic development.

The question naturally arises as to why the industrial countries have not been able to adjust to the oil crisis as well as the ADCs. Four factors seem to be of greatest importance. First of all, the greater wealth of the industrial countries gave them the option of delaying their adjustment to the rise of oil prices – the United States is the extreme example of this policy. But an adjustment that is delayed is also made more difficult. Poorer countries living closer to the line were unable to avoid the loss of current consumption and thus made a faster and more complete adjustment. Secondly, industrial countries are more dependent on petroleum to run their economies and in general, the life styles in advanced countries revolve around the automobile to a greater extent. Thus the rise in the price of oil was more disruptive to their economies.

Thirdly, industrial countries almost by definition had much greater investment in physical capital in 1973. The increase in the relative price of energy destroyed the economic usefulness of much of the capital invested in industry. Energy-intensive technology was imbedded in the older capital stock and made it non-competitive with newer energy-saving technology put in place subsequently. Thus by having more investment in place, industrial countries had a greater loss. This loss was reflected in business firms. For private firms, the asset side of their balance sheets lost economic value, but their liabilities were not reduced. Thus many firms have run into financial difficulties. This is most evident in Japan, but is also seen elsewhere and has complicated the task of economic recovery.

Finally, over the decades since World War II, industrial countries have witnessed an increase in various protections against income loss for members of their societies. Legislation and other government action generally protect the income of the retired and the elderly through indexation of pensions and the like. Similar indexation is applied to unemployment compensation for those able to work, but unable to find a job. Civil servants have similar protection for their real purchasing power. Farmers have also had their position strengthened by various government actions. In private industry, union contracts often contain cost-of-living clauses for workers or wage bargaining itself accomplishes the same task. These mechanisms work reasonably well when a domestic disturbance occurs, as the winners and losers are within the same country so redistribution is theoretically possible. When the problem is caused from abroad as was the rise of oil prices, internal redistribution cannot overcome the equity problem because there are no domestic gainers, just losers. The mechanisms are still at work, however, and by shifting the burden from one group to another, they merely increase inflation and worsen overall economic performance. They add inflexibility to the economy and make adjustment very difficult. Since these social mechanisms are much more widespread in Europe than elsewhere, the problem is greatest there. By way of contrast, the ADCs and other LDCs as well have few such mechanisms and thus retain greater flexibility in their economies.

The inflation produced by the oil crisis set off an inflationary spiral in those industrial countries unwilling to take restrictive measures. But inflation itself undermines the economies of advanced countries with large asset – liability structures and undermines financial institutions as well. Some countries, such as Germany, took strong restraining measures and stopped the inflation and suffered stagnation in its place. The United Kingdom experienced both inflation and stagnation. Because of this, pessimism concerning economic prospects pervades Europe and many Europeans believe that the stagnation that has gripped that continent will be perpetuated for some time. The European countries have managed only a very weak recovery from the deep 1974–5 recession, achieving much lower growth than the United States and Japan. Gloomy forecasts for future growth have been based on a host of factors and the forecasts themselves tend to generate a self-fulfilling prophecy.

IMPLICATION OF DIVERGENT ECONOMIC TRENDS

A number of developments can be foreseen if stagnation should be perpetuated in Europe, while economic progress continues in the rest of the world – albeit at a somewhat reduced pace in the United States and Japan. The growth of world trade, for instance, is likely to be subdued. European countries are major traders and if they grow slowly, they will not provide expanding markets for exports from other countries and particularly from each other. Also trade liberalisation in Europe is unlikely to make much headway if economies are stagnant; in fact protectionist forces could become stronger. Thus world trade expansion, which in the past has been faster than real income growth because of trade liberalisation, is unlikely to be helped and may be retarded. Of course some countries can proceed with trade liberalisation even if others will not go along. These countries could recognise that their own economic welfare in the post-war period was greatly furthered by being able to import products at reduced costs in terms of domestic resources. This is certainly true for the United States. Selective trade liberalisation is made easier by the existence of the floating exchange rate system which permits a country's currency to depreciate if it begins to import too much. Thus countries with better growth records could have weaker currencies. Nevertheless it will be difficult for some countries to liberalise trade if others do not.

All trends will come to an end in time, including economic stagnation in Europe. Europe could be saved by developments in other parts of the world, although that is less likely. Europeans will likely seek change themselves because a stagnant economy is not a very pleasant place in which to live. Gains for one group can only be made at the expense of another – a classic zero-sum game. Stagnation will present a challenge to European societies which sooner or later must be faced. Continued inaction forces most burdens onto the unprotected members of society; namely foreign workers, young people or other new entrants into the labour market (for example women). The challenge can be met by re-evaluating and changing the societal mechanisms that have made European economies so inflexible.

Two diametrically opposite alternatives exist. European countries could rescind those social protections which are not doing their job or reduce those that have been overdone. For example, rules which prevent the discharge of unproductive workers could be eliminated; unemployment compensation could be reduced so that it no longer so closely approaches wage earnings; marginal tax rates would have to be reduced; and business firms would have to be permitted to fail. Failure is the discipline of the market and without failure there can be no growth. Command over resources must be given up so that they can be attracted to new uses without destructive inflation. The other alternative is to extend social control over the remaining areas of the economy. Government decisions would replace market incentives and flexibility would be restored by government direction. Thus direct controls would replace incentives with the resulting loss of individual choice. Possibly some countries will choose one path and some the other. The choice must be faced soonest by countries with naturally expanding labour forces, such as France. The pattern of choice might well be visible within the next five years.

The ADCs will be on a much different economic path from that of Europe. Success breeds success. Rapid per capita growth in the ADCs permits and encourages larger savings and also the creation of economic entities to convert those savings into productive investment; and thus the growth process is perpetuated. There are natural limits to rapid growth but they are unlikely to be reached within the foreseeable future. The ADCs will broaden and deepen their industrial capabilities as they invest more and more over time. This is bound to improve their international competitiveness and they will be supplying goods to the world market that once were the preserve of industrial countries.

Larger societal changes will also occur in the ADCs as they become wealthier with more mature economies. They will face choices of equity as they will be able to afford some redistribution of income even at the expense of efficiency, if they choose to do so. One is also likely to see a decline in ideological politics within the ADCs as the extremes of left and right are out-competed by the pragmatism of the centre. Furthermore these societies will be exciting places to be as change will be so evident. This atmosphere will attract energetic people from all over the world to the benefit of the ADCs and to the loss of the societies from which they came.

The continuation of stagnation in Europe and rapid growth in the ADCs will change relative economic power and is bound to have consequences for international relations. The ADCs will have a larger role in world decision-making at the expense of the industrial countries, principally those in Europe. For instance, the current Tokyo Round of trade negotiations under the aegis of GATT will be the last one that is essentially a negotiation between the United States and the European Community with the Japanese participating as almost an equal partner. Further negotiations will involve the ADCs in a central way since they will have the most to gain from a successful negotiation and the greatest bargaining chips to ensure a success. Moreover greater pluralism and diversity will reduce the value of economic summits as a way of promoting economic cooperation. There will be too many important countries to bring their heads of state together to discuss economic matters. There may be just enough time left to let all summit countries host one before they are discontinued.

The world economy is likely to be less tidy and less manageable in the future. Institutional changes are likely to occur, reflecting the new constellation of power and new methods of negotiations may have to be developed. The OECD, for instance, may recede in importance because of its restricted membership. A new OECD-like organisation may have to be created for the Pacific Basin to promote economic cooperation and coordination in that area. Some universal institutions such as the United Nations and UNCTAD will become even less important in economic matters than they are now because they are so unwieldy as to be useless; and the ADCs no longer will be satisfied with empty rhetoric. The functional institutions such as the IMF and the World Bank will continue to have an important role in their area of expertise, but with greater control going to the ADCs. Also further efforts will have to be made to create an effective forum where economic issues of various sorts can be discussed and decisions taken, possibly utilising the principle of representative democracy to get around the weaknesses of universal institutions.

OUTLOOK FOR FUNCTIONAL ISSUES

Of the traditional functional areas of international economics – trade, investment, aid and the monetary system – international trade is likely to be the most altered by changes in the world economy. Many ADCs have specialised in the production and export of commodities (raw materials) and commodity policy will continue to be of great interest to them as well as to industrial countries. The ADCs will increasingly process more of their own raw materials and progressively become dependent on imports for other raw materials. This means that much greater stress will be placed by them on obtaining market access for processed materials which implies a direct assault on tariff escalation now employed by industrial countries to protect domestic processors. Also the ADCs will take a more mature view of commodity agreements making them possible for the first time. As long as all parties recognise the deficiencies of existing arrangements due to excess price fluctuations and desire price stabilisation as a remedy, then a mutually beneficial commodity agreement is conceivable. Up to now the ADCs have wanted price-raising agreements which are bound to fail. The altered position of the ADCs in the commodity market will change their perception of self-interest; this should make an agreement possible.

The increased industrial capabilities of the ADCs will permit them to export a wide range of manufactured products rather than just labour-intensive products as in the past. The Korean entry as a competitor in the world shipbuilding market is a harbinger of the future. As the ADCs become more competitive in more sophisticated products, the relative price of those products will decline.

Meanwhile they will vacate the market for labour-intensive products leaving them for other LDCs such as those in South Asia (India, Pakistan, Bangladesh, Sri Lanka and China). For older industrial countries that must compete to buy relatively scarcer raw materials and to sell relatively more abundant manufactures, the international terms of trade are likely to move against them. An escape from this trend exists through the development of new technology, but not all industrial countries have talent in producing or quickly adopting new technology.

The greatest growth of international trade will involve the ADCs both as exporters and importers. Much trade will be among the ADCs themselves and institutional arrangements such as ASEAN will be developed to increase it. Industrial countries will have to be aware that discrimination against their products in ADC markets is a possibility and will be a serious matter for them, and thus they must adopt an appropriate negotiating posture to prevent it. This is similar to the challenge presented to the United States by the formation of the EEC in the 1950s. In a larger sense, the ADCs will obtain a greater share of the benefits of international trade and will have to accept a corresponding share of the responsibilities.

International investment, both portfolio and direct, will remain an important element in international commerce. Few business firms will remain competitive, whether large or small, unless they have an international dimension. Commercial banks, for instance, will have to be able to operate in a number of different currencies (both assets and liabilities) and in a number of locations or they will be reduced to merely exploiting a local monopoly. Producing firms will have to be very flexible to survive and make profits in the complex environment of the ADCs, but effort in this direction will be worthwhile. Of course firms located in, and owned by, ADCs will become more international and will compete everywhere. This can already be seen in the Middle East where Korean and Philippine companies compete successfully for public work contracts. Diversity will make the international scene as joint ventures among different countries and between public and private enterprise become more common. Imagination may well be the key to business success in this environment.

International aid efforts will become more diffuse as distinctions blur between aid givers and aid receivers. Some poor countries, qualifying for concessional assistance by world income standards, will also be fast-growing and without need for such assistance to sustain their growth process. However, continued access to world capital markets will remain of great importance to such countries and thus there is a role for government efforts. Other poor countries will remain in a 'low income trap' and require continued concessional aid. The trick will be to distinguish between the two without seeming to penalise success. As more countries rise from low income levels, a more pragmatic thrust will be given aid policy. The current tendency is to emphasise 'basic human needs', but this is likely to give way to efficiency criteria and more aid will be given to those who utilise it most efficiently. When ADCs graduate into aid givers, they are likely to be hard-nosed and demand that their aid be used wisely.

The international monetary system will continue to go through evolutionary changes in the future. The world rejected the Bretton Woods system when it proved it could no longer cope with the reality of economic relationships and adopted the managed floating exchange rate system in March 1973. This system was endorsed because there was no alternative and not because it represented a well-designed and theoretically superior construct. There were no agreed rules of management in 1973 and subsequently there has been little real consensus among governments on what the rules should be (although a verbal formula was worked out to revise the Articles of Agreement of the International Monetary Fund).

One form of evolution that will be necessary is to revise the way ADCs are incorporated into the system. Up to now the ADCs have been free to set exchange rates as they wish and many have chosen to peg their currencies to that of an industrial country, most commonly the US dollar. This would make sense if the US was the only large trading partner of the country, but this is seldom the case. The country's currency thus fluctuates along with the dollar, leaving the ADC with a disequilibrium exchange rate and making it more difficult for the United States to attain a sustainable balance of payments position.

Another change that might well occur in the international monetary system will be expanded use of the mark and the yen for official reserves, and possibly other currencies could join them. In a world in which economic power is more equal and wealth widespread, exclusive use of the US dollar as a reserve currency makes little sense. For instance the countries of the 'European snake' hold dollars almost exclusively when they should hold primarily marks and only Germany need hold dollars, yen, etc. A number of currency areas might develop in the future with orderly exchange relations within the area and greater variance between areas.

NOTES

1. The views are those of the author and should not be attributed to other staff members, officers or trustees of the Brookings Institution. An excerpt from this paper has appeared in the *Sunday Times* (of London), 30 July 1978.
2. The countries of southern Europe are not included, although they could qualify by some definitions, because their economic performance was too greatly influenced by internal political change during this period. Few developing countries in Africa have yet reached ADC status and those that have are tremendously influenced by the fate of copper which must be considered a special case.
3. The ADCs trade performance is compared with industrial countries rather than world totals to avoid the distortion of the rise of oil prices.

12 Multinational Enterprises as a New Form of International Industrial Integration

Jack N. Behrman

Multinational enterprises have been both praised and maligned for their role in changing the international economy over the past 15 years. They are seen as deserving praise or blame, neither or both, according to the viewpoint of the observer. They have been seen as creating new levels of efficiency and growth by some; while others dislike the composition of the products produced, despite the growth. Some see the MEs as having created closer international economic integration, while others do not desire this closeness; still others desire closer integration, but not at the hands of the MEs. Some see these companies as a challenge to the control of the host economy on the part of the government; while others see them as too greatly subject to governmental controls all over the world. Some see the MEs as making significant economic and technical contributions; while others see these contributions redounding to the benefit of the companies rather than the host countries. Still others assess the political and social consequences as undesirable.

Most of the same observations could have been adduced to the advent of the automobile. It has had both good and bad impacts, depending on the time, the situation, and the view of the observer. There are some further similarities: both have tended to increase mobility and to raise integration among and within economies; both have undoubtedly increased economic production, while adding to some of the problems of environmental protection; both tend to liberate individuals from governmental controls, yet both have been subject to increasing control; both are essentially techniques, leaving the ethical and proper use thereof to the decisions of people acting as individuals or groups.

The purpose of these comments is to demonstrate that the multinational enterprise is an institution, and is neither good nor bad *per se*; it depends on the use made of it. The purport of the rest of this presentation is that the multinational enterprise is uniquely capable of being used to achieve desirable objectives in the international economy, and that it is up to the officials of the companies and governments to make certain that this good is sought and accomplished. Otherwise, what is a unique institution for the pursuit of international economic integration will be gradually destroyed by governmental regulations and interferences, which were not necessarily intended to cause economic disintegration but which will have that effect. Not to understand the ME's potential for international economic integration will likely lead to greater disintegration. Governments have begun to treat the ME as a distinct (desirable or undesirable) entity – rather than assessing it according to its effects on desired goals. Consequently, much attention has been given to the writing of 'codes of conduct' for transnational corporations (TNCs) in an effort to ameliorate their less desirable impacts without making certain that the positive results are those desired.

Many people have observed that the multinational enterprise form of TNC – that which operates under a policy of integration of affiliates (among themselves and with the parent) to serve a standardised market around the world from least-cost sources, under a common strategy determined at the centre – has been a catalyst to industrial integration among the OECD countries at least. In the sixties these companies were a stimulus to economic integration within the European Community especially, and in the seventies that integration has spread throughout the North Atlantic countries and, more lately, between them and Japan. This integration was encouraged by a reduction of barriers to trade, finance and the movement of personnel; a system of transportation which provided low cost (per value) movement of materials, components and final products; the increasing standardisation of markets; and the possibilities of economies of scale in production, marketing, and management.

Similar integrative impacts could be achieved between the North and the South and even the East and the West, if similar preconditions were met. Presently, there are too many obstacles to the free flow of goods, capital and manpower to permit the MEs to employ fully their unique capabilities. One of the reasons why these obstacles remain is governmental concern over the distribution of benefits (ownership, control, profits, technical improvements, etc.), which they see as redounding principally to the benefit of the companies themselves.

There are many economic or even political goals which the MEs might be used to serve or accomplish. One is that of international economic integration, which is the main method by which productivity is increased and progress maximised around the world at least cost. It is an objective which governments still espouse, but which has increasingly been honoured in word rather than deed. Governments have rather injected themselves into the process of integration under what is called the 'new nationalism'; as a result there are increasing pressures towards the adoption of 'industrial policies' which can be used as surrogates to protection. However, even within such a policy orientation, the MEs can be employed effectively to gain the objective of economic integration, as well as to help meet some of the very difficult problems which cannot be achieved through policies of freer trade. The policy decisions which are being taken are complicated by the fact that the criteria of acceptability of both the ends and the means are shifting and have become multi-faceted. Fortunately, the ME is capable of being both flexible and multi-faceted itself; it therefore provides an effective means of achieving our goals. It is up to the companies and governments to recognise this possibility and help to design the future.

I) INTERNATIONAL ECONOMIC INTEGRATION

International economic integration (as opposed to disintegration) has long been praised as a desirable objective among nations – even by those who temporarily wish to separate themselves in order to strengthen their national wealth and future bargaining power. The basic desirability of such integration stems from the advantages of specialistion, which provides greater productivity and therefore greater output. More *can* be produced, therefore, to meet the world's needs. The present problems of poverty, energy consumption, hunger, squalor, ignorance and disease are so vast and deep that the capabilities of individual countries acting alone are insufficient. Cooperative efforts would be necessary, and some form of integration is required. Further, to induce the large-scale efforts required to meet these problems will require the pull of larger markets, so that companies can produce at scales which are efficient. Otherwise, continued low standards of living will have to be sustained.

There are several modes by which integration can be achieved. The one which is most widely praised by classical and neo-classical economists is that of 'multilateral, non-discriminatory trade and payments', under which the determination of the international division of labour would be guided by free market signals. Few governmental restrictions or interferences would be countenanced, and a free flow of information would provide signals as to where the comparative advantages lay in both production and marketing. The problem with this mechanism is that it says nothing about the distribution of benefits, and these can be altered to the advantage of one or more parties by various interferences. Changes in exchange rates, trade barriers of various sorts, and even internal developmental policies can change either the nature or use of the underlying factors of production, altering the comparative advantages which would determine the location of production and the patterns of trade. This being the case, governments are not likely to leave the determination of the nature and extent of economic integration to the market. In any case, the market is itself nothing but a technique, and its value depends on the setting within which it is used and the applications permitted.

A second mode is through bilateral agreements among countries to establish the nature and extent of integration. This form permits trade-offs among countries on a one-on-one basis. Though it is likely to reduce the size of the total pie, it conceivably can maximise the gains to one of the parties. These gains are seen as especially important when one of the countries is seeking to increase its employment levels. This mode is sometimes accompanied by a rise in barter trade among countries – as we are seeing today. The fact that this bilateral approach is being used emphasises the significance of the problem of the gains from trade as distinct from the size of the pie.

An offshoot of bilateralism, which is 'multi-bilateralism', seeks to achieve some of the gains of both bilateralism and multilateralism. This approach occurs when several countries agree on mutual patterns of trade on a one-on-one basis, hoping to increase the advantages of specialisation and economies of scale while not losing control over the gains. If one of the countries is dominant over the other two or three, it can increase its gains at the expense of the others, which will still enter in order to obtain a slightly larger slice than they would have otherwise, but still not equal proportionately to the returns to the dominant countries.

An approach even closer to multilateralism occurs under regional economic integration. Here, greater productivity and wealth is sought through the expansion of the market and economies of scale, but the success of this technique still depends upon the acceptability of the distribution of gains. In the case of countries such as in the European Community, these gains may be specified by a series of agreements (such as the Common Agricultural Policy). Where such agreements are not feasible, the association tends to atrophy – as is the case with the Central American Common Market, the ANDEAN Pact and the East African Community. Expansions of these regions – as between Europe and Africa – are also acceptable only if the distribution of benefits is carefully stipulated.

A final mode for determining the location of production internationally, and the markets to be served, is through permitting TNCs to decide where they will operate and where they will market their products. These company criteria, of course, are set within existing policies of government and existing economic conditions – modified by expectations of company officials. However, the criteria of decision-making as to the location of production and the patterns of trade employed by the TNCs are not the same as would be applied by governments in seeking to determine these same relationships. Consequently, since the governments are charged with responsibility for economic progress and social welfare, they are unlikely to leave to the TNCs the decisions about international economic integration.

Instead, we have seen in the past few years an increasing injection of governmental goals and procedures into the determination of the international division of labour. One of the key modes of doing so has been through sectoral approaches, segmenting different economic activities for diverse treatment. Thus, agricultural policies are determined largely with reference to the interests of national groups, and then modified somewhat to take into account international integration goals. The energy and extractive sectors tend to be dominated by national security interest, which again are modified only to the extent necessary to accommodate international pressures. And some industrial sectors are seen as so critical as to be considered 'key' sectors or 'poles of development', requiring differential treatment.

In sum, it can be seen from the ways in which governments are increasingly attempting to guide the nature and extent of international economic integration that they consider this facet of their economic and political life too important to be determined by any outside group or technical mechanism. Instead, international economic integration has become a political decision, having to meet those criteria of acceptability which include an equitable distribution of benefits.

2) THE EFFECTS OF THE NEW NATIONALISM ON INTEGRATION

Governments have taken the above stance largely as a result of domestic pressures as well as changes in the international scene. Since World War II, governments have been under increasing pressure to assume responsibility for a variety of aspects of economic and social life. These include not only the level and composition of employment, and the multiple social goals of housing, urbanisation, security and safety, but also price stability, regional development and environmental protection – to name a few. All of these are impacted – sometimes favourably and sometimes adversely – by shifts in international relations. In order to achieve greater control over the domestic economy, governments have tended to seek means of insulating it from adverse international impacts.

Among the shifts in the international economy which have continued to disturb domestic governmental policy are the pressures on the exchange rate, shifts in the composition of trade and payments, the movement of capital, shifts in the structure of capital markets, the movement of labour, and the increasingly important transfers of technology. All of these continue to provide shocks to the domestic systems, causing governments to seek means of insulating themselves. At the same time, governments have sought the benefits of greater international integration, and at least in the advanced countries have permitted the expansion of the multinational enterprises. They remain ambivalent, however, as to whether or not specific governmental objectives are appropriately served by the activities of these companies.

In addition, governments have found traditional, aggregate policies ineffective in meeting some of the multiple pressures under which they live. The post-war rules of the game have been seen as inadequate, and we are now moving into a new 'transitional' period.

3) INDUSTRIAL POLICIES

The nations of even the industrial world have become dissatisfied with the Bretton Woods rules over the past several years. This dissatisfaction has added to that of the developing countries, who have long felt that the rules were biased against them. This dissatisfaction is evidenced by the breaking of some of the rules and the absence of formation of substitutes. In almost every case, the breaking of the rules has been done in a way to cause greater disintegration of the world economy. Thus, to protect domestic economic policies of growth and stability, currencies have been floated (more or less cleanly); to protect specific industries and to maintain their location within the home country, orderly marketing agreements have been promulgated; to maintain local employment, pressures have arisen to restrain technology transfers abroad; to reserve capital and raw materials for local use, restrictions have been imposed on the outflow of both; and to alter the international division of labour, inducements have been offered to foreign investors to enter the host country.

In each of the above changes, it can be seen that there is one major issue – the distribution of the benefits, achieved through a changed location of industrial activity and the resulting patterns of trade. Consequently, industrial policies are being formed on an *ad hoc* basis, without a careful assessment of the total impacts. Presently, and over the past several decades, state governments have had industrial policies seeking to attract various types of industry into their jurisdictions and into various regions within the state (province or laender). On a slightly larger scale, regional development programs have been adopted by Italy, the United Kingdom, France and others – all seeking to move the location of industrial activity within the country and as well as attracting it from abroad. These *ad hoc* policies affect not only national industrial structures but also the international division of labour. Similarly, at the national level, a variety of *ad hoc* industrial approaches have been adopted: reserving specific industries for nationals, preventing the outflow of industries, accelerating the elimination of certain activities – all of which alter the nature of international industrial integration. There is no evidence that these various techniques or approaches have been coordinated in any significant fashion internationally.

A review of the *ad hoc* efforts undertaken demonstrates that the governments are looking at the distribution of costs and benefits reflected in a variety of gains – the maintenance of technological advantage, development of key industrial sectors, preservation of mobilised capital, an appropriate mix between agricultural and industrial sectors, maintenance or expansion of tax revenue, acquisition of technical advances elsewhere, regional dispersion of industry and employment, gestation of indigenous R&D activities, etc. There is no single benefit sought above all others, and the diversity of gains permits the pursuit of *ad hoc* policies towards industry for distinct benefits.

Consequently, we see a variety of nationally-oriented industrial policies, beginning with some of the techniques adopted by Japan and extending through those used by France under its 'indicative planning', to those adopted by Mexico, Brazil, Taiwan and Korea (the last of which has stressed the development of an infrastructure for the attraction of a variety of industries). All of these activities have altered the international division of labour. The mere fact of alteration does not mean that the result is either good or bad. To make such an assessment would require application of agreed criteria; this has not been done at the international level.

Some effort has been made at the regional level to focus on the effects of industrial policies, and even to use them in a more rational manner. The Central American Common Market was one of the first to adopt a policy of forming 'integration industries', which would rationalise the division of labour among the members – though no attention was paid to the effects of these policies at the international level. Great difficulties were found in balancing off the benefits of one industry located in each country, and the scheme virtually broke down over the problem of reciprocity. The Andean Pact has formed sectoral integration agreements, hopefully to be implemented by regional multinational enterprises which will invest in the countries designated and take advantage of the free movement of goods and services across the borders of the member countries. However, the difficulties of agreeing to reciprocal benefits have been compounded by the even greater difficulties of implementing the plans through investments by local or international companies. These sectoral agreements would in fact constitute an extensive industrial policy for the Andean members, the results of which was a reason why Chile withdrew.

Although the ASEAN countries have provided for a substantial integration of industrial activities among the members, they have not in practice developed appropriate methods of doing so. Industrial development policies remain highly nationalistic, despite the regional agreement.

Similarly, the European Community has sought to integrate key sectors among the European-owned companies, but the efforts to determine the distribution of benefits and costs beforehand have led to an increasing cartelisation of industry – as has been widely noted in the business press.

The orientation of the UNCTAD members has been to encourage (or even force if possible) a redeployment of industry from the advanced to the developing countries, altering significantly the international division of labour in an effort to redress the imbalances of the past. For its part, the OECD has essentially called for nothing more than an expansion of information exchange so that better policies toward the MEs can be made in the future. No serious effort has yet been made to adopt new industrial policies, despite the shift away from the aggregate policies of the postwar world.

The shift from macro–aggregate to micro–sectoral policies is opposed by many who see the latter as too specific an interference and who fear inappropriate decisions and goals and inefficient mechanisms arising from such interventions by governments. The US is clearly among those taking this view. Others, such as France, the UK and Italy have adopted *ad hoc* policies in critical sectors, but are unwilling to introduce this set of policies into the highest echelons of the OECD or the highest policy priorities. Undoubtably, such an approach would be complex and difficult, but, then again, so are the goals being sought.

4) NATURE OF INDUSTRIAL POLICIES

One of the reasons for the timorous approaches to industrial policies is the fact that so many facets of economic activity are involved, and the trade-offs are difficult to discern in advance. Among the different aspects of industrial policy possible at least the following would be found:

Selection of specific industries to foster;
Decisions on appropriate location of industries within, or among, countries;
Provision of appropriate infrastructure for the industrial development sought;
Encouragement of appropriate technologies and technology transfers;
Facilitation of indigenous R&D activities;
Promotion of innovation in the leading industrial sectors;
Determination of appropriate concentration and rationalisation within each sector;
Determination of the nature and extent of governmental guidance of each sector;
Determination of the mix between private and state-owned enterprises in each sector;
Selection of 'industrial champions' to lead a sector;
Amelioration of impacts on employment – sectoral or regional;
Acceptable modes of discrimination among entrants (domestic or foreign) into specific sectors;
Means of eliminating redundancy in a sector;
Means of encouraging redeployment into other geographic regions for given sectors; and
Mean of determining the country membership in the cooperative determination of industrial policies.

This list shows only some of the difficulties. It is quickly seen that there are no neat and cleanly measurable criteria by which to determine what is the best way of implementing any decision that might be taken – much less how to come to the decision. Fortunately, the multinational enterprise is a business form which helps to resolve these problems.

5) POTENTIAL ROLE OF MULTINATIONAL ENTERPRISES

Transnational corporations can be divided for analytical purposes into three basic types: resource-seekers, market-seekers and efficiency-seekers. Only the last fits into the concept of the multinational enterprise as previously defined. Resource-seekers include the extractive sectors and those plants established overseas which are solely based on low-cost labour and whose product will be brought back into the parent company for either further processing or final sale. The location of such plants has nothing to do with the market and is strictly based on the availability of the resource – either natural or human. The market-seekers move the physical plant into the local market area in order to be close to it and be able to serve it – frequently behind tariff protection or under local government requiring a high local content for a product. In a sense, these activities are disintegrating in terms of the international economy, because they potentially limit the economies of scale and therefore world-wide productivity. However, of course, if the size of the local market is sufficient to permit appropriate economies of scale, then there is no gain to further world-wide integration as compared with serving only the national market. There are few markets which fit this characteristic in any but a few industrial sectors.

The efficiency-seekers are interested in locating their activities not only where a substantial local market exists but also where it is possible to serve the wider markets abroad. Thus they are interested in economies of scale, permitting high levels of efficiency and low-cost production and distribution. These activities are the most integrative among those of the transnational companies. This potential of the ME-form either is not recognised by many governments or is discounted in favour of greater local control – this seems to be the explanation for the pressure for joint ventures, which tend to prevent the ME from operating in an integrative fashion.

Where the multinational enterprise has not been under governmental constraints altering its basic characteristics, it has produced significant levels of economic integration. It has the same potential among all OECD members, which is a reason why that body should seriously examine the sectoral approach to economic integration, focusing on the attributes of the multinational enterprises. Similarly, these enterprises have a potential for assisting in the integration among the North–South countries and even among the developing countries themselves.

For example, in the development of the sectoral agreements in the Andean Pact, the MEs could be used to implement the sectoral arrangements by locating segments of their activities among the different countries, as stipulated, and trading across national boundaries in the form of both components and final products. The Andean requirement that companies benefiting from the elimination of barriers among members should sell a majority of their equity to citizens of the Andean countries has prevented this development from taking place. That is, the MEs have retained 100 per cent of their affiliates in these countries, restricting their operations to the national markets in each case. Integration has, therefore, not taken place; and the transnational corporations are operating as market-seekers rather than efficiency-seekers (MEs), with the result that the objective of regional integration is not being effectively pursued. Although the MEs could not be left wholly alone to produce appropriate integration, the Andean agreements provide quite appropriate governmental umbrellas under which the companies could carry out the desired objectives.

6) SPECIAL PROBLEMS REQUIRING ME CAPABILITIES

In addition to the goal of international economic integration, there are a number of problems facing the world which can be met by the capabilities of multinational enterprises, and which cannot be resolved appropriately without cooperative efforts. They include the problems of exploration of the seabed and aerospace, cross-national regional development, hunger and nutrition, agro-business development, pollution control, environmental protection, transportation and communication and development of alternate energy sources. None of these is readily tractable with the institutional structures at hand. Rather, world-wide problems require world-wide institutions, and the ME is just that at the industrial level.

However, as indicated earlier, it will not be acceptable to turn these problems over to the MEs for solution in ways which they themselves desire. In fact, MEs would not take the initiative in grasping them because the customers in each case are governments. Governments will have to take the initiative, set the guidelines, and then induce appropriate responses on the part of the companies. The types of guidelines which the governments will need to establish are not 'codes of behavior' at all, but are rather procedures for the entrance of companies and implementation of contractual arrangements. For example, bidding procedures will be required to establish appropriate competition among MEs or among consortia of MEs, depending on the nature of the project involved. Cooperative management structures will be required – not only among companies if there are consortia but also between governments and companies, so that it is clear that the specific guidelines have been complied with. In addition, a variety of trade-offs among the cost and benefits will have to be determined – not only among the member countries facing these international problems but also between the governments and companies and among the companies themselves. This will require substantial negotiations – as with the development of 'The Enterprise' in the exploration of the seabed.

But, once all of these negotiations have taken place, the MEs are most capable of achieving the desired efficiency and the goals sought. If the industrial form now known as the multinational enterprise did not exist, we would have to develop some such institution in order to meet the international problems requiring cooperative efforts. Fortunately, the companies exist. Unfortunately, we seem to be unable to imagine how to use them and are, conversely, attempting to dismember them.

7) CRITERIA OF ACCEPTABILITY OF NEW INSTITUTIONS

It has become commonplace for speakers to proclaim the need for new institutions to meet new problems. It is, however, clear that new institutional forms and new modes of behaviour will be required under a new set of international rules. None of these can come full-blown; they will be developed only out of a discussion of the numerous criteria which will be applied to determine their acceptability. Divergent criteria will emerge from a number of sources and concerns, but at the least the following will be involved:

Economic criteria of *efficiency* and progress will be applied to any new set of institutions or rules, since all countries of any persuasion are concerned with improving the material well-being of the populace.

Political criteria of *participation* will be significant, as shown by the increasing effort on the part of the new entrants into the world community to express their views; they will insist that they be able to help form any new institution, to negotiate new rules and to continue to participate in decision-making.

Social criteria of *equity* in the distribution of benefits has emerged as one of the most significant issues in all international policy-making, and one of the basic reasons for the demand for new rules and institutions stems from this concern of imbalance of the gains.

Cultural criteria are being imposed also in the form of a continued *autonomy* among countries so as to maintain diversities in behavioural patterns – which is necessary both for the satisfaction of national groups and the maintenance of national distinctions.

Ecclesiastical criteria arise from the concept that man is a creative animal, made in the image of God, and both representing and sharing in His creation; in the industrial realm, this criterion is exemplified in the process of *research* and *development*, leading to innovation; countries will increasingly insist on a participation in this process in order to progress toward the goal of designing their own future.

Correlative with these criteria is a shift from measurement of success by 'values in the market' to success in achieving power relationships. Power has become a means to prestige – rather than mere material wealth (although it may be a means to material wealth also). It is also a means to the preservation of individual or group interests (rather than material status). And it is the means of protecting or achieving perquisites for particular groups (élites) within and among countries. Thus, any new institutions will have to reflect the new power relationships among countries.

These new concerns can be described under different concepts of justice. Distributive justice will focus on the redistribution of benefits of employment and trade and the redeployment of industrial activity. Commutative justice will focus on equality of opportunity and participation in the process of decision-making. Judicial justice will focus on the process of the setting of the new rules and the settlement of disputes within the new international economic order. The process of coordinating these different concepts is difficult, despite the fact that we have been working at it for over 4000 years.

What is new on the scene is that the institutions of capitalism, which have existed in the dominant economies for some 200 years, are now increasingly strained. Capitalism has not been legitimised over the entire world, nor have the corporations which have arisen from its concepts of private property and free enterprise. In order for any institution to be legitimised, it must demonstrate its pursuit of agreed social goals, and these have been shifting over the past decade. The new mechanisms need to achieve the concepts of distributive and commutative justice demanded by the society, without losing desirable elements of flexibility, innovation, competitiveness and motivation. This will not be easy, especially since it will come in a form which appears to alter the power relationships. In addition, the stress on these institutions is increased by a widening of the arena in which the decisions are made to include countries not formally acquainted with capitalism internally and who have seen it only as a form of exploitation from outside. Consequently, the former institutions (including the multinational enterprise) must bend to fit the new molds, or they will either break under stress or be broken by governmental rules and regulations.

8) THE ME – A FLEXIBLE, EFFICIENT MECHANISM FOR NEW GOALS

Fortunately, the multinational enterprise has shown itself to be a highly flexible and effective means of pursuing mutual economic objectives by quite different means in diverse social and political settings. It has operated effectively among the countries of the OECD as well as between the East and the West. The numerous and varied affiliates permit trade-offs among national interests to be made within a single company. MEs have many product lines not only within an industry but within a single company, again permitting trade-offs among the products, as may be required by social and political changes. Some of them even have multi-industry sectors – conglomerated within a single company – permitting trade-offs among industrial sectors within a single company. They exist in many different types of markets – ranging from raw materials and industrial supply to final consumers and services (both private and public) – thus permitting trade-offs among market sectors if desired. They are also involved in markets for human and natural resources as well as in capital markets, thus permitting trade-offs among the sources of factor inputs.

They have shown themselves to be adaptable to rules imposed within socialist, capitalist, democratic, or *dirigiste* societies, permitting economic integration among ideologically diverse countries.

Guidelines can be established so that competition will remain among the multinational enterprises, preventing monopoly at the international level – though it will appear at times that monopolistic elements exist within any one country. The wider the integration at the international level, the less monopolistic will the situation be, however. Maintenance of international competition will itself accelerate innovation, as it is needed to meet new problems and provide the cooperative solutions required in the areas mentioned above.

Without the use of the capabilities of the multinational enterprises, the search for nationalistic gains and a redistribution of the benefits will push the world still further toward mercantilism – a system which has tended more towards stagnation than progress. To make the shift in orientation, governments must perceive MEs as a unique means towards a solution of world economic problems, rather than as itself a major problem.

13 Technology and Economic Nationalism

Keichi Oshima

Throughout scientific history, nationalism has served as a major incentive for the development of technology. In Japan, for example, satellites are being launched by a group at the University of Tokyo for apparently scientific reasons, but, perhaps, if one were to look more closely, the real motivation behind this project would turn out to be the nationalism of the researchers. Of course, when the researchers submitted their request for a budget, the objective of the project was expressed in scientific terms, such as studying the upper layer of the atmosphere. In reality, however, engineers engaged in the project are more interested in launching a satellite through indigenous technology than in studying anything in the upper atmosphere. When people talk about technological development, they usually proffer some objective, but in many cases the researchers involved in the development are primarily motivated by nationalistic feelings.

However, what I am going to discuss here is not just the role of nationalism in technology in general, but nationalism related to industrial technology. Technology policy and technological development have always been important elements contributing to industrial development, but government technology policies aimed at specific national objectives (other than defense or national prestige) are rather new in history. In many cases, technology policies for industry are aimed not at some well-defined industrial objective, but rather at promoting the whole technological capacity of industry in general. The concept of technology policies aimed at some specific objective – such as technological innovation in order to adapt the industrial structure to altered external conditions – represents a relatively new approach. In many cases, present policies are based on intuitive judgment and still require further study and analysis.

In the past, technology and economic nationalism were issues related to technology transfer from advanced countries to developing countries, with the latter trying to maintain their autonomy or reduce the constraints and restrictions which they faced in connection with technology. The developing countries tried to build their own technological capacity in order to cope with the dominance of the advanced countries in the field of technology transfer. Recently, however, the whole issue of economic nationalism and technology in the advanced countries has come under a new light. I propose to deal here with two different aspects of this new approach.

The first point touches on the restrictions on technology transfer ostensibly for purposes of national interest. It is argued that technology transfer through multilateral and bilateral aid to countries of low labour cost is unadvantageous to the donor countries; it promotes competition in domestic and international markets and the donor country may ultimately suffer unemployment as a result of this new competition from abroad. This argument was originally voiced in the United States by the labour unions; it now prevails in both Europe and Japan due to the stiff competition they are facing from rapidly industrialising developing countries.

The other argument for economic nationalism, or even protectionism, is the use of technology policies to bring about industrial restructuring or adaptation. Technology policy can, in fact, be used to protect domestic industries in the international trade arena. It has been argued, for example in the Tokyo Round negotiations, that government procurement policies and technical and industrial standards discriminate against imported goods, and there have been calls for greater freedom in these areas. These two measures, however, are considered today as the most effective government policy tools for the development of innovative industrial technology. This has created a very delicate situation because government aid in the development of industrial technology is becoming increasingly important. On the one hand, government assistance allows industry to adjust its structure to social and resource constraints. On the other hand, it can be used to protect weak industries from international competition, especially through indirect measures which serve as non-tariff barriers.

It might be useful at this point to examine some figures illustrating the role of technology in Japanese industry. One important fact is that even with the present decrease in our overall economic growth rate, there has been fairly rapid growth in the technology-dependent part of the economy. For example, between 1955 and 1960, the average annual growth figure for the Japanese economy was 8.5 per cent of which 1.7 per cent, or 20 per cent of the total, could be attributed to technological innovation. This proportion is gradually increasing and during the high growth period of 1965–70, when the average annual growth rate reached 11.6 per cent, the contribution of technology was 4.4 per cent, or 38 per cent of the total. Even since 1970, when the overall growth rate began to decline, the contribution of technological innovation has been increasing. For 1970–2, of the 8.5 per cent total growth rate, the contribution of technology was 47 per cent. According to the estimates of the Economic Planning Agency of Japan, for 1975–85, the total growth rate will be around 6 per cent, of which 3.9 per cent, or 65 per cent of the total, will be attributable to technological innovation.

Figures such as these would seem to indicate why many governments, like the Japanese, are reinforcing technology policy, not only to promote economic growth but also to adjust the industrial structure.

One important factor here is the international flow of technology. In this estimate of the contribution of technology to the economy, technology does not mean only domestic technology but it also includes a substantial contribution of technology transferred from abroad. According to a survey of 645 Japanese companies in 1977, 57.7 per cent of the technology used by these companies was of domestic origin; out of this 57.7 per cent, 52 per cent had been developed within the company itself, while 5.9 per cent had been transferred from other companies within Japan. Imported technology accounted for the remaining 42.3 per cent and of this, only 4.8 per cent (or about 10 per cent of the total) was purely foreign, while the remainder (i.e. 90 per cent of the imported technology) had been improved by (43 per cent), or combined with the existing technology of, the recipient company (46 per cent). These figures serve to illustrate the important role of international technology transfer as well as the strong mixing of transferred technology and indigenous development. Development of technology for industry thus turns out to be a rather complicated process.

There is a very close correlation in Japan, and perhaps in all advanced industrial countries, between the level of technology imports and the R & D expenditure of industry. In Japan, for example, electrical equipment and electronics, chemicals, transport vehicles and machinery are the four sectors which have the highest R & D expenditure; they are also the four major technology-importing sectors. It is interesting to note that no similar correlation exists, at least in Japan, between exports of technology and R & D expenditure.

Now I would like to turn to government policy for technological development. As I pointed out in the beginning, technology policy is a rather new concept. Traditional science policy is a government tool for the promotion of intellectual activity or for the enhancement of the knowledge of mankind. In its early stages, technology policy was considered to be just a part of science. After World War II, there were strong arguments for government to adopt a policy to develop technology aimed at specific national goals or objectives. There were two reasons for this new policy direction. The first reason stems from the fact that after World War II, the major sciences, such as nuclear energy and aircraft and space research, developed rapidly, particularly in the United States. The second reason is somewhat related to the first. In the beginning of the 1960s, in the OECD countries, there was strong concern about the technology gap between the United States, on the one hand, and Europe and Japan, on the other. This new situation required a new approach to technology policy. In the latter part of the 1960s, around 1967–8, the OECD came to define technology policy as government policy using technology to promote economic growth: in other words not just promoting the development of technology but using it as part of a programme of specific goals for industry.

Between 1968 and 1973, the emphasis of government technology policy shifted from mere economic growth to much broader social needs. This was the first symptom that government technology policy might direct industrial sectors towards some national or social objectives which do not necessarily coincide with the profit motive of industry. In this case, technology assessment was introduced to evaluate the impact of technology in a comprehensive manner. At the present time, in most countries, government technology-development activities are oriented towards areas in which profit incentives are not very strong; this is the case, for example, of welfare, medical and other social services.

Since the oil crisis, because of the recession and what appears to be structural unemployment, governments have tried to use technology policy to promote structural change in industry. I think this can be regarded as an extension of the policies of the late 1960s: what governments are actually concerned with here are national long-term objectives which do not necessarily coincide with the short-term interests of the private sector or the market place.

Such trends in technology policy can easily be identified, but I should emphasise that there are still very few studies on how to develop and implement effective technology policies. For example, in the 1960s, when the European governments tried to narrow the technological gap, most efforts were focused upon a few strategic sectors, such as aircraft, space, nuclear research and computers. Statistics show that government expenditure on these sectors came to almost 80 per cent; in the aircraft industry, for example, government funds accounted for 72 to 80 per cent of total R & D expenditure. Today, however, there exist strong arguments to the effect that such a policy may have been ineffective in trying to strengthen technology-intensive industries in Europe or may have been even counter-productive.

But during this period, Japan proved to be an exception. Japanese policy gave more emphasis to the whole technology-intensive 'industrial structure' or 'heavy and chemical industry' than to specific projects or technology. This is why about 94 per cent of Japanese industrial R & D is financed by industry itself. The corresponding figure in West Germany is 78 per cent, in France 62 or 63 per cent, in the United States also 62 per cent and in the UK, it is 60 per cent. These are only average figures and in some countries, industry expenditure is much lower in certain strategic sectors.

These are some of the main aspects of modern technology policy. Recently, however, there have been some characteristic changes in technology development. In the first place, the technology capacity of countries, on the basis of an international comparison, has changed. For example the technology gap between the United States and Europe or Japan has narrowed. One Japanese study compares the technological level and R & D capacity of several countries. This study shows that, in the late 1960s, the technological development capacity of the United States was 100, West Germany 40.4, UK 25.0, France 23.9 and Japan 22.2. But early in the 1970s, these figures changed: the USA 100, West Germany 49.4, Japan 41.0, France 31.7 and the UK 25.3. The predominance of American technology has been declining and there are also shifts between the various countries.

The second major change noticeable in the technological field is the so-called 'decreasing rate of technological innovation'. One source of data on this phenomenon is 'Science Indicators, 1974', published by the National Science Board, which compares technologies of very highly innovative advancement, remarkable advancement, and improvement. The figures show that between 1953 and 1959, there were 22 highly innovative advancements, 23 between 1960 and 1966, but only 12 between 1967 and 1973. The total for the three categories taken together was 62 between 1953 and 1959, 80 between 1960 and 1966, and only 66 between 1967 and 1973. One can observe a similar decline in the ratio of R & D expenditures to GNP. Between 1971 and 1975, this figure increased only in the Soviet Union, while in all other countries there was a decrease. One other element to be considered in this regard is the strong correlation between the sales of a company and its R & D expenditure. This implies that the decline of sales due to the recession will substantially reduce R & D expenditure in industry, particularly in smaller companies.

Turning now to the transfer of technology in general, Japanese figures would tend to indicate that technology transfer is increasingly accompanied by restrictive conditions. These conditions include market regulations, higher royalties, the requirement for cross-licensing and capital participation. In 1968, for example, imports of technology with no market regulations constituted 36 per cent of the total; this figure was reduced to 21 per cent in 1976. On the other hand, imported technology with a market restricted only to Japan was 10 per cent in 1968 but increased to 40 per cent in 1976. Such a trend is natural at a time when the world market is becoming saturated; the development of technology is becoming more expensive and the companies want to get more profit out of the technology transfer itself.

Set against this background, there are two rationales for increased government intervention in the development of technology. The first stems from the lack of economic incentives for private industry; the risk in developing more innovative technology is becoming greater because of the higher costs involved, while profit tends to be more limited because of market saturation. There is less risk involved in a period of high growth since, in any case, industry has to expand its production capacity. New technological innovations can be embodied in these new investments which can also be improved through subsequent expansion. The other relevant factor here is the fast diffusion of technology. Because the technological capacity of countries and companies is rising and becoming more equilibrated, the diffusion of technology to competitors takes place very rapidly. For example, when Dupont invented nylon, the company had a monopoly on this product for several years, but when it developed synthetic leather, which was publicised as an innovation of almost the same order of importance as the development of nylon, other companies started similar production within a few months' time. With such a high technology-diffusion rate, profit incentives will fall. Such trends, moreover, are being accelerated by government anti-trust policy which restricts the monopoly of patents and encourages licensing.

The second point is the current insecurity about the future. We are faced with increasingly greater social constraints, as well as trade and resource uncertainties, and so companies cannot decide whether long-term investment, such as that required for technology development, can be justified. For example, in the case of emission-control regulations, the emission standard was changed not because of scientific evidence, but because of strong political pressure. This example would seem to indicate that uncertain government policies only serve to bring about confusion and discourage technological development.

Above, I have attempted to outline some of the main reasons why governments are supporting industry-oriented technology policy. It is now becoming increasingly clear that if government is going to play a major role in the development of industrial technology, then an effective technology policy can only be achieved through an integrated approach, including marketing and investment measures at the commercialisation stage. Government aid given mainly in the R & D phase has turned out to be ineffective, because technological innovation itself is an integrated process. This has been demonstrated by various cases in the past in Japan. When Nippon Telephone and Telecommunication Corporation developed electronic-switching technology, this was accomplished not only through cooperation with private companies at the R & D phase, but also by procurement policy at the commercial phase. NTT introduced new technology very quickly by adopting a new system of electronic switching before the entire mechanical-switching equipment was amortised. This could only be done by government agencies and turned out, in fact, to be very successful. This shows that once a market is created, new technology can be developed very quickly. Similarly industrial standards can also strongly affect the development of technology.

Government procurement and industrial standards are two items often raised in trade negotiations as presenting an obstacle to the free access of domestic markets. Such important government measures aimed at technological development can now bring about conflict in international trade.

The point here is that technology is becoming increasingly important as a tool or policy measure for industrial adaptation, in both the LDCs and the industrialised countries. Because technology is a most dynamic element in industry, there can be extensive room for improvement. However, if technology policy is applied in a conservative way, it can easily be used to protect weak industries or employment, either through the restriction of technology transfer, or though government intervention in technological development. In other words, it can be used as a tool of protectionism.

However, complete restrictions on technology transfer are not possible because in the long term, no country can limit the transfer or diffusion of technology completely, although in the short run, such measures may appear to be effective. Some people say the most important know-how aspect of a technology is the fact that a given technology, or process, simply exists. For example, nuclear technology is highly restricted, but once the discovery of the atomic bomb, for example, was made known, then even a country like China, with a low technological capacity, could develop such a bomb. Most of the information is public, and although one can limit the transfer of the technology or of the process itself, the basic elements and principles are generally available in public literature and reports.

If we admit that there will be increasing government intervention in the development of technology aimed at achieving national or social goals, the fundamental question that should be asked is whether these goals are likely to cause international conflict. If the goals or objectives conflict, then technology policy has to be conflictual. If the goals or objectives of nations are harmonised, then the technology policy of these nations can be used for the benefit of other parties, whether in international trade or in any other sphere of international relations. This point is not sufficiently taken into account in government technology policy because, in most countries, such policy is not yet very mature. I would urge that studies on the international impact of government technology policy be made in a comprehensive way, rather than on the present basis of fragmented and short-term considerations, such as trade or unemployment in one sector of industry. I feel that there should be studies and discussion of specific measures that governments plan to take, as well as of how these measure will affect other countries. One cannot reach any concrete outcome by discussing general philosophy and principles, since there is no clear understanding of the impact of government intervention on the implementation of technology policy.

I would conclude by saying that there is an element of economic nationalism in technology policy aimed at industrial adaptation and structural change because such policy sets out to achieve national objectives. However, technology is an important and dynamic element for changing the future. Today, even the OECD countries have only limited resources for research and technological development. Investment on technology, in government and private sectors, is declining.

Clearly, nationalistic conflict over technology will be detrimental to all concerned, since it will lead to the impossibility of sharing an already limited market. Similarly, resources which could be otherwise used to build up mutually beneficial industrial and commercial relations will be wasted in international competition. If, on the other hand, the countries involved can manage to harmonise their national objectives, then technological developments in one country can be of benefit to others. This, in turn may lead to a new approach to technology policy, which would be aimed at serving common international interests and goals.

14 Nationalism: Notes Towards a Reappraisal

André Reszler

The philosophical groundwork of *economic nationalism*[1] can best be highlighted by two metaphors: the seedling and the infant child. Both are exposed to the harshness or the open hostility of their environment and need care and affection if they are to develop into healthy, self-supporting organisms. The period of protection they require is defined by the time they need to adapt themselves to the adult world of strife and competition. It is no accident that two of the foremost theoreticians of economic nationalism, of self-sufficiency and protectionism–Johann Gottlieb Fichte and Friedrich List–are citizens of the 'young' Germanic world which is industrially backward and politically disunited and which is surrounded by the industrially and politically 'mature' nations of Europe—England and France.

Economic nationalism cannot be assessed, of course, on purely economic grounds. It is part of a complex body of ideas elaborated by some of the most prominent philosophers, historians and statesmen of the nineteenth century and which has been popularised by several generations of *instituteurs* and newspaper editors. Industrialists, bankers and tradesmen played only a relatively minor role in its emergence. Their contribution to the modern cult of the nation – and the nation-state – is not more important than the share of the poets, painters and composers who came to see in national genius (*Volksgeist*) the main inspiration of artistic creation. Nationalism is first of all a quasi-mystical mass phenomenon which aims at providing the psychologically, culturally and socially uprooted populations of modern Europe with a new feeling of identity. Now identity has to do with roots – tradition, language and history – and it involves a clear perception of future evolution.

Principles of economic organisation – tools and equipment quotas and tariffs – have hardly anything to do with the unifying myths of the past and they can hardly be turned into the building materials of a nationalistic Utopia.

Let us begin this tentative reappraisal of nationalism with a brief analysis of its most radical and certainly most short-lived form, cultural nationalism.

CULTURAL NATIONALISM

Among the various attempts at establishing the nation as the unique center of values and as the mainspring of all creativity, whether political, intellectual or technological, cultural nationalism is the last to appear. It is also, as far as we can tell from our experience, the most ephemeral one. In fact, cultural nationalism emerges only when the spiritual and intellectual unity of Europe is already on its decline. For centuries, from the formative period of Western civilisation to the early years of Romanticism, the intellectual and artistic culture of Europe has been essentially cross-national, deriving its specificity from values and aspirations shared by the peoples that had settled between the Atlantic on the West and the Eastern borders of Poland and Hungary. As long as European culture was in the ascendant phase of its history, there was no room for the development of a specifically French or German art or literature. (Let us note that European culture maintains strong ties, throughout its 'continental' phase, with popular culture which is always 'local' or 'regional' in character. When it enters into its 'decadent', 'universalist' phase, it loses all contact with popular music and art).

It is with Wagner's address at the opening ceremony of the Bayreuth Festival Theatre that cultural nationalism comes of age in Germany. When the composer of the *Ring of the Niebelungen* presents his music dramas as the founding acts of a new era in the history of 'German art', the ideals of cosmopolitanism in German music are already on the defensive. The example of Gluck composing Italian operas in Paris – a German musician at home in the various music capitals of the continent—is forgotten. Half a century after Wagner celebrates his art as Germany's return to the idols of her origins, a French composer decides also to create an *oeuvre* capable of acting as a counterforce to German musical 'imperialism'. In an age when music becomes an instrument of foreign policy and a propaganda weapon of the first magnitude, Claude Debussy signs the scores of his latest musical compositions as 'Claude Debussy, *Musicien français*'. It is not altogether surprising that in the nationalistic press of the period – we are afterall in 1914! – the composer is referred to as 'Claude de France'. If, during this period, Debussy speaks in unfriendly terms about Arnold Schönberg's twelve-tone system of composition, it is partly because Schönberg is the citizen of a country which had established a military alliance with imperial Germany.[2]

It is in Hitler's Germany that cultural nationalism reaches its height. During the twelve years of Nazi dictatorship, German art and literature are profoundly reshaped in conformity with the guidelines of a totalitarian cultural policy (*Gleichschaltung*). In order to 'purify' German cultural life from alien influences that had allegedly diverted it from its original path, the new masters of Germany put a ban on all modern artistic creation branded as 'Jewish', 'Bolshevik' or simply 'degenerate'. They are not satisfied with protecting German artistic life against the alien elements that threaten it from within; in order to defend it from the prevailing cosmopolitanism of European art, they isolate it from the outside world so that it can thrive on the purely Germanic values of 'soil' and 'blood'. (Nazi literature is habitually referred to as *Blut und Boden Literature*, sarcastically rebaptised *Blubo* by its anti-Nazi opponents.)

When Hitler inaugurates in 1937, the newly built *Haus der Kunst* in Munich, he dedicates it to a 'true and everlasting German art'. Freed of its degenerate elements, this art must be understood henceforth in its 'integral relationship' with its ethnic heritage. 'National Socialist Germany . . . wants again a "German art", and this art shall and will be of eternal value, as are truly creative values of a people', proclaims the Führer.[3]

In spite of Wagner's support of Bismarck's Germany – and the revival of the Nordic saga of the Nibelungen in which he hoped to discover the 'purely human element' he had been unable to find in contemporary society – the composer's music dramas have, in the past 30 years, lost much of their nationalistic connotation. They appear rather as early experiences in 'modern' musical composition and, thus, as works of a truly universal character. Very few people, if any, see in Debussy's musical world, manifestations of a purely 'French' spirit. His art is generally interpreted as the artist's breakthrough – alongside Cézanne's and Mallarmé's accomplishments – towards the uncharted lands of modernity. It is established beyond any doubt that modernity dissolves the purely national distinctions in artistic creation. It appears to us today more and more clearly that cultural nationalism was a brief interlude leading to the progressive de-nationalisation – and de-Europeanisation – of the creative spirit in contemporary Europe.

TOWARDS A DEFINITION OF NATIONALISM

Let us now discuss the central phenomenon of which protectionism and cultural nationalism are the late and somewhat odd variants – nationalism.

In a lecture delivered in 1959 at Santa Barbara, Aldous Huxley defined nationalism as a 'divisive religion' that places 'absolute values in fragmentary parts of humanity and positively condemns those who accept it to chronic strife with their neighbours'.[4] (We have seen how Wagner's music dramas and Debussy's ideology-free musical compositions have been turned into weapons when the age-old Franco-German conflicts degenerated once more into a generalised European war.) Nationalism is based, writes the well-known writer and essayist, on a pseudo-religious system – a coherent body of concepts, ideals and ethical commandments – based upon a

> natural and instinctive attachment to our place of origin and to familiar people but extended, by means of our capacity for abstraction and generalization, far from the natural piety of the native place and the familiar folk. Nationalism uses all the devices of education to create an artificial loyalty to areas with which the individual is quite unacquainted and to people that he has never seen.[5]

Huxley's last remark drives home a point that we tend to forget in an age that takes for granted the solidarity of a planet seen in its fundamental unity (the idea of One World). As individuals, we are limited in our capacity to establish meaningful ties with other people by the natural boundaries of our perception. Our memory is confined to a few hundred or thousand individuals *and* we can be acquainted with – by having talked to them or by having seen them at school or elsewhere – a few hundred or, at most, a few thousand other individuals. This natural limitation of the circle drawn around ourselves by our 'finitude' makes us part of a community that does not extend far beyond this limited number of people: the members of our family, friends, classmates, colleagues or members of a political party. (Let us keep in mind that in Goethe's time, Weimar had about 6000 inhabitants, all of whom had the opportunity to know each other at least by sight, and that any citizen could be familiar with the city-landscape made up of some 700 houses built around the Ducal Castle.) We can say, by extending this rather narrow sphere to a vaster geographic area, that anyone can *be* the citizen of a 'canton', a *Land* or a 'région' – and assume the distinctive traits of an Auvergnat or a Corsican.[6] One can, however, *become* a German, a Frenchman or a Swiss only after having followed a complex educational and socialisation process based on the fiction-building of a cultural and social 'encadrement' throughout one's lifetime.

Nationalism as a historical phenomenon appears in Europe for the first time during the year of the revolutionary upheaval in France. In Germany it arises in the wake of the Napoleonic wars and partly as a response to the nationalistic expansionism of post-revolutionary France. (Nationalism is practically unknown in Latin America before 1821, and it spreads to Asia only after the end of World War I. In Africa, it is imported and closely modelled on European nationalism in the same way that African novels of today are adaptations to local circumstances of a European literary genre.) Nationalism is born of the disintegration of traditional societies and thrives only where the familiar network of 'fragmented' loyalties – the family, church, race, tradition, etc. – has been weakened or destroyed by the pressure of industrial society.

If nationalism assumes the function of the secular theology[7] of modern Europe as it emerges from the crisis of the pluralistic cultural and social patterns of the Ancien Régime, it is at the same time a thoroughly revolutionary force bent on the destruction of all traditional loyalties that stand in its way. During most of the nineteenth century – in many respects, a century of Restoration – creativity is founded upon a compromise with traditional hierarchic and religious principles. It is only in our century, qualified in advance by Nietzsche as the 'century of nationalism', that it progresses freely and can be rightly presented as a cancerous phenomenon that destroys all the beliefs and ideas it encounters on its road to supremacy. (Nationalism as a modern phenomenon cannot be lastingly identified with any social class or any political ideology. In many countries, it is, at its start, a fundamentally bourgeois movement.[8] In other countries, however, it is led, in its initial phase at least, by members of the nobility. Turned into a mass movement in our century, it cuts across all social boundaries and appears as one of the major movements that carries the principle of egalitarianism.[9] Politically, the nationalist credo often has liberal undertones, although its alliance with various totalitarian ideologies is a historically established fact.[10]

WHERE DIFFICULTIES BEGIN . . .

If, in spite of its fundamental transparency, nationalism eludes any easy definition, it is because it never appears in isolation. Its history is intertwined with the emergence of *race thinking* and anti-Semitism. It becomes synonymous with the creation of the *nation-state* (the more or less exact coincidence of state frontiers with the geographic extension of a nation) and the spectacular growth of political and administrative *centralisation*. The Revolution and the Napoleonic wars incited Frenchmen – and consequently the 'patriots' of most European nations – to combat all local and regional particularisms in the name of a progressive unitary principle. They favoured the concentration of political power in the hands of a central government – and the concomitant localisation of all intellectual and artistic activities in the increasingly overpopulated capital cities.[11] As a consequence, all over Europe, provincial cities which had long been the centres of a flourishing and largely decentralised cultural life, became the simple transmission gears of a centrally organised official culture, losing most of their vitality and initiative. The history of nationalism becomes therefore the history of *étatisme* and of cultural and administrative centralisation.

NATIONALISM: A BALANCE-SHEET

No single philosophical creed or political movement has contributed more to the destruction of the idea of Europe, nor accelerated more the decline of the continent, than has nationalism. All its critics recognise, however, the beneficial role it has played in the modern centuries in the fight by small nations against the hegemonic drives of their big-power neighbours.

In his carefully balanced analysis of the nationalist phenomenon, Hans Kohn credits nationalism with both positive and negative values.[12] To each of the conflicting sets of values he enumerates, we can oppose, however, qualities which seem to contradict his findings.

According to Kohn – and we begin by the 'liabilities' column of the balance-sheet – nationalism is

– a divisive force in a world growing more and more interdependent;
– a force capable of producing bitter tensions and one-sided self-righteous judgments that threaten the rational solution of international conflicts.

On the 'assets' side, nationalism appears to him as

– an important factor in preventing any one or two of the strongest powers from establishing their hegemony over the whole globe or a large part of it:
– a bulwark of the beneficial diversity, individuality, and liberty of collective groups.

We can offer in opposition to Kohn's analyses a set of arguments which show that nationalism is

– an ideal which obliges modern man deprived of his particularism, to challenge the often self-explanatory claims of internationalism;
– a source of great power aggressiveness which creates tension and produces war;
– a coercive power that tends to reduce the various human, ethnic and cultural factors to uniformity;
– 'a melting-pot' which deprives the individual of his freedom and paralyses him in the exercise of his responsibility.

The alternate realities of nationalism can easily be integrated into a unified vision if we consider separately the purely 'internal' function of nationalism, in which it acts as a unifying factor, and its impact upon the international or inter-European arena, where it appears as a divisive force. In this way, we understand that although nationalism acts among nations as the arch-enemy of all uniformity, within the frontiers of the unified nation-state, it is the agent of self-imposed conformity and uniformity. It fosters great power aggressiveness and at the same time, it encourages the victims of power-politics to oppose national resistance to the disguised 'internationalism' of imperialism.

BY WAY OF A CONCLUSION

We live in a world where a more or less fixed set of values make up the foundations of 'civil society'. Some of the values upon which our institutions are founded are well established and openly vindicated. Other values however are undeclared. They are at the basis of fundamental policy-making, yet they never appear in the open. The will to power of organised groups, political movements and power-thirsty individuals, as well as the desire to dominate, are never mentioned among our openly declared values. We know nevertheless that we must never forget about their existence, if we want to understand the society in which we live.

Nationalism is beyond any doubt one of the openly declared values of our society. In the thirties, it was fashionable in Western Europe to be known as a champion of nationalist goals. Even in those times, however, nationalism was essentially a mask under which were hidden the 'qualities' of imperialism, racial hatred, anti-Semitism and class warfare. For all these reasons, the issue of nationalism cannot be settled by rational, historical arguments. Nationalism never appears in isolation. It is often the facade of policies and aggressions which never bear their name.

NOTES

1. For a comprehensive treatment of the theoretical aspects of economic nationalism, see Michael A. Heilperin, *Studies in Economic Nationalism* (Geneva: Publications of the Graduate Institute of International Studies, 1962).
2. In a letter to Durand, dated 18 August 1914, Debussy gives way to his deep-seated distrust of all cosmopolitan elements in French culture: 'Depuis qu'on a nettoyé Paris de tous ses métèques, soit en les fusillant, soit en les expulsant, c'est immédiatement devenu un endroit charmant.' (Quoted by Jean Barraqué, *Debussy*, Paris: Seuil, 1975, p. 175).
3. Next to the exhibition devoted to new German art, a second exhibition

featuring contemporary 'degenerate art' (*entartete Kunst*) was organised so that visitors could immediately grasp the vitality and superiority of racially pure German art over the decadent works of Kandinsky, Klee, Chagall, etc.

4. Aldous Huxley, *The Human Situation* (London: Chatto & Windus, 1978) p. 80 – 'The only definition which the old League of Nations was ever able to find for a nation . . . was that a nation is a society possessing the means of making war. Thus the feeblest and smallest nation which has some kind of a war-making machine – Libya, for example – is a nation, but an immense geographic unit with a huge population, such as California, is not a nation because it does not have a war-making machine', remarks Huxley (p. 77).
5. Ibid, p. 76.
6. Until the beginning of the seventeenth century, the word *nation* was used in order to describe the geographical entity we today call *région* or *province*, observes Philippe Ariès. 'L'opinion commune désigna...par patrie, dans la langue courante, la terre natale, le pays des ancêtres. Le mot de nation nous ramène aussi à la même conception restreinte. La Faculté des Arts était divisée en *nations*, mais on n'opposait pas une nation française à des nations étrangères, on distinguait seulement une *nation picarde*, une *nation normande*, etc.' ('Nationalisme d'hier et nationalisme d'aujourd'hui,' in *La Table Ronde*, March 1960, p. 48).
7. Carlton J. H. Hayes' 1960 essay bears the significant title of *Nationalism: A Religion.* (New York: The McMillan Company).
8. 'On a . . . l'impression qu'il faut chercher l'origine de l'idée nationale dans ce milieu de clercs et d'officiers, qui constituera peu à peu la noblesse de robe – ou la bourgeoisie d'offices – *grammatici certant*. Ils ont été les premiers à prendre conscience de la solidarité qui lie tous les habitants d'un même pays, d'un même Etat, du roi au plus petit des sujects.' (Philippe Ariès, op. cit., p. 50).
9. 'The twentieth century has added another revolutionary dimension to nationalism', writes in this respect Hans Kohn. 'Nationalism has also become a socially revolutionary movement, demanding equal economic and educational opportunities for all members of the national group and the active promotion of the welfare of the socially underpriviledged classes. Its aims have become the establishment of a classless, theoretically egalitarian national society.' ('Nationalism', *International Encyclopaedia of the Social Sciences*, New York, 1968).
10. English nationalism seems to be largely devoid of the egalitarian undertones noticeable on the continent. 'Equality was never a part of English nationalism as it was of the German or the French national tradition,' writes George L. Mosse. 'As Burke has said, the development of liberty was traditional, but ideas of equality smacked of a foreign ideology. England had neither the tradition of Jacobin rule nor the problem of achieving unity in a nation which had been disunited since the Middle Ages.' (*The Culture of Western Europe. The Nineteenth and Twentieth Centuries*, London: John Murray, 1963, p. 61).
11. The Versailles Palace is an early example of state culture and the architectural symbol of pre-Jacobin centralisation.
12. Hans Kohn, op. cit.

Index